Studies in Ethics

edited by
Robert Nozick
Pellegrino University Professor
at Harvard University

A Garland Series

THE BOUNDS OF CHOICE

Unchosen Virtues, Unchosen Commitments

TALBOT BREWER

GARLAND PUBLISHING, Inc.
A MEMBER OF THE TAYLOR & FRANCIS GROUP
NEW YORK & LONDON/2000

Published in 2000 by
Garland Publishing Inc.
A Member of the Taylor & Francis Group
19 Union Square West
New York, NY 10003

10 9 8 7 6 5 4 3 2 1

Library of Congress Cataloging-in-Publication Data
Library of Congress-in-Publication Data is available from
the Library of Congress

Brewer, Talbot.
        The bounds of choice : unchosen virtues, unchosen
    commitments / Talbot Brewer
    Includes bibliographical references and index.
    ISBN: 0-8153-3667-5 (alk paper)

Printed on acid-free, 250-year-life paper
Manufactured in the United States of America

Contents

Preface

This book is a modified version of *Character, Desire and Moral Commitment*, a Ph.D. thesis presented to the Harvard Philosophy Department in January of 1998. In the book, I develop two related facets of a single, sustained challenge to what might be called the "voluntarist" understanding of morality. According to the voluntarist, we are morally responsible only for those aspects of our character which we ourselves have authored or chosen, and we can enter into particular, non-universal moral obligations only by voluntarily agreeing or consenting to them. I reject both claims. In the first two chapters, I argue that we are sometimes morally responsible for aspects of our character that we have not chosen or otherwise authored; in the last two chapters, I argue that we are sometimes subject to particular, interpersonal obligations to which we have not voluntarily agreed. The principal aim of this book, then, is to show that the boundaries of the moral self are more ample than the choosing will. From the moral point of view, who we are and what we owe to others is not merely a matter of what we have chosen to make of ourselves, but also, inescapably, a matter of what our socio-cultural inheritance has made of us.

Stated in this bald form, these twin theses concerning "the bounds of choice" are far from original. I believe, however, that (for better or worse) I do have something quite distinctive to say both about "unchosen virtues" and about "unchosen commitments."

The most distinctive aspect of my discussion of "unchosen virtues" is that I begin with a paradigmatic voluntarist position—Kantianism—and try to show that it unravels in the face of a serious effort to spell out the central Kantian notions that each morally assessable action has a maxim, and that we are assessable only for the moral acceptability of the maxims to which we are committed. The heart of my argument (as elaborated in Chapter II, sections iii-v) is that Kantians make two key uses of the notion of a maxim, and that these uses are in tension with each other. On the one hand, Kantians claim that bits of behavior must have maxims if they are to count as actions, hence fall subject to moral assessment. On the other hand, Kantians portray maxims as subjective principles of action that can be read off of our practical deliberations. The idea is that in the practical deliberation that precedes any action, we judge certain features of our circumstances to be sufficient warrant for the action, and this implicitly commits us to the maxim that counts such circumstances as a justification for actions of that type.[1] The trouble with this picture is that there are many bits of behavior which are widely believed to be morally assessable, yet are not preceded by anything recognizable as deliberation. This means that the Kantian must either implausibly restrict the scope of behavior open to moral assessment or find some way of making sense of the categories of unreflective and impulsive actions. I argue that the latter course is preferable, and that the most straightforward way is to reconstruct the maxims of these actions by attending to the agent's characteristic patterns of attentiveness and responsiveness to changing features of her circumstances. I also argue that this will often require attentiveness to characteristic emotions and desires. The Kantian cannot make good sense of the core ideas that every action has a maxim, and that the action's moral worth depends entirely upon the moral acceptability of its maxim, without jettisoning the voluntarist dogma that we are morally responsible only for that which we have voluntarily chosen or authored. My argument does not require an abandonment of the central Kantian thesis that only the will is morally assessable, nor of the thesis that the will is practical reason. It does, however, require a salutary widening of the boundaries of the will and of the "faculty" of practical reason, to reflect the fact that sometimes, our reasons for action are encoded in our characteristic feelings and desires.

---

1 Or, more specifically: for some action-type that includes the action we judge to be choice-worthy.

As noted above, the second half of this book addresses the topic of particularistic obligations—i.e., obligations that we have in virtue of particular, contingent facts about ourselves and our relations to others. I claim that many such obligations are grounded not on past voluntary choices, but on unchosen facts about ourselves and our circumstances. My argument for this claim is, in its broad form, structurally similar to my argument against Kantian voluntarism: just as the Kantian must either distort the phenomenology of deliberation or implausibly restrict the range of morally assessable behavior, so too the voluntarist about obligations must either distort the phenomenology of interpersonal obligation or implausibly restrict the range of such obligations. The trouble is that there are many interpersonal relations—ranging from family relations to friendships to bonds of fellow citizenship—which we take to be the source of obligations, yet which cannot persuasively be traced to anything resembling a promise or voluntary agreement. This insight has prompted some theorists to deny that we have moral obligations to friends, family, and/or fellow citizens, and this would be a reasonable conclusion if voluntary agreement were indeed the only possible source of particular obligations. The burden of Chapters 3 and 4 is to show how we might make sense of special, non-voluntarist obligations.

In re-editing this discussion of "unchosen commitments," I have come to believe that its most distinctive contribution to contemporary philosophical debate is the reconciliation it affords between communitarians and voluntarist liberals. I argue that the familiar voluntarist analysis of interpersonal obligations is true of one sort of social group, which I call an aggregation, while an alternative, broadly communitarian model of interpersonal obligation best captures the normative structure of a different sort of social group, which I call an association. This distinction puts me in a position to claim that liberals and communitarians are both right, only about different social groups; they err only to the extent that they take their pictures of interpersonal obligation, and of the normative structure of social groups, to be exhaustive. The communitarian worry can then be understood as a plaintive reaction to the replacement of associations by aggregations in many arenas of social life, and to the erosion of the valuable forms of shared activity that are possible only within associations.

So much for my retrospective assessment of the text's contributions to contemporary philosophical debate. I turn now to a chapter-by-chapter summary of the text, for the convenience of readers who may be interested only in specific themes.

In the first chapter I argue, as against Kant, that desires and emotions have a cognitive element that leaves them open to direct moral assessment. I maintain that a wide range of affects enter into moral reasoning as initial mappings of practical reasons onto the world. This suggests a way of characterizing conflicts between persistent desires and all-things-considered practical judgments. Such conflicts indicate that our considered judgments lack the status of wholehearted convictions.

Kant maintained that dutiful action can have the fullest measure of moral worth even if chosen in the face of powerful inclination to act immorally, and indeed that opposing inclinations only highlight the worth of the action. This claim, I believe, owes its plausibility in part to the intuitive belief that we are not responsible for what we cannot voluntarily control. If we think of feelings and desires as arising in us unbidden and pressing upon us even against our will, it seems to follow that we are not responsible for them. It is then natural to locate moral worth in that for which we can plausibly be held accountable: the firmness of the rational will's attachment to morality. This intuitive understanding of moral responsibility goes hand-in-hand with a compelling picture of practical reason. On this picture, desires provide un-cognized raw materials for deliberation. The cognitive work lies in assessing our desires and determining whether they are to count as reasons for action. If moral assessment is an assessment of the adequacy of our reasons for action, this implies that it need not concern itself directly with sentiments and desires.

I begin to unravel these pictures of moral responsibility and practical reasoning in Chapter I, by examining the conception of moral worth and the companion conception of virtue at work in Kant's seminal moral writings. I argue that these conceptions leave Kant without resources to explain the critical distinction between self-interested and malicious violations of duty. In my view, we can only properly account for this fundamental moral distinction after we have grasped the intimacy of the connection between desire and practical judgment. I follow Kant in maintaining that persons are morally assessable only for their practical judgments, but I argue that practical judgment is already in mid-stride when certain desires arise. For instance, certain persistent desires to harm others are open to moral censure because they manifest the prima-facie judgment that the suffering of another is good. This implies that malice ought to count on Kant's own terms as a moral failing of the deepest sort, since it manifests that one does not fully acknowledge the equal standing of other persons as ends in themselves. I argue that this insight helps us to rescue what is most plausible and to jettison what is more implausible from Kant's discussion of morally worthy action.

In Chapter II, I ask how significant a revision must be made to Kantian moral theory in order to answer these criticisms. I argue that there are demanding affective preconditions for the full recognition of the equal moral standing of other humans, and that these provide the core of a more plausible conception of moral virtue than is usually associated with Kant. I find fruitful suggestions for developing this conception of virtue in Kant's later moral writings and in Barbara Herman's recent attempts to expand the Kantian conception of virtue by introducing character-shaping Rules of Moral Salience. I agree with Herman that acuity in moral judgment depends upon a quasi-perceptual capacity to highlight certain features of our situation as prima-facie reasons for action. I take issue, however, with Herman's contention that this capacity can be conceived in isolation from the maxims on which we act. I argue that in many cases, our maxims are partly determined by the "Rules of Moral Salience" which we have internalized. Since the maxims of our actions are subject to moral assessment and criticism, I argue that the Rules of Moral Salience which we internalize in the course of our socialization are also subject to direct moral praise and blame. As I see it, these insights provide grounds for insisting that the boundaries which the Kantian imposes on practical reasoning are overly restrictive. Once we expand the boundaries of the "faculty" of practical reasoning, we will see that the deliverance of practical reason is sometimes manifest in our characteristic emotions. I maintain that the Kantian who accepts this picture of virtue must give up the attractive claim that we can always voluntarily will to do whatever morality requires. Such a Kantian might still preserve the essential Kantian equation of dutiful action and autonomy—here understood as self-governance in accordance with laws we wholeheartedly accept

In the course of Chapters I and II, I argue for a particular understanding of conflicts between our desires and our all-things considered judgments of what we have reason to do. Such conflicts often show that our considered beliefs are not wholehearted—they lack the status of convictions. In Chapters III and IV, I work out an account of moral commitment and obligation that clarifies the moral importance of wholehearted conviction in interpersonal relations. The basic claim is that the obligations which bind together intimates and fellow members of certain face-to-face communities are best analyzed in terms of wholehearted convictions. I argue that this approach is truer to the phenomenology of moral deliberation than rival analyses.

In Chapter III, I distinguish two kinds of interpersonal commitments which might bind individuals together and structure their coordinated activities. I begin with an investigation of the words and actions by which we undertake commitments, and I argue that it is impossible to analyze all commissive performances on the model of promises or contracts. Unlike promises and contracts, which cannot straightforwardly be construed as descriptions of the world, some utterances and actions commit us by making known our basic goals, ideals and values. I argue that this sort of speech has its paradigm function in creating and sustaining a fragile and extremely valuable kind of social group—a kind which, following Rousseau, I will call the association. This sort of social group is distinguished by the fact that its members are united by self-consciously shared values, and not—as in some other social groups—by a mere overlap of self-interest.

In the last chapter, I try to show that certain political obligations, including the putative political obligation to risk one's life in defense of the state, are most convincingly understood as associative commitments of the sort specified in Chapter III. If this is right, it implies that such "ultimate obligations" are far rarer than has often been supposed. I also try to show that marital obligations are best understood as associative commitments. This also has a somewhat radical implication: it implies that marital obligations are far more provisional and tenuous than has often been supposed.

Acknowledgments

Thomas Scanlon advised the dissertation that appears here in modified form. He was extremely generous with his time and energy, and his comments on successive drafts of this text have made it far more interesting and defensible than it would otherwise have been. This work has also been greatly improved by Christine Korsgaard's and Gisela Striker's thoughtful comments on earlier drafts. I am deeply grateful to both of them.

Many of the ideas in this book were shaped by my studies with other Harvard professors, in particular Stanley Cavell, John Rawls, Fred Neuhouser and Richard Moran. I wish to express my appreciation of their fine teaching and even finer philosophical example. I have also benefited greatly from conversations with fellow graduate students, particularly Tony Laden and Sanjay Tikku. I thank them.

In my last year of graduate study, while teaching at the University of Pennsylvania, I benefited greatly from the input of several of my colleagues, especially Gary Ebbs, Tom Ricketts, Sam Freeman and Paul Guyer. I have also been given valuable feedback on portions of my dissertation by several of my current colleagues at the University of Virginia, including John Marshall, James Cargile, Jorge Secada, John Simmons and Bill Diggs. I am deeply appreciative that they have taken an interest in my thoughts.

I wish to thank the Whiting Foundation, the University of Virginia Summer Grants Program, and the Program in Ethics and the Professions at Harvard's Kennedy School of Government, for invaluable financial support. I also wish to thank my wife, Saphira and my sons Benjamin and Ethan for their patience and good cheer during my long stretches of immersion in philosophical speculation.

A Difficulty with Kant's Account of Desire

INTRODUCTION

Many doubts have been raised about Kant's view of the place of sentiments and desires in morally worthy actions and in the virtuous moral character. However, I think that we still lack an adequate account of precisely what is amiss with Kant's view. I will attempt to show that Kant goes awry because his moral psychology leaves him with a deficient conception of commitment to principles, and with a corresponding deficiency in his conception of virtue.

In this chapter, I will take for granted the Kantian notion that moral virtue can be conceived of as commitment to maxims, or subjective principles of action, which reflect the equal, unconditional worth of all beings imbued with practical reason. What I will argue is that there are affective preconditions for commitment to such moral principles, and that Kant does not bring these out sufficiently clearly. I believe this problem stems ultimately from Kant's insistence on a strict separation between the faculty of judgment, whose operations we must conceive of as spontaneous or uncaused, and the faculty of desire, whose impulses Kant reduces to brute mechanical forces. I will call this separation into question by bringing out the benefits of conceiving of practical judgment as an ongoing activity that is already in mid-stride, so to speak, when certain sentiments and desires arise.

My argument makes use of a philosophical thesis concerning characteristic emotions and desires—that in many cases they give us clues about the depth of our commitment to moral principles. I do not rely upon the more controversial thesis –associated with certain stoics and with a handful of contemporary philosophers[1]—that emotions are evaluative judgments. I make use only of the much weaker thesis that characteristic desires and emotions sometimes provide us with grounds for doubting the strength, or whole-heartedness, of our commitment to our avowed principles and values. While I do not here provide a full philosophical justification of this picture of emotion and desire, I try to show that it is implicit in our intuitive moral assessments, hence is part of what might be called our "folk moral psychology." For the purposes of this paper, this is all I need to do. This is because my aim is to critique passages in the *Groundwork* and *Second Critique* where Kant's explicit aim is to extrapolate philosophical conclusions about moral worth or virtue from the "ordinary" or "common" knowledge of morality.[2]

My discussion of Kant will span two chapters, neither of which can stand entirely alone. In this chapter, I will identify and explore tensions in Kant's conceptions of moral worth and virtue as they arise in the *Groundwork of the Metaphysics of Morals*. In the second chapter, I will consider certain elements of Kant's later moral writings, and the writings of certain contemporary Kant scholars, in order to determine whether there are Kantian resources for resolving these tensions.

---

1   See e.g. Robert C. Solomon, *The Passions* (New York; Doubleday: 1976)
2   One passage is found in the first section of Kant's Groundwork for the Metaphysics of Morals, which is entitled "Transition from the Ordinary Rational Knowledge of Morality to the Philosophical." The German word here rendered with the English "ordinary" is "gemeinen," which connotes the popular or common (it can also mean the vulgar or low, but these latter connotations seems to be canceled by Kant's insistence on the rationality of the knowledge in question). The second key passage is found in the penultimate section of the second Critique, "The Methodology of Pure Practical Reason," where Kant's concern is to derive an attestation of the true nature of virtue from the common-sense understanding of morality possessed even by young children. (Critique of Practical Reason, Ak. 155-6.)

PART 1: KANT ON MORAL WORTH AND GOODNESS OF WILL

I begin with a *prima-facie* difficulty in Kant's moral theory—one that Kant's defenders generally acknowledge at least to the extent that they feel compelled to clear it up in one way or another. The difficulty I have in mind arises from Kant's well-known claim, in the first section of the *Groundwork*, that moral worth—the highest sort of worth that an action can have—is clearly manifest in the dutiful actions of those who feel no inclination to fulfill their duty.[3] Kant presents a series of sketchy cases through which he hopes to elicit this conclusion from his readers' "common rational knowledge of morality."[4] Perhaps the most notorious of these cases is that of the constitutionally unsympathetic person who helps others despite his lack of any inclination to do so. Kant supposes it to be particularly evident that the helping actions of this person are morally worthy, yet it has seemed to many readers of the *Groundwork* that this purportedly exemplary agent is at best uninspiring and perhaps even morally deficient.

Before attempting to make sense of this widespread, inchoate doubt about Kant's appeal to common knowledge, it will help to situate Kant's discussion of moral worth in the broader argument of *Groundwork I*. Kant's aim here is to attain philosophical insight into the supreme principle of morality by bringing out what is implicit in the common-sense understanding of the good-willed agent. His strategy is to identify what morality requires of us by identifying the principles which structure morally exemplary wills. In general terms, what morality requires of us is that we make our own wills good by adopting the principles which govern the actions of the good-willed agent.[5]

Like Hume before him, Kant believes that moral praise of actions

---

3 Immanuel Kant, *Groundwork for the Metaphysics of Morals*, Ak. 399.
4 *Ibid*, Ak. 393.
5 This general interpretive approach has been taken by Christine Korsgaard and Keith Simmons, among other Kant scholars. See Korsgaard, "Kant's Analysis of Obligation: The Argument of Groundwork I," reprinted in Korsgaard, *Creating the Kingdom of Ends* (Cambridge; Cambridge University Press: 1996), pp. 43–76. See also Keith Simmons, "Kant on Moral Worth," *History of Philosophy Quarterly*, Volume 6, No. 1, January 1989, pp. 85–100.

is directed at the agent and is sensitive to the agent's *motive* for acting as she does. Kant disagrees with Hume, however, about *which*
motives we find morally praiseworthy. Hume maintained that we
praise people for enduring passions that dispose them to act in ways
which are beneficial either to themselves or to others. What Kant
attempts to show in the first section of the *Groundwork* is that in fact
we are prone to attribute moral worth to those whose dutiful actions
arise from the motive of duty itself.[6] Kant attempts to demonstrate
this conclusion first by gaining his readers' intuitive attestation that
moral worth is most clearly manifest by dutiful actions performed
without any supporting inclinations, then by pointing out that the
only possible motive for such actions is the motive of duty.

Kant opens the first section of the *Groundwork* by asserting
that nothing is unconditionally good except a good will, and that
it is good quite apart from any purpose that might be attained by
it. These insights, he maintains, "already dwells in the natural
sound understanding and needs not so much to be taught as merely to be elucidated."[7] Kant examples of morally worthy actions are
presented as a way of elucidating our pre-philosophical grasp of
the good will. What these examples do, according to Kant, is to
"bring [the good will] out by contrast and make it shine forth
more brightly."[8] This is done by describing cases of persons who
act dutifully in the absence of any inclination to do so, and even in
the presence of powerful inclinations to act immorally. These cases
are meant to lead us to the conclusion that what distinguishes the
dutiful actions of the good-willed person is that they are motivated by a recognition that they are obligatory, or lawful.

---

6   Now, Hume had offered a striking argument against the notion that
    the motive at which we aim our moral praise is the motive of duty
    itself. Hume argued that morality could not require us to do what is
    right out of recognition that it is right, unless there is some way of
    characterizing right action independent of the stipulation that it be
    chosen out of a regard for its rightness. Otherwise, Hume reasoned,
    there would be no way for us to discern our duty. If we are told that
    we must perform right actions out of regard for their rightness, this
    will not tell us what concrete actions we must choose, and it seems as
    if it will not help at all to be told that right actions are those which
    are performed out of regard for their rightness. (See Hume, *A
    Treatise of Human Nature*, Bk. III, Part II, Section 1.) In order to
    answer this Humean challenge, Kant must show that respect for the
    moral law as such has content—that it determines what we must do.
    Kant attempts to discharge this task in *Groundwork II*.
7   *Groundwork*, Ak. 397.
8   *Ibid.*

In concluding that the good-willed person is one who is responsive to lawfulness as such, Kant rejects at least two other hypotheses. One rejected hypothesis is that the good-willed person is one whose purposes or ends are laudable. This hypotheses is rejected on the ground that the purposes of the good-willed person can be shared by others whose wills are not morally good. The second rejected hypothesis is that the good-willed person is distinguished at least in part by her characteristic emotions or desires—perhaps because these affective states tend to generate morally praiseworthy actions, or perhaps because they manifest one's commitment to that which is morally good. One form or another of this thesis is affirmed by theorists as varied as Plato, Aristotle and Hume. Kant claims to have shown that the presence or absence of certain inclinations cannot be a *sine qua non* of moral worth when he writes, "We have also shown above how neither fear nor inclination, but solely respect for the law, is the incentive which can give an action moral worth."[9] Though this passage comes in *Groundwork II*, It is hard to see where Kant might believe that this has been demonstrated if not in his prior illustrations of morally worthy action, which aims implicitly to show that inclinations lend nothing to the moral worth of actions.[10]

PART II: DIFFICULTIES WITH KANT'S NOTION OF MORAL WORTH

Given Kant's methodology in *Groundwork I*, what he says about the moral worth of particular actions must meet with assent from the "common rational knowledge of morality." I will argue that Kant cannot draw upon "common" knowledge to support the rejection of the second hypothesis noted above—that is, the hypothesis that the good-willed person is characterized at least in part by morally praiseworthy inclinations and desires. I will proceed by attempting to cast doubt on Kant's claim that the source of moral worth is most clearly displayed to our ordinary lights

---

9 *Ibid.*, Ak. 440.
10 One of Kant's main reasons for rejecting the notion that people can be assessed morally for their affective states seems to be that such states cannot be commanded, presumably because they cannot be produced at will. One implication of this, for Kant, is that the scriptural invocation to love one's neighbor can be salvaged only if we conceive of it as the requirement that we determine our will to act beneficently towards others. See *Groundwork*, Ak. 399.

when we imagine someone who acts dutifully in the absence of any
inclination to do so, and even in the presence of powerful contrary
inclinations. Indeed, I will argue that such cases sometimes cast
into doubt the goodness or purity of the agent's will.[11]

In order to elicit intuitions supportive of his position, Kant
presents the reader with four separate characters who act dutifully in the absence of any inclination to do so. I am particularly
interested in two of these figures, each of whom acts benevolently
even though he has no sympathy for others, and hence no inclination to help them. These two differ in the following way: one
"friend of mankind" characteristically takes pleasure in helping
others to achieve their aims, but temporarily loses his considerable
sympathy for others because he is burdened by his own woes; the
other figure is constitutionally cold and unsympathetic, hence not
what Kant would call a "friend of mankind."[12] Kant claims that
if the first (the friend of mankind) were to tear himself free from
his temporary insensibility and act beneficently in the absence of
any inclination to do so, then for the first time his beneficent
action would have genuine moral worth.[13] Along the same lines,
Kant claims that if the second (the constitutionally unsympathetic
character) acted beneficently because he acknowledged such action
to be his duty, he would thereby "find in himself a source from
which he might give himself a worth far higher than any that a
good-natured temperament might have..."[14]

---

11 I do not mean to suggest that at the end of the day, this claim is sup-
    ported only by common-sense intuitions. Once these intuitions have
    been developed into a moral theory, Kant's theoretical insights into
    the nature of freedom, the moral law, moral judgment and the
    virtues of character might lend added credence to these starting
    points. In fact I think that any really plausible development of Kant
    tends to undermine these starting points. Still, Kant presents this as
    a starting point on the road to philosophical knowledge of the
    supreme principle of morality, and my immediate interest is to try to
    say whether those who are not already convinced by Kant's moral
    theory have any reason to assent to his starting point.
12 Immanuel Kant, *The Metaphysics of Morals*, translated by Mary
    Gregor (Cambridge; Cambridge University Press: 1991), Ak. 472.
    Here Kant identifies the "friend of mankind" as one who takes an
    affective interest in the well-being of all men, rejoicing with them,
    while also acknowledging their equality.
13 *Groundwork*, Ak. 398.
14 *Ibid.* I will provisionally grant that there could be figures of this
    sort, in order to explore our reactions to them. By the end of this
    chapter, I will raise doubts about whether Kant's cases describe real
    possibilities.

Now, these passages have often been read in ways that make Kant's claims unappealing, and that throw into doubt his warrant for drawing support from the "common rational knowledge" of morality. Kant has variously been misunderstood as suggesting that we ought to purge ourselves of feelings of sympathy, or that those who lack sympathy are better than those who have it, or even that those who feel sympathy could never be properly responsive to the moral duty of benevolence. Schiller gives expression to just this sort of misunderstanding in the following verse parody of Kant:

> Gladly I serve my friends, but alas I do it with pleasure.
> Hence I am plagued with doubt that I am not a virtuous person. Surely your only resource is to try to despise them entirely, And then with aversion do what your duty enjoins you.[15]

I will interpret Kant's treatment of moral worth in the way that seems to me to render the view most plausible—though, as I will indicate below, there are serious difficulties with this reading. On the (hardly novel) reading that I have in mind, Kant is not denying that an action can have moral worth if one has an immediate inclination to do the action. What he is denying is that an action done *from* inclination can have moral worth. Kant directs our attention to dutiful actions unaccompanied by harmonious inclinations only because it is particularly clear that such actions are done from duty and not from inclination.

What is it, then, to act from inclination? An action is done from inclination if one's reason for choosing the action is that one is inclined to do it. This leaves open the possibility that one might do something one is inclined to do, yet not act from inclination; In order to know whether someone has acted *from* inclination, one must know why the person judged the action in question to be choiceworthy. In more recognizably Kantian terms, one must know the maxim of the action.

One might object that this is an overly rationalist construal of action from inclination, and that it is possible to act from inclination immediately, without any deliberation or reflection at all. As I understand it, Kant does not deny this. Rather, Kant holds that

---

15 From Friedrich Schiller, "The Philosophers." Quoted from Paul Guyer, *Kant and the Experience of Freedom* (Cambridge; Cambridge University Press: 1996), p. 336.

when one acts immediately from inclination, one *implicitly* takes the inclination to be a sufficient reason to act. The idea behind this claim is that a rational agent cannot give an account of his actions as unreflective effects of inclinations. To think of one's actions as following immediately from inclinations, without attributing to oneself the (implicit) judgment that the inclinations give one reason to act, is to think of oneself not as an agent but as a locus of causally determined events.[16]

Moral worth, then, is entirely a matter of one's motives, or reasons for action, and these are given by the maxims on which one acts. Since the structure of one's will is given by the maxims to which one is committed, moral worth is entirely a matter of the structure of one's will. Kant does not specify what he takes the maxims of the sympathetic and unsympathetic helpers to be, but I believe that they can be reconstructed as follows. The maxim of the sympathetic helper's action is presumably: 'When I feel inclined to help someone, I will endeavor to help.'[17] The maxim of the unsympathetic helper's action would presumably run something like this: 'When someone needs help in order to pursue his/her ends effectively, and I can help without great sacrifice and without violating any perfect duties, I will endeavor to help.' Each of these

---

16 As I see it, we can *imagine* a rational being offering such an explanation, but we would count such an explanation neither as a justification nor an excuse. When the justifiability of an action is in question, to say that one acted immediately on inclination is to apologize ("I just didn't think about what I was doing."). This implies that we are under some sort of obligation to think before we act. These thoughts lead to the puzzling question of the moral status of justifiable actions whose justifiability is recognized only in retrospect and not explicitly brought out in judgment prior to action. On the Kantian account, they seem deeply flawed, as it is only by happenstance that they are in agreement with morality. It does not seem to me that their agreement with morality can be reduced to dumb luck. Further, I believe that such actions have an important sort of value which the Kantian does not adequately account for, since they manifest or express laudable character traits. I hope that the force of these claims will become clear over the next two chapters.

17 I believe that this is how Kant would formulate the maxim, but it shows how unusual a person the sympathetic helper really is. Most sympathetic people, it seems, would take their sympathy as a sensitivity to real reasons for action; they would act on it because it reliably sensitizes them to real reasons for action. This extra level of deliberative sophistication is missing from the figure portrayed by Kant, at least on the interpretation of that figure which makes his argument most compelling.

maxims has the following general form: 'When reason R, I will adopt purpose P.' These maxims do not differ in their purposes: both agents aim to help someone. Thus, if Kant is right that only the unsympathetic helper's actions clearly manifest a good will, this shows that the will's goodness is not solely a function of its purposes. It is clear, however, that moral worth cannot depend entirely on one's reasons, since no reason can justify the adoption of all conceivable purposes. Thus, moral worth must be a function of the relationship between one's reasons and one's purposes.[18] The sympathetic helper's motive, or reason for action, is that he feels inclined to help, and the unsympathetic helper's motive is that someone needs help. If the unsympathetic helper's action is morally worthy while the symnpathetic helper's is not, this can only be because it is the unmet needs of others, and not our own unfulfilled inclinations, which lie behind the duty of beneficence.

The first thing to note about Kant's cases is the oddness of his view of acting from sympathy. To say that someone is sympathetic, I think, is to say that they tend to be vividly aware of the suffering of others, and that they tend to see this suffering not, *a la Sade*, as something to be brought about, but rather as something to be eliminated or avoided. Put another way, they have a vivid awareness of suffering as a reason to help. If this is right, then to act out of sympathy is not generally to take one's *feelings* as a reason to help, but rather to take *suffering* as a reason to help. This is not a direct objection to Kant, who is free to stipulate any conceivable psychology for his particular sympathetic helper. My reason for mentioning this point is that later in this essay, when I attempt to bring out the moral importance of sympathy, I do not wish to be misunderstood as championing the maxim of helping when and only when one feels like it. My point, instead, will be that there is good reason to doubt that Kant's unsympathetic helper could truly be *committed* to the maxim that Kant attributes to him. For in order to be truly committed to helping those when they need it, it would not be enough simply to *avow* a commitment to do so, however sincere that avowal might be; one must also be

---

18 The "second proposition" that Kant attempts to extract from his exemplars of morally worthy actions is this: "An action done from duty has its moral worth, not in the purpose that is to be attained by it, but in the maxim according to which the action is determined." *Groundwork*, Ak. 399.

constituted so as actually to notice the suffering of others and respond to that suffering by attempting to alleviate it. To say that someone is sympathetic is, to my ear, just to say that someone is so constituted.

It is worth noting another oddity—this one in my interpretation of Kant. I have said that the unsympathetic helper's reason for helping is that someone needs help, yet Kant seems to suggest that his reason for helping is that he has a duty to help. Since a maxim is supposed to display one's reason for helping, we might suppose that the unsympathetic helper's maxim is: Whenever it is my duty to help, I will help. There are two problems with this suggestion. The first problem is that this maxim is not stated in terms fit to guide deliberation, since it does not indicate what circumstances might occasion a duty to help. The second, closely related problem is that this maxim could not play one of the key roles which Kant assigns to maxims—that of providing an appropriate input for the universalizability test, which after all is supposed to help us to identify our duties, and not to sanction maxims that direct us to perform independently identifiable duties.

The best way of reconstructing Kant's view, I think, is that typically there are multiple maxims of different orders which guide our actions, and these maxims specify multiple reasons of different depths for the action in question.[19] The unsympathetic helper, then, has multiple reasons for acting as he does. His deepest reason is presumably that the maxim of *not* helping under such circumstances cannot be universalized, hence is contrary to duty. This reason is embedded in the agent's highest-order maxim—a maxim which governs the good-willed agent's acceptance of all other maxims. The highest-order maxim is this: When the maxim of an action cannot be willed as universal law, I will not act on it. This can be rephrased as follows: I will act only on those maxims that

---

19 On this point as on several other interpretive questions, I have taken my bearings from Christine Korsgaard, "Kant's Analysis of Obligation: The Argument of Groundwork I," *Op. Cit.*, p. 58. I believe that the strongest textual evidence for this interpretation is found in *Religion within the Limits of Reason Alone*, where Kant makes clear that maxims are not only adopted but also ordered in a hierarchy of authority, and that the good will is the will that adopts the moral law as its supreme maxim. See Kant, *Religion within the Limits of Reason Alone*, translated by Theodore M. Greene and Hoyt H. Hudson (New York; Harper Torchbooks: 1960), pp. 19–20; 31–32.

can at the same time be willed as universal laws. This is simply the categorical imperative taken up as a subjective principle of volition—that is, as a maxim. And in this maxim, we can see that the deepest motive of the good-willed agent is to act only on lawful maxims, which is just what Kant concludes in the first section of the *Groundwork*.[20]

On the reading I have offered, morally required actions are performed on the motive of duty, hence are morally worthy, whenever the highest-level maxim of the action is the subjective formulation of the categorical imperative. By contrast, one acts from inclination whenever one acts on a maxim that counts the occurrence of any inclination as a necessary condition for choosing the action.[21] One of the principal attractions of this reading is that it leaves room for morally worthy actions which are *accompanied* by an inclination to do them, since one might feel inclined to do one's duty yet choose to do it on principles which would direct one to do the same thing irrespective of one's inclinations.

All else equal, it counts in favor of this interpretation that it leaves room for this class of actions, since Kant dismisses actions accompanied by inclinations from his attention only because it is difficult to tell whether such actions are done from duty. If it is dif-

---

20 *Groundwork*, Ak. 401–2. I have not attempted to reconstruct Kant's derivation of the categorical imperative. That would take us beyond the scope of this paper. I have only reconstructed the maxims of the various figures he discusses in light of his considered views about the moral law.

21 It is not clear to me whether moral worth can be attributed to actions that are permitted but not required by duty. If this is possible, then it seems to me that moral worth would be attributed to such actions only if the inclination to do the action is not regarded as a sufficient condition for performing the action (since permissibility would also have to be taken as a necessary condition). The really complicated case, though, is that of actions which are duties under one description but not under another. For instance, according to Kant I have a duty to develop my talents, but no duty to develop my philosophical talents. Thus, my efforts to develop my philosophical talents are not required by duty, but if I describe these same efforts more generically as efforts to develop my talents, they are required by duty. In this case, I take it, it does not detract from the moral worth of my efforts if I count my inclination to develop my philosophical talent as a necessary condition for deciding to develop this particular talent (rather than some other). However, my efforts to develop my talents lack moral worth if I take any inclination or class of inclinations as a necessary condition for choosing to develop my talents.

ficult to tell, then presumably it is possible for such actions to be done from duty, hence possible for them to have moral worth.[22] But it is one thing for an interpretation to *leave open* the possibility that this class of actions might have moral worth; it is quite another thing to *explain* this possibility in terms consistent with Kant's text.

One initially plausible option is to think of Kant's cases as models of counterfactual tests for the presence of moral worth. The key question, as indicated by these cases, is this: If one found oneself without any inclination to fulfill some duty, would one still fulfill it? If so, then one's dutiful actions can be said to have moral worth, even if one has an inclination to do them. But while this line of interpretation might seem plausible, it fits uneasily with Kant's actual descriptions of the cases. Kant writes that when the previously sympathetic person loses his sympathy and yet continues to act morally, "then for the *first* time his action has genuine moral worth." (my emphasis)[23] He says the same thing of the gout patient who finds himself suddenly without his usual inclination to provide for his future health, yet does so from duty.[24] However, both of these figures have proven to be the sort of people who would continue to do their duty even absent all inclination. So why, if *this* is the test of moral worth, would Kant have held that their previous dutiful actions lacked moral worth?

This question might be answered by reading Kant as simply positing, for the purpose of his cases, that the sympathetically constituted person and the gout sufferer had previously been meeting their duty from inclination. However, this has an odd implication. It means that up until the point at which they were put to the test, they would have failed to do act in conformity with duty if they lost any inclination to do so. Otherwise they would have passed the counterfactual test for moral worth. Yet at the moment Kant describes, in which they actually lost their inclination to act dutifully, they had a sudden change of background commitments such that it became true of them that they would act dutifully even in the absence of any inclination to do so. We must think of Kant's

---

22 *Ibid.*, Ak. 397. This point is made by Henry E. Allison in *Kant's Theory of Freedom* (Cambridge; Cambridge University Press: 1990), p. 111.
23 *Groundwork*, Ak. 398.
24 *Ibid.*, Ak. 399.

cases precisely as not revealing how these same people would have acted at any earlier point in their lives, had they lost their inclination to do their duty then. On this interpretation of the text, it seems a glaring omission that Kant makes no reference to any sudden moral conversion.

A second interpretive strategy is to reject the notion that moral worth can be understood in terms of what one would do in a time-extended range of counterfactual circumstances, and to trace it instead to an ordinarily inscrutable fact about the action at hand— namely, the highest-level maxim governing the choice of the action.[25] This interpretation is also subject to a serious difficulty, arising from the very notion of action on a maxim. A maxim is the subjective principle according to which one acts. Now, we ordinarily tend to use diachronic criteria for attributing principles to agents. We are prone to reject the notion that someone acted yesterday on a given principle if that same person's actions two days ago and again today are clearly at odds with the same principle. We attribute principles to people in order to codify what they stand ready to take as reasons for action—that is, in order to codify their evaluative commitments—and we do this by identifying the general patterns of their actions over time. It is because we attribute principles of action in this way that we are prone to think that the sympathetic person who finds himself without his previous sympathy, who yet dutifully helps another, must all along have accepted the principle of helping others irrespective of inclination.[26]

The present interpretation suggests that the maxim or principle of an action is an entirely synchronic fact, contemporaneous with the action, and that we are constrained to use an inferior set of diachronic indicators only because this synchronic fact (i.e. the

---

25 Barbara Herman favors this interpretation of Kant. See Herman, "On the Value of Acting from the Motive of Duty," in *The Practice of Moral Judgment* (Cambridge; Harvard University Press: 1993), pp. 1–22; especially pp. 18–21.
26 One might object that this is an overly third-personal view of principled action, and that from the first-person point of view we have purely synchronic criteria for the principles on which we act. While there is something to this suggestion, it is not one that Kant could have adopted, since he held that actual motives cannot reliably be identified even in the first-person case, and in Religion within the Limits of Reason Alone, he claimed that the best indication we can have of the actual maxims of our is our entire personal history of action. See Kant, Religion..., Op. Cit., p. 71.

actual highest-level motive for the action) is opaque to us. This suggestion seems to me misguided, for the reasons I suggested in he previous paragraph. Having a principle is in a certain key respect akin to being reliable. It would be odd to say of something that it was reliable for but a single moment, and unreliable before and after that moment. In order to make such a claim, we would have to explain the changes which ushered in and ended this moment of reliability, and there are precious few such explanations which would not call into question the thing's reliability. It is even odder to say of a person, "She has only been a reliable promise-keeper on several isolated occasions." In the case of personal reliability, it is dubious that there are any changes which could usher in and end discrete moments of reliability without calling into question the person's reliability. And just as a person or thing cannot be deemed reliable on a smattering of isolated instances, so an agent cannot act on a principle on sporadic occasions. To act in this way is simply to be unprincipled.[27] This helps to show why the counterfactual analysis of moral worth is philosophically attractive in the first place.

Even if we could make philosophical sense of this second analysis of moral worth, it would not clear up all of the interpretive difficulties with Kant's examples. The trouble is that this interpretation would give us no good reason to suppose that the sympathetic helper is not helping from duty, since the highest-level maxim structuring his will could be the subjective version of the categorical imperative. Here again, it is hard to see why Kant would have asserted, without further explanation, that this person's actions for the first time take on moral worth when he ceases to feel any inclination to help. It begins to seem that we must either read this as a mistake, or attribute to Kant the implausible view that dutiful actions accompanied by supporting inclinations must lack moral worth.

This leads to another interpretive question. On Kant's view, we can never actually know an action to have moral worth, since we

27 It is perhaps true that Kant did not think of the principles of practical judgment in this way. One of the perplexities of thinking of practical judgment as absolutely spontaneous, hence entirely unbound by all prior determinants, is that it seems at least conceptually possible for an agent to act on a new principle with each new action. This seems to me an affront to the notion of principled action.

can never know the fundamental motives even of our own will, much less of the wills of others. We can only have this knowledge with regard to hypothetical actions like those represented by the *Groundwork* cases, which are spun from an omniscient vantage point on human motivation. This suggests that the evaluative category of moral worth cannot be the central moral standard to which we hold others in our actual evaluations of them, for although we may have persuasive reasons for believing moral worth to be absent, we can never know it to be present. And this is a congenial suggestion, since it seems at least churlish if not downright offensive to preoccupy ourselves with the motivational purity of others, especially when their actions conform with duty. However, our moral assessment of the dutiful actions of others *does* seem to *shift* when we imagine ourselves to have normally unavailable insights into motivations. To what, then, do we owe our evident familiarity with this sort of moral assessment?

I think there is a persuasive answer to this question: our familiarity with this sort of assessment stems from the domain of self-evaluation. While we cannot know even in our own case that our actions have moral worth, we do have greater insight into our own motivations than into the motivations of others. To this extent we are in a better position to identify instances in which we do our duty from inclination and not from duty. More importantly, the Kantian agent has good reason to attempt to assess the purity of her own motivations. In Kant's view, "the first command of all duties to oneself"[28] is to know oneself, and this requires that we seek to "...penetrate into the depths (the abyss) of one's heart that are quite difficult to fathom..."[29] From this first command follows the requirement of "...uprightness in confessing one's inner moral worth or lack thereof...."[30] This suggests the following answer to the difficulty at hand: we owe our grasp of moral worth, and our familiarity with the omniscient viewpoint from which it can be discerned, to our concern with the purity of our commitment to morality. In other words, we owe it to our moral conscience. We do not actually enjoy this omniscience even with respect to our own motivations, but our pursuit of our own moral perfection requires us to approximate it as nearly as possible, and hence

---

28 *The Metaphysics of Morals*, Ak. 441.
29 *Ibid.*
30 *Ibid.*, Ak. 441–2.

familiarizes us with this perspective as a constitutive element of our actual ideal of moral self-knowledge.[31]

It strikes me as intuitively plausible to suppose that the proper place for a concern for motivational purity is in the domain of self-evaluation. I would add, though, that this concern might also have a proper place in the evaluation of intimates—in particular that class of intimates whose moral education and development is in some significant measure our responsibility or concern. I will return to this point in later chapters.

PART III: MORAL WORTH AND VIRTUE

While moral worth is not our central concern in our moral evaluations of others, it seems clear to me that it *is* a central element of Kant's moral theory. As I understand it, Kant conceives of moral worth as virtuous character manifest in action. Now, some Kant scholars have insisted that Kant's conceptions of moral worth and virtue must be more sharply differentiated than this. They argue that moral worth is a property of single actions while virtue is an attribute of an enduring character, and they deny that morally worthy action presupposes a virtuous character. After all, this line of interpretation continues, even the most vicious and self-interested person might on a single occasion act from duty, and Kant would be bound to grant that this action had moral worth, but he would hardly be bound to call the person virtuous.[32] Why, then, do I reject this interpretation?[33]

---

31 I believe that this helps to illuminate Kant's claim that the idea of God as a scrutinizer of hearts is always contained, even if only obscurely, in the moral conscience. See *The Metaphysics of Morals*, Ak. 439.

32 Christine Korsgaard has objected to the present paper on this interpretive ground. Barbara Herman also favors this interpretation. See "On the Value of Acting from the Motive of Duty," in The Practice of Moral Judgment , Op. Cit., p. 13n.

33 There is one immediate reason for doubting this interpretation, which I will not pursue. It is that Kant sometimes refers not only to actions but to persons as having moral worth. This has been noted by several interpreters, including Karl Ameriks and Keith Simmons. It can be seen, among other places, in the following passage drawn from Kant's assessment of the constitutionally unsympathetic individual who acts beneficently:

> ...would he not yet find in himself a source from which he might give himself a worth far higher than any that a good-

We have seen that dutiful actions have moral worth when their highest-level maxim is the moral law, expressed as a subjective principle of volition (i.e. I will act only on those maxims that I can at the same time will to be universal laws). Now, Kant writes that his entire discussion of morally worthy action is meant to serve as an elucidation of the good will and its unconditional value.[34] It is natural to suppose, then, that morally worthy actions are particularly clear manifestations of goodness of will. This makes sense, since for Kant the good will is the one that adopts the moral law as its supreme maxim, and this is precisely the precondition for morally worthy action. But this implies either that morally worthy actions are particularly clear manifestations of virtuous character, as I believe, or that virtuous character is something quite different from goodness of will.

There is considerable evidence that at least in the case of humans, Kant simply equates goodness of will with virtuousness of character.[35] Kant opens the first section of the *Groundwork* by asserting that the good will is the only thing we can conceive of that is good unconditionally, and that it is the condition of the value of all other human goods, and even of happiness.[36] In the second section of the *Groundwork*, Kant equates virtue with "the morally good disposition," and maintains that it has "dignity"— which Kant defines as "unconditional and incomparable worth."[37] Since Kant maintains that the good will is the only conceivable thing that has unconditional worth, he must equate goodness of will and virtue. Again, Kant maintains in the *Second*

---

natured temperament might have? By all means, because just here does *the worth of the character* come out: this worth is moral and incomparably the highest of all, viz., that he is beneficent, not from inclination, but from duty. (*Groundwork*, Ak. 398–9; emphasis mine.)

For further discussion, see Karl Ameriks, "Kant on the Good Will," in ed. Ottfried Hoffe, *Grundlegung zur Metaphysik der Sitten: Eine Kooperativer Kommentar* (Frankfurt; Vittorio Klostermann: 1989), pp. 45–65. See also Keith Simmons, "Kant on Moral Worth," *Op. Cit.*, p. 88.

34 Groundwork, Ak. 397.

35 This equation does not hold for all rational beings, since virtue is possible (and morally necessary) only for those rational beings who must overcome resistance from the inclinations in order to conform their will to the demands of morality.

36 *Groundwork*, Ak. 393.

37 *Ibid.*, Ak. 435–6.

Critique that virtue is the unconditional good, and that it is the condition of the goodness of all other human goods, including even happiness.[38] This precisely what he says of goodness of will in the first section of the *Groundwork*.

Still another confirmation of my interpretation can be found late in the *Second Critique*, where Kant writes, "I have said above that in the mere course of nature happiness exactly proportionate to moral worth is not to be expected and is indeed impossible and that therefore the possibility of the highest good from this side cannot be granted except under the presupposition of a moral Author of the world."[39] Now Kant has earlier identified the highest good as perfect virtue conjoined with perfect happiness, and thus it seems that he is here equating moral worth with virtue. For those interpreters who think of moral worth as a property only of actions and never of persons, and who insist that morally worthy actions do not necessarily indicate a virtuous character, this passage remains highly perplexing. On my interpretation, it is precisely what one would expect Kant to say.

There is yet another piece of powerful textual evidence for my interpretation in the "Methodology of Pure Practical Reason"— the final section of the *Second Critique*, in which Kant outlines the appropriate method of expounding morality to youths in order to secure their attachment to the moral law. Here Kant maintains that the appropriate procedure is to present youths with an "exhibition of pure virtue,"[40] and this is precisely what he goes on to present. He does this by devising an example of an action in which "the distinctive mark of pure virtue" is particularly evident, and can be

---

38 Immanuel Kant, *Critique of Practical Reason*, translated by Lewis Beck White (New York; MacMillan Publishing Company; 1956), Ak. 110–111.

39 *Ibid.*, Ak. 145.

40 The relevant passage reads: "Now it is clear that those grounds of determination of the will, the direct thought of the law and objective obedience to it as duty, which alone make the maxims really moral and give them a moral worth, must be thought of as the real incentive of actions, for otherwise legality of actions but not morality of intentions would result. But it is not so clear—in fact, it must appear highly improbably at first glance—that even subjectively the exhibition of pure virtue can have more power over the human mind ... than all allurements arising from enjoyment and everything which may be counted as happiness or from all threats of pain and harm. But it is really so..." (*Critique of Practical Reason*, Ak. 151–2; emphasis added)

41 Kant, *Critique of Practical Reason*, Ak. 155.

pointed out even to a boy of ten years of age.[41] The example is almost precisely the sort of case of morally worthy action that Kant uses in the *Groundwork* to illuminate the concept of the good will. It is a case of dutiful action chosen in the face of powerful temptations to violate one's duty, and it displays the purity of the agent's will precisely by stripping away any possible incentive to act morally which might be counted as a part of his happiness.[42] Here we get a very clear indication that Kant thinks that only the virtuous agent could possibly act in a morally worthy way, so that moral worth is indeed properly conceived of as virtue in action.

Having seen the textual basis for asserting that moral worth is virtue in action, it remains to be seen *why* they are related in this way. In numerous passages, Kant conceives of virtue as the strength of the will's attachment to the moral law which permits one to "overcome the vice-breeding inclinations" insofar as they conflict with duty.[43] Morally worthy actions manifest precisely this power of the rational will to affirm the supreme authority of the moral law and to act in accordance with desires only on the condition that such action is morally permissible. Given this, it seems to me that one could only insist that a non-virtuous person could perform a morally worthy action if one believed that one could momentarily make the categorical imperative one's highest-level principle of action.

When we attend to the actual limitations of human moral assessments, we can see that we would not actually attribute moral worth to any dutiful action that was isolated and entirely uncharacteristic. The best indication we can actually have of the principles on which an agent actually acts is the characteristic behavior of the agent. At least in his late moral writings, Kant explicitly acknowledges this point even in the first-person case. In *Religion within the Limits of Reason Alone*, he traces the worth of one's character to the relatively priority that one gives to the two principles which compete for dominance in one's willful decisions: the principle of self-love and the moral principle. Kant writes that when the individual examines his life to determine what he may hope for or fear at life's close, "...he can form no certain and defi-

42 Kant, *Critique of Practical Reason*, Ak. 156.
43 The quoted passage is found in the Metaphysics of Morals, Ak. 376. For other relevant passages, see the *Critique of Practical Reason*, Ak. 118 and the *Metaphysics of Morals*, Ak. 376, 380, 394, 397 and 405.

nite conception of his real disposition through an immediate consciousness thereof and can only abstract it from the way of life he has actually followed."[44] In particular, he must examine his *actions* in order to identify the fundamental disposition of his will. Thus, to the extent that judgments of moral worth figure at all into our actual judgments, we would not assign moral worth to the actions of anyone who characteristically displays a disregard for moral principles. We would only assign moral worth to the actions of those whom we take to be virtuous; conversely, we would not judge anyone to be virtuous if we believe that they ordinarily act from inclination (where, as specified above, this means that they take some inclination as a necessary condition for fulfilling their duty). Thus, the imagined conflict will not arise in any case that respects the epistemic limits which constrain human moral assessment.

Still, a critic of my position might continue, we can *imagine* a person who acts from duty but is not characteristically committed to moral principles, and this shows that the two ideas are conceptually distinct. I indicated above why I do not think that this objection is persuasive. We will only recognize the possibility of such a case if we can imagine ourselves acting on a principle only once, then so to speak discarding it. I argued above that this is simply too whimsical to count as the adoption of a principle. In adopting a practical principle, an agent accepts the principle as an authoritative guide to action in some range of relevantly similar cases. I do not know what momentary and immediately canceled mental event could count as the acceptance of the authority of a principle.[45] If there were such a mental event, then it would seem at least conceivable that we could change principles with each new act. For humorous effect, we might perhaps imagine an agent adopting new principles of action at every turn and gravely attempting to ferret out their practical implications, only to abandon them in the

---

44 Kant, *Religion within the Limits of Reason Alone*, Op. Cit., p. 71.
45 Here I am in agreement with Marcia Baron, who argues that actions have moral worth only if they are done from a commitment to moral principles, and that such a commitment must endure over time, showing up not only in one's characteristic actions but also in one's reflections and one's readiness to revise one's beliefs, plans and aims in light of these reflections. See Baron, "The Alleged Moral Repugnance of Acting from Duty," in *The Journal of Philosophy*, Vol. LXXXI, No. 4, April 1984.

next moment. This, however, would be a burlesque of the life of principle and not a portrait of a principled agent.

If we imagine our case differently, so that the morally worthy action of the characteristically vicious person really does stem from an earnest, wholehearted resolution to regulate future actions in accordance with moral principles, then it does not seem nearly so odd to say that this first morally worthy action marks a deep moral conversion, and that the formerly vicious person has become virtuous in the moment of his first morally worthy action. If we follow Kant in conceiving of virtue as the strength of will needed to determine the will to action as morality requires, even in the face of resistance from the inclinations, then this will seem like a very natural thing to say.

As I see it, Kant's own position on these matters changed over time. However, neither of the views that I find in Kant's post-*Groundwork* writings seems to me to lend support to the objection I have been considering. In *Anthropology from a Pragmatic Point of View*, Kant seeks to distinguish between having a character and having character *tout court*. He explains, ". . .if we say that [someone] has character simply, then we mean the property of will by which he binds himself to definite practical principles that he has prescribed to himself irrevocably by his own reason."[46] Kant proceeds to trace the attainment of character to a definite biographical moment (one that rarely precedes the 30th birthday) in which one makes a silent vow to regulate one's actions in accordance with moral principles. This new commitment may not be firmly consolidated for many years (it is rarely consolidated before the 40th birthday, Kant says). However, if the vow is made with due solemnity, it immediately effects a "rebirth" or "revolution" in which one acquires moral character.[47] This same rebirth cannot be effected by any less solemn or more piecemeal commitment to moral principles. This suggests that the first morally worthy action of the formerly vicious person must mark the moment of a revolutionary reform of character. If it did not, then this could only be because his commitment to moral principles is incomplete or piecemeal, and thus that he would not have taken himself to have rea-

---

46 Kant, *Anthropology from a Pragmatic Point of View*, translated by
  Mary J. Gregor (The Hague; Martinus Nijhoff: 1974), Ak. 292.
47 *Ibid.*, Ak. 294.

son to do his duty under some conceivable circumstance. In that case, we could not exhaustively characterize his reasoning by saying that he chose the action because it was his duty; we must add that other conditions were also met. This means that, contrary to supposition, his action lacked moral worth.

In the *Anthropology* passage cited above, Kant conceives of "character" as something that originates in a temporal act and that can be consolidated in biographical time. We may doubt whether Kant would really equate this attainment with virtue, since in other works Kant speaks of virtue as a continual *progressus* towards an ideal endpoint that can never be attained. Kant puts it as follows:

> Virtue is always *in progress* and yet always starts *from the beginning*. It is always in progress because, considered *objectively*, it is an ideal and unattainable, while yet constant approximation to it is a duty. That it always starts from the beginning has a subjective basis in human nature, which is affected by inclinations because of which virtue can never settle down in peace and quiet with its maxims adopted once and for all but, if it is not rising, is unavoidably sinking.[48]

On this view, it is an illusion to see virtue as an enduring state of our temporal or worldly character. Virtue is an ideal that remains forever beyond our reach, and none of us exemplify that ideal. Our duty is to reestablish our progress towards virtue with each successive act, presumably by a fresh apprehension of the authority of moral principles and by a fresh humiliation of the competing principle of self-love (i.e. the principle that takes one's own inclinations as all-things-considered reasons for action). On this view, it does seem possible to imagine an isolated action of true moral worth. What does not seem possible is to attribute such an action to a vicious person. This is because insofar as the notions of virtue and vice are applied to humans at all, they are not to be thought of as enduring states of character, but as instantaneous vectors of direction in a progression or a regression. To borrow Kant's metaphor from the above-quoted passage, the person who performs a morally worthy action is "rising" towards the ideal of virtue from the "beginning" at which we all start in each of our actions. This means that either virtue is never exhibited by humans, or it is exhibited in all and only morally worthy acts.

---

48 Kant, *The Metaphysics of Morals*, Ak. 409.

PART IV: SPECIFYING OUR RESERVATION ABOUT KANT'S CASES

Let me now put aside the interpretive questions that I have been pursuing, and turn to an evaluation of what I take to be the central message of Kant's cases. Kant's claim is that the unsympathetic helper, and others who do their duty in the absence of any inclination to do so, provide us with a particularly clear view of the true source of moral worth. The true source of moral worth is a commitment of the will to the moral law, where this commitment is understood as a capacity of the will to determine itself to dutiful action even when the inclinations are in revolt. Thus, while the actions of these figures may be lacking in *other* sorts of values— for example, in aesthetic or prudential value—they display all the *moral* value that an action can have.

This central claim has a certain intuitive appeal, which might be traced to our awareness that those who act in accordance with duty only because they are inclined to do so cannot be counted on to do their duty when they are not so inclined. Their dutiful actions do not manifest any real attachment to duty; rather, they signal a contingent overlap between what they want and what duty requires. The figures in which Kant locates moral worth also have a more direct or intrinsic appeal. They demonstrate an admirable strength of character. To my lights, this is particularly true of the first of Kant's two unsympathetic benefactors—the woe-struck friend of mankind. Since his lack of sympathy can be traced to his misfortunes, we are tempted to trace his lack of fellow feeling to external causes, and not view it as characteristic of him. We might fear, or know, that we too would lack sympathy for others if our own circumstances were difficult and our own prospects bleak. Given these considerations, we might view his case as analogous to other cases of people who navigate adversity with self-control, if not exactly with grace.

At the same time, we are likely to have the persistent sense that there is something unappealing about Kant's unsympathetic benefactors. This sense is, I think, particularly cogent in the case of the *constitutionally* unsympathetic benefactor, partly because his lack of sympathy cannot so easily be seen as the result of a merely contingent misfortune, but stems instead from an enduring character trait. Still, we may wonder whether our reservations about this figure are really *moral*. Our judgment might, for instance, be merely aesthetic—e.g. we might be put off by a certain stiffness and severity that mars his interpersonal dealings. This might lead us to conclude that he is an unattractive person, someone we would not want to befriend, but this judgment might imply no moral reproach.

Along these lines, Kant sometimes speaks of the social graces such as courtesy, gentleness and affability (which Kant also calls by the Latin *humanitas aesthetica*, suggesting that it includes an affective attachment to other humans), as the proper garb for virtue.[49] Though these social graces are not properly part of virtue, still they make virtue attractive and promote a feeling for it. As such, the social graces have a derivative moral value, and we have a duty to associate them with virtue.[50] This value owes to the fragility of real human virtue, for presumably it is because the hold of the moral law on humans is tenuous that it must be bolstered by what Kant calls the "beautiful illusion resembling virtue"[51] that attends the social graces. Still, we have here the seeds of a Kantian account of our persistent sense that there is something morally amiss with the constitutionally unsympathetic benefactor. If we think of him as lacking the social grace of affability that helps to make virtuous action attractive to humans, then we can make a certain kind of moral objection to him on purely Kantian grounds. The objection is that his insensibility gives to his virtuous action an unattractive garb, and hence makes virtue itself unattractive to our eyes. This provides a possible explanation of our reservations about Kant's cases, and it is perfectly consistent with his central claim. For presumably it is only insofar as we have not discerned, or do not properly attend to, "virtue in her proper form" (i.e. virtue stripped of all sensuous adornment)[52] that our attachment to morality must be secured by beautiful illusions. When we begin to engage in moral philosophy, we must purge these illusions from our minds—and this is just what the opening of the *Groundwork* aims to do.

As I said, this seems to me to offer an interesting Kantian

---

49 Kant makes this point in several places. See e.g. *The Metaphysics of Morals*, Ak. 473–4 and *Anthropology from a Pragmatic Point of View*, Ak. 282.
50 Kant, *The Metaphysics of Morals*, Ak. 473.
51 *Ibid.*
52 Kant, *Groundwork*, Ak. 426n.

incorporation of the intuitions that I have been attempting to tweak. (I will consider the adequacy of this and other Kantian responses to these intuitive objections in the next chapter.) However, I wish to argue for a different interpretation of our sense of these figures as unappealing—an interpretation under which this persistent sense *does* present a *prima-facie* problem for the beginnings of Kant's theory-building in the *Groundwork*. The interpretation is this: we sense that these figures do not fully recognize the worth of those whom they are helping. It is true that they offer one very important sort of recognition: they take the needs and interests of others as reasons for action. But there is a further kind of recognition—a more full-blooded varietal—that they do not extend. This further stretch consists precisely in sympathy, understood as a tendency to take pleasure in the good of others and to be pained by their misfortunes.[53] For the unsympathetic helper portrayed by Kant, the prospect of attaining another's good is not as such pleasant. In fact, it is just this feature of the case that permits it to serve Kant's purposes of illuminating the operation of the moral incentive by stripping away all possible sensuous motivations.

On Kant's moral theory, what the moral law requires of us is that we acknowledge the equal worth of all rational beings as ends in themselves.[54] To value a person as an end in him/herself is to recognize that the person has the standing to confer value on oth-

---

53 This is not precisely what Kant means by 'sympathy.' Kant (and Hume before him) characterized sympathy as a susceptibility to feeling the pleasures and pains that are actually felt by others. This seems to be a mischaracterization of sympathy. As Derek Parfit has pointed out to me, a surgeon might remain sympathetic even though he has numbed himself to the pains of his patients, and even if he has learned to inflict pain without recoiling. It seems to me that Kant would be forced to deny that such a doctor remains sympathetic, since he is not receptive to the contagion of his patient's pleasures and pains. On Kant's view, the doctor should be described as someone who has overcome his sympathetic feelings in order to increase his rational control over his actions, thus increasing his capacity to further the good of others. It seems to me, however, that Parfit's benumbed doctor does exhibit sympathetic, provided that he is pleased by the real long-term good of his patients, and pained by real harms to others.

54 As is well known, the categorical imperative can be formulated as the requirement that we act in such a way as to treat rational nature, whether in ourselves or in others, always at the same time as an end in itself and never merely as a means. (See *Groundwork*, Ak. 429.)

erwise indifferent ends simply by adopting these ends. In order to make sense of the notion that one has reason to pursue one's ends, one has to view oneself as having this standing. Kant argues that since all other rational beings have equally persuasive grounds for viewing themselves as having this standing, we must recognize that the attainment of the ends of others is every bit as important as the attainment of our own ends. What this implies, according to Kant, is that we have a duty to adopt the happiness of others as our end, and to contribute to the fulfillment of those of their particular aims which we agree would contribute to their happiness.[55] This we must do if we are to recognize others as having the same intrinsic value that we must think of ourselves as having.

What I wish to argue, then, is that to *recognize* another as having equal moral standing requires that we ordinarily experience the successful attainment of their ends as pleasurable and the frustration of their ends as painful, at least insofar as we think that the attainment of their ends really would count as a constitutive part of their happiness.[56] Here, I am using 'recognition' to refer to an awareness that is quite direct, almost perceptual, and not to a conscious cognitive judgment. Kantian judgment is, in general, a matter of taking something as something else.[57] In Kant's view, one recognizes another by taking the other to have a certain kind of worth or standing. This recognition consists negatively in restricting one's own actions so as not to interfere with their rights; more positively, it consists in taking their aims as reasons for action. I think that the difficulty with the cases under consideration stems from our sense that when we take someone as valuable in the same way that we are valuable, our sentiments cannot be unmoved by their successes and failures. There is an intimate link—a link that I will explore and attempt to specify more completely in the course of this thesis—between taking the fulfillment of their aims as something valuable or good, and being pleased by it.

Here I am drawing upon the idea that pleasure is a kind of perception of goodness. I follow Christine Korsgaard in taking this to

---

55 *Metaphysics of Morals*, Ak. 388.
56 This slightly complicated rider must be attached, since we need not revel in the satisfaction of the cravings of the drug addict, or in the satisfaction of other desires that we judge to be self-destructive, in order to manifest a commitment to the furtherance of the happiness of another.
57 Allison, *Op. Cit.*, pp. 36–41.

be Aristotle's view of pleasure, and also in singling this out as a key point of disagreement between Kant and Aristotle.[58] Of course, I do not wish to rule out the possibility that one might not take pleasure in something, and hence might not in this sense perceive it as good, yet might still judge it to be good. There are all sorts of instances in which we correct, in our all-things-considered judgments, for what we take to be distortions or illusions in our perceptions, and there is no reason why perceptions of goodness should not also be viewed as fallible. What I do wish to claim is that we have not fully digested the judgment that some state of affairs is good—we have not reconceived the world in line with this judgment, and hence have not solidified our belief in it—until we have come to take pleasure in the state of affairs in question. I do not deny that we can give a full account of what it means to take other persons as sources of value, on an equal footing with ourselves, purely in terms of our willful decisions and the evaluative judgments implicit in them. My objection, which is developed in detail in the next chapter, is that we cannot identify the evaluative judgments implicit in our willful decisions without reference to our characteristic sentiments and desires.

Korsgaard holds that the differing views of pleasure in Kant and Aristotle mark a disagreement only in their views of moral psychology and not in their "basic *ethical* outlooks."[59] I believe that the difference is more fundamental than this would suggest. As I see it, the difference is best spelled out in terms of differing conceptions of moral commitment. The question, I think, is whether moral commitment can be understood purely in terms of the principles which determine the practical judgment which immediately precedes and leads to an action, or whether our standing affects and inclinations are partially constitutive of our practical commitments. I wish to argue that if a principle carries conviction—if we are really committed to it—then it must be embodied not only in our actions but also in our characteristic sentimental reactions and in our mode of discerning the social world around us.

This sheds further light on the claim I made above that we

---

58 See Christine M. Korsgaard, "From Duty and for the Sake of the Noble: Kant and Aristotle on Morally Good Action" in *Aristotle, Kant and the Stoics: Rethinking Happiness and Duty*, edited by Stephen Engstrom and Jennifer Whiting (Cambridge; Cambridge University Press: 1996), pp. 203–236, especially pp. 223–227.

59 *Ibid.*, pp. 2 and 19.

cannot hold a principle fleetingly. One might think that this limitation arises because we only attribute principles where we see
long-term regularities in action, and this indeed may be part of the
logic of our talk of principles. However, this holds not only for
attributions of practical principles but also for attributions of
other sorts of principles, including those principles of physics
which govern events in the natural world. The particular distinction of practical principles is that they are in some sense *the agent's
own*—they define a mode of self-control or self-governance. This
seems to me to lead to a more fundamental reason why practical
principles cannot be held fleetingly: we do not *hold* a principle as
our own unless our fundamental character has been made or
remade in line with it, at least to some considerable extent.

As I see it, Kant's conception of autonomous action, and his
equation of autonomy and morality, prompt him to understand
moral commitment entirely in terms of the governing principles of
the will. I do not wish to deny this so much as to call into question
Kant's conception of the boundaries of the will. If we conceive of
the will in the broadest sense, so that it embraces all those elements
of one's mental life which determine one's practical commitments,
then this is perfectly correct. This is the conception of the boundaries of the will, and also of the boundaries of the domain of the
morally assessible, that I favor and will argue for.[60]

This critique of Kant is broadly Aristotelian. As I see it,
Aristotle conceives of feelings of pleasure themselves as partial
embodiments, or revelations, of our evaluative commitments.
This is why our dispositions to feel pleasure and pain are con-
stituents of the moral virtues and hence of moral perfection. This
means that the Aristotelian and the Kantian differ in their under-
standings of what would have to be true of someone in order to
justify the claim that they assign value to something, that they
count it as good. It also suggests that the Aristotelian account of

---

60 I believe that Philippa Foot has something like this conception of the
will in mind when she maintains that the virtues are properties of the
will, where 'will is "understood in its widest sense, to cover what is
wished for as well as what is sought." Foot goes on to note that
wishes and wants are part of the will, hence morally assessable only
if they manifest the values of the agent. I accept and attempt to
develop this point in this and subsequent chapters. See Foot,
"Virtues and Vices" in *Virtues and Vices* (Oxford: Blackwell; 1978),
pp. 1–18, especially p. 5.

moral perfection will contain character requirements which Kant would deem extraneous to morality, since these character traits are beyond our voluntary control. I will argue that the Kantian notion of moral character ought to be expanded in order to encompass these Aristotelian insights concerning the affects. As I see matters, we cannot accept the Aristotelian conception of pleasure without giving up one of two Kantian doctrines: the doctrine that the moral law is the law of autonomy, or the doctrine that autonomy can be conceived purely in terms of the principles that govern our voluntary willing. I will argue in succeeding chapters that the Kantian ought to reject this latter doctrine, and that this leads to a revisionist Kantianism that preserves the equation of the moral and the autonomous, and that contains a more plausible conception of moral virtue than is normally associated with Kant.

On an intuitive level, this interpretation of our reservation about Kant's cases helps to account for our sense that there is something amiss about the help of those who find no pleasure in helping us but do so because they believe it to be their duty. Since there is an affective element to true commitment to (moral) principles, there is reason to doubt that their action really is motivated by a commitment to the moral law, which after all entails full recognition of the equal moral standing of others. Their help carries a trace of condescension—a suggestion that they think themselves above our predicament.[61] I think that this is particularly tempting as a way of viewing the second unsympathetic benefactor—the one who is constitutionally inured to the sufferings of others. It seems to me no accident that as soon as Kant attempts to tell a plausible story of this person's psychology, he is pressed to the idea of a person who approves of stoicism and who "expects or even requires" the same of others.[62] This suggests that in helping others, he treats them in a way that he would not wish to be

---

61 I am not suggesting that we actually do size up the motives of all those who offer us help, much less that we ought to. Kant's cases require a greater abstraction from our actual moral reactions and assessments, since they presuppose an omniscience about motives that we do not enjoy even with respect to ourselves. I find that I can produce the intuition that I offer here only by imagining the benefactor telling me to my face that he intends to help me only because duty requires it of him, and perhaps adding that he strongly desires not to help me.

62 *Groundwork*, Ak. 398.

treated, and implicitly exempts others from his normal expectations or requirements. There is, to my ear, more than a hint here of what Nietzsche would call mercy (to distinguish it from the pity that he found so distasteful or unmanly), where mercy is the luxury of the powerful, expressing a consciousness of their superior power and hence announcing or reconfirming an inequality between themselves and those who need and accept their mercy.

Kant offers only a measured praise of this constitutionally unsympathetic benefactor: he "would truly not be nature's worse product."[63] This is hardly a recommendation that anyone aspire to be like this person (though elsewhere Kant characterizes sympathy as a mixed blessing that the true sage might wish to dispense with, since it clouds moral judgment[64]). And in his later writings, Kant evidenced a nuanced awareness that beneficence can create damaging inequalities in human relations.[65] Still, Kant's claim in the passages we have been examining is that the unsympathetic

---

63 *Ibid.*

64 See for instance *Anthropology from a Pragmatic Point of View, Op Cit.*, Ak. 253 (section 75). Kant here maintains that the Stoics were correct in their contention that apathy is the proper mental state of the sage, since all emotional agitation—even sympathetic sorrow over the misfortunes of one's best friend—interfere with sound practical deliberation. (Note that in the same passage, Kant offers a measured praise of sympathy, which he characterizes as a gift of nature that gives provisional moral guidance until reason has achieved the necessary strength to take the reins.)
See also *Critique of Practical Reason*, Ak. 118. Here Kant writes: "Even the feeling of sympathy and warm-hearted fellow feeling, when preceding the determination of what is duty and serving as a determining ground, is burdensome even to right-thinking persons, confusing their considered maxims and creating the wish to be free from them and subject only to law-giving reasons."

65 Kant held that the true friend of mankind is distinguished not only by his affective (*asthetisch*) interest in the well-being of others, by virtue of which he shares in their joys and sorrows, but also by his active concern for the equality of men, which leads him to conceive of himself as *obligated to others* by his own beneficent deeds. Otherwise, his help might be thought to create special obligations owed particularly to him—obligations which, because they are owed uniquely to him, upset the rightful equality of persons. (*The Metaphysics of Morals*, Ak. 472–3.) Kant also traces the great fragility of perfect friendship (i.e. perfect, hence equal, mutual love and respect) in part to the inequalities in respect that are necessarily introduced when one friend helps the other in need and hence obligates him, while the other is unable to offer reciprocal help and hence to maintain an equal balance of obligations. (*Metaphysics of Morals*, Ak. 470–1.)

benefactor's action displays the full measure of moral worth, and I believe there is reason to doubt this.

If I am correct in maintaining that there is some stretch of recognition of the worth of others which the unsympathetic benefactor does not extend, then this is potentially very troubling for Kant. Kantian ethics is built upon the recognition of the worth of self and other rational beings. For Kant, to act dutifully is to give practical recognition of that worth, and violations of duty are practical denials of that worth. If the Kantian conception of moral worth leaves out preconditions for the full recognition of the worth of another, then it requires some sort of supplementation.

I have already suggested, and will go on to argue further, that what is called for is a reconsideration of the Kantian limitation of the domain of moral assessment to the principles implicit in willful decision. But one might accept that there is some stretch of recognition that actual unsympathetic benefactors generally do not extend, yet trace this to ordinary empirical correlations between the will's principles, on the one hand, and characteristic affects and inclinations, on the other. There are numerous passages in Kant's later writings that suggest this sort of response to the difficulties I have been pressing. There are also some extremely intriguing passages that seem to count certain standing sentiments as preconditions of real commitment to the moral law, and hence seem to contradict the *Groundwork* view of moral worth. I will examine these passages in the next chapter, after having set the stage for them by showing more clearly what lacuna they must fill.

PART V: RECASTING THE *GROUNDWORK* CASES

I do not expect that the argument I have given to this point will prove convincing to all readers. However, I believe that I can make the same point more forcefully by recasting Kant's cases in a way that it might seem Kant would have to accept.

Broadly speaking, Kant's cases can be characterized as follows: they are all cases of dutiful action performed without any support from the inclinations. This sort of action can be imagined in two importantly different ways: first, one might *have* strong inclinations to *violate* one's duty; and second, one might simply *lack* any inclination to *fulfill* one's duty. Notably, Kant portrays the morally worthy fulfillment of duties to oneself in the first way, and the morally worthy fulfillment of duties to others in the second way. Thus, when Kant attempts to portray a person who preserves his own life from duty, he imagines a man so beset by adversity and sorrow as to wish for death (hence presumably to want to kill himself), who yet preserves his life from duty.[66] Similarly, when he portrays a person who provides for his own happiness from duty, he imagines a gout sufferer who is strongly inclined to secure some immediate pleasure which would interfere with the recovery of his health.[67] By contrast, when Kant considers the morally worthy fulfillment of duties to others, he focuses on cases marked by a simple absence of inclinations to do what duty requires.

As I have tried to show, Kant holds in the *Groundwork* that all dutiful actions which are done from duty have moral worth, and that their moral worth consists solely in this: that they were done out of respect for the law. Given Kant's understanding of what it is to have and to act on a principle, this implies that one's actions could display moral worth even if one's inclinations were entirely opposed to morality. If this were not the case, the presence or absence of certain inclinations would be a *sine qua non* of moral worth, and Kant makes clear that he takes himself to have rejected this possibility.[68]

When summarizing the lessons of his discussion of action from duty, Kant takes himself to have shed light on the paradoxical Christian duty of neighborly love:

> Undoubtedly in this way are to be understood are also to be understood those passages of Scripture which command us to love our neighbor, and even our enemy. For love as an inclination cannot be commanded; but beneficence from duty, when no inclination impels us, and *even when a natural and unconquerable aversion opposes such beneficence*, is practical, and not pathological, love. Such love resides in the will and not in the propensities of feeling, in principles of action and not in tender sympathy; and only this practical love can be commanded. [69] (emphasis mine)

Kant's suggestion, as I read him, is that the duty of neighbor-

---

66 *Groundwork*, Ak. 397–8.
67 *Ibid.*, Ak. 399.
68 The passage in which Kant makes this clear is found at *Groundwork* Ak. 440: "We have also shown above how neither fear nor inclination, but solely respect for the law, is the incentive which can give an action moral worth."
69 *Ibid.*

ly love really boils down to the duty of beneficence, and can be discharged in a morally worthy way even if one has natural and conquerable aversions to one's neighbors. If this is correct, however, it raises the question whether Kant's discussion of unsympathetic beneficence would not be far less persuasive if recast so as to include such "natural and unconquerable aversion(s)." It is a peculiarity of Kant's discussion of moral worth that he includes such active resistance from inclination in his portrayal of the morally worthy fulfillment of duties to oneself, yet when he turns to duties to others he portrays the inclinations simply as silent. Thus the person who preserves his own life from duty is so beset by adversity and sorrow as to wish for death (hence presumably to desire to kill himself), and the gout suffer who provides for his own happiness from duty is strongly inclined to secure some immediate pleasure which would be ruinous to his health and happiness.[70] If the case of the unsympathetic helper were recast so as to bring it into closer parallel with these cases, I believe we would be far less convinced that it manifests goodness of will.

This recasting might be done in one of two ways. First, one could imagine an unsympathetic benefactor who has powerful inclinations to further his own interests even where this will frustrate the interests of others and/or cause others to suffer. This, as I see it, would provide the closest possible parallel to the first-person case of the gout patient. Second, we might imagine the benefactor as beset with enduring desires to harm, frustrate or bring grief to those he is helping. This would be the closest possible parallel to the case of the person who resists suicide.[71]

This brings to the fore the question whether we disapprove morally of *feelings* of spite, malice and envy, even when they have no influence on deliberate action. There are grounds for reading Kant as denying that there is any *direct* moral objection to such feelings.[72] After all, if it is possible for practical reason to override

---

70 *Ibid.*, Ak. 397–9.
71 The gout patient is in effect inclined to do this to himself, but he is not inclined to do it under this description.
72 It is clear that Kant countenances *indirect* moral objections to such feelings. In his later moral writings, he denounces them for their tendency to erode our commitment to moral principles (*Metaphysics of Morals*, Ak. 473 and 484–5). However, many commentators have believed that Kant had no direct moral objection to such feelings. See for instance Thomas Nagel, "Moral Luck" in *Mortal Questions* (Cambridge; Cambridge University Press: 1979), pp. 24–38 (especially pp. 32–3).

any inclinations arising from these feelings and to determine the will to benevolent action out of the pure thought of duty, then it seems that Kant must acknowledge the possibility that benevolent actions accompanied by such feelings might have the full measure of moral worth. If I am right to interpret moral worth as virtuous character in action, then Kant must also conclude that such actions also make moral virtue manifest.

This conclusion is not just an idiosyncratic stepchild of Kantian moral theory; it also arises rather directly from powerful pre-theoretical intuitions about the attribution of moral responsibility. Intuitively, it seems that we cannot be held morally responsible for what we do not voluntarily control. Since it is plausible to suppose that we cannot alter our feelings and inclinations simply by choosing to do so, it seems to follow that we are not morally responsible for our feelings and inclinations, and hence that they are not open to moral assessment.[73] This, I think, is the intuition that lends to Kant's conception of moral worth whatever support it does draw from the ordinary understanding of morality.[74] However, I side with Thomas Nagel in thinking that this intuition leads not to a clear starting place for moral theory-building, but rather to a deep paradox. As Nagel observes, we also have a stubborn intuition that there is something morally wrong with feelings such as envy or spite, and this intuition returns as soon as we cease to attend to the conditions of moral responsibility.[75] Kant tends to view the resistance to his conception of moral worth, and its inde-

---

73 Derek Parfit has suggested to me that the last claim need not follow from the first, for there may be moral assessments which neither presuppose responsibility nor imply blame. For instance, we might assess a person as cruel, selfish or prejudiced without implying that they are responsible and hence to blame for their cruelty, selfishness or prejudices. I will return to this interesting proposition in future chapters. At this stage, suffice it to say that our intuitions are likely to tug different ways in different domains of judgment. Thus, in the domain of self-assessment, we are most likely to find these mere feelings blameworthy. I believe that this is because these feelings manifest a tendency to see cruel and self-serving actions as valuable. What we blame ourselves for, I believe, is the proto-judgment that gives shape to, and is implied by, this perceptual tendency. By contrast, in the domain of third-person judgment, we often do excuse others for such feelings. When we do so, however, I believe that we take a diminished view of the status of the agent whom we are judging

74 I have suggested that Kant draws directly upon this intuition in at least one passage of Groundwork I. See footnote #7 above.

75 Nagel, "Moral Luck," *Op. Cit.* p. 33.

pendence from feeling and inclination, as arising from distortions wrought by past engagement with, or exposure to, bad moral theories.[76] In other words, the resistance is supposed to come from philosophy and not from common sense. But Nagel's claim, which seems to me quite right, is that the resistance comes from the same fund of common-sense judgments which spawns the claim being resisted. The target of my inquiry is precisely this intuitive resistance; my aim is to characterize it in a philosophically revealing manner.

It seems to me that our moral disapproval of feelings such as envy, spite, and malice is clearest and most cogent in the domain of self-assessment. In a wide range of circumstances, we count our own feelings of this sort as defects in moral character, quite apart from whether we give them deliberative weight as reasons for action. If I am right that Kant's illustrations of moral worth draw forth intuitions that originate in the moral conscience, then this leads to an objection to Kant's discussion of moral worth. We will not count Kant's cases as paradigms of moral worth if we believe that the feelings which must be overcome in these cases are in themselves moral defects.[77] To put the matter another way, our conscience does not provide clear grounds for discriminating, in advance of moral theory, between a pure core of moral commitment embodied in the principles according to which the will determines itself to action, and a sensuous garb that typically adorns (and partially obscures) this moral commitment in the human case.

There is a second and I think closely related peculiarity in the

---

76 See for example *Critique of Practical Reason*, Ak. 155, where Kant writes: "If one asks, however, what pure morality really is, by which, as the touchstone, the moral import of each actions must be tested, I must confess that only philosophers can put the decision on this question in doubt. For by common sense it is long since decided..."

77 Nagel and Kant begin with quite different questions, but Nagel's inquiry has a relatively direct bearing on Kant's. Nagel asks whether we count felt temptations to immorality as moral defects in themselves, while Kant sets out to isolate the distinctive characteristic that gives to actions whatever moral value they have. If Nagel is right in his claim that we are irrevocably (though paradoxically) drawn to the conclusion that these sorts of feelings are moral blemishes, then this casts into doubt Kant's claim that moral worth is best illustrated by dutiful actions which are done in the face of powerful resistance from the sentiments. I have been attempting to follow out this strategy.

set of cases that Kant chooses in order to illustrate his conception of moral worth. These cases fall into three categories: perfect duties to self, imperfect duties to self, and imperfect duties to others. The typology of duties used in the *Groundwork* includes a fourth category: perfect duties to others. Kant does not give us a vignette of the morally worthy observance of a perfect duty to another. (As we will see below, he does give us such a case in the *Second Critique*, but this case is importantly different from the *Groundwork* cases.) The question is: Why not?

The first thing to note about such duties is that they are *prohibitions*. They do not require that we *do* certain things but that we *refrain* from certain actions (e.g. acts of deception or coercion). In order to display the pure operation of the motive of duty in the observance of this sort of prohibition, it would not do simply to imagine the inclinations as silent. Where there is no temptation to violate such a prohibition, there is no practical decision before the will, and hence no way in which the will might be thought to determine itself to do its duty from duty alone. The morally worthy fulfillment of a perfect duty to others could only be displayed by imagining an agent who is inclined to violate his duty.

We might think that it is this general feature of perfect duties which makes it implausible to think of inclinations to violate them as morally unobjectionable. This, however, does not appear to be Kant's view, for Kant does present us with an example of the morally worthy observance of a perfect duty to oneself: the case of the individual who longs for his own death but who yet refuses to kill himself. If we imagine the parallel case of a person who longs for the death of another, who yet overcomes his inclinations and refrains from murder, we run into a particularly pointed version of the difficulty that, I think, plagues all of Kant's examples to one degree or another. The problem is that in a wide range of circumstances, the very presence of this persistent longing for the death of another, and of the associated inclination to kill the other, would reflect a failure to assign proper value to others; in many circumstances it would represent a failure to recognize the moral standing of the other as a person equal in worth to oneself. A persistent longing of this sort cannot be viewed merely as a force of nature that assails us and partly determines the context within which our practical reasoning must *begin*. Our practical judgment is already in *mid-stride*, so to speak, when we feel these longings. Such longings reveal a *prima-facie* judgment that something (here the death of another) is a good outcome.

As I imagine it, this longing might be more or less engaged with our inclinations; that is, it might be a mere idle fantasy or a continual incitement to action. If we are inclined to act so as to bring about the longed-for outcome, and if this inclination proves persistent, then it evidences the proto-judgment that we have reason to bring about the outcome in question.[78] We are implicated in these affections and inclinations *in our capacity as judges*.[79] We cannot wash our hands of them entirely by overruling them in our practical deliberations, hence denying them any influence on action. If we do overrule them and they stubbornly reemerge, their reemergence reveals that we have not fully accepted our own all-things-considered practical judgment about what we have reason to do. Put another way, they reveal that we are not fully committed to the values that guide our deliberate actions.

For my part, these ruminations do not lead me to hold morally blameworthy those who long for their own death yet do not kill themselves. I think of this sort of desperation-born suicide as tragic yet not in itself immoral. In general, I am unconvinced that there

---

78 Derek Parfit has suggested in correspondence that this is true only of some subset of our standing desires—a subset he dubs "persistent desires." Parfit gives the example of "A 19th century daughter whose life will be wrecked if her tyrannical, ailing father lives long enough to blight her only chance of marriage to the man she loves." As Parfit sees it, "Perhaps she oughtn't to have any longing that her father die. But she could have that while still both regarding her father as having equal moral standing, and (even) continuing to love him."
I don't think that Parfit's case tells against the general claim that desires reveal *prima-facie* judgments. Rather, I think that he has constructed a case in which we can see the *reasonableness* of the woman's prima-facie judgment that her father's death would be a substantial good, even if it would not be an all-things-considered good. In general, we need to know quite a lot about the provenance of a desire that stands in conflict with morality before we are in a position to evaluate it. I hope to illustrate this point in the remainder of this chapter and in succeeding chapters.

79 I owe to Tim Scanlon the suggestion that my point might best be captured by thinking of involuntary character elements as morally assessable because, and insofar as, they contain proto-judgments or tendencies to judge in particular ways, hence because they implicate us in our capacity as judges.

are duties to oneself.[80] But if I were entirely convinced of the immorality of killing oneself when one has lost all hope of happiness—that is, if I really saw it as wrong in the same way and for the same fundamental reasons that killing someone else is wrong—then I suppose that I *would* see a sustained desire to kill oneself as an occasion for moral guilt.

As before, so here it is implausible to trace our moral censure of such inclinations to the possibility that they might tempt us to act immorally in the future. This consideration alone could not account for the guilt we feel in our own case when we feel such inclinations—a guilt which is not extinguished by an inner assurance of sufficient strength to resist the temptation presented by these inclinations. Imagine, for example, an aging man who finds himself beset by persistent desires to rape a younger woman. It seems to me that this persistent longing is an occasion for a morally directed self-criticism and self-reform, and that this would remain true even if the man were entirely confident that he would never permit himself to rape anyone. Persistent inclinations of this sort are appropriate occasion for moral censure because they reveal that one has not fully accepted the equal worth of others—that in some sense one does not accord them full respect.[81] (The

---

80 I do believe that suicide might be morally wrong, insofar as it might wrong others. This seems to me possible not only in the relatively obvious cases where some dependent (e.g. a child) is left helpless in the world, but also in the more subtle and far more common cases where one's decision to kill oneself damages the fragile belief of one's intimates in the value of the patterns of life they have established together, in cooperation with friends and family, and in the thin defense against absurdity that these life patterns provide. There are certain kinds of hard mental stares, emanating from the thought of death and in particular from the thought of chosen death, under which one's conviction in the meaningfulness of one's life can evaporate entirely. And while there seems to me to be a certain nobility in enduring this sort of hard stare—and even in purging oneself of banal, self-demeaning and life-dissipating habits by confronting one's life periodically with this sort of hard stare—still I think that there is at least some *prima-facie* wrongness in upsetting innocent confidence and contentment where it still has some hold.

81 I realize that this is a bit of a crude interpretation of the case at hand, and that matters would almost certainly be more complex. Perhaps the desire in question evidences an inability to accept one's own diminishing virility—an inability which prompts the exertion in fantasy of the raw physical potency that is no longer actually one's own. Thus, while the fantasy manifests a failure to recognize the true value of others, it also suggests a misidentification of the true

qualifier "in some sense" is important here, for the pathological pleasure of rape may require that the rapist view his victim as fully human in some sense, precisely so that he can view his deed as the subjugation of a free and independent being of great worth. In other words, the rapist simultaneously recognizes and denies the worth of another.[82]) In terms more proper to Kant, they reveal a tendency to see others as mere means to one's own ends. If there is a standing conflict between this *prima-facie* view of others and one's all-things-considered judgment of their worth (i.e. the judgment that determines one's willful decisions), this cannot be conceived as a conflict between practical reason and something foreign to it. The conflict is internal to practical reason.[83]

In his later moral writings, Kant locates the root of evil in the disposition of the will to give undue weight to one's own inclinations simply because they are one's own.[84] In the same vein, Kant tends to represent violations of duty such as coercion or deception as tempting only insofar as they provide a means for securing tangible benefits for oneself. If this were the exclusive source of the temptation to immorality, then it would make sense to think of evil as a kind of over-indulgence towards one's own inclinations. It seems to me, though, that this is a deficient view of the source of evil. Its inadequacy is perhaps nowhere more evident than in Kant's shallow analysis of the pathology of suicide. Kant portrays the suicide as motivated by a desire to spare himself from future frustrations, and he argues that killing oneself on such a maxim is wrong.[85] Few have been convinced by his argument that this maxim fails the test of universalizability, and I will not visit that debate here. What is most striking about the example from my point of view is the sheer improbability of suicide driven by self-

---

source of one's own value—and it may be that exploring and correcting this latter misidentification is the key to moral growth for this individual.

82 This was pointed out to me by Christine Korsgaard.

83 To use Wittgenstein's evocative phrase, we might say that seeing something under a particular aspect—that is, *seeing* it *as* something or another—is " 'The echo of a thought in sight.' " Ludwig Wittgenstein, *Philosophical Investigations* (Third Edition), translated by G.E.M. Anscombe (New York; Macmillan Publishing Company, Inc., 1958), p. 212e.

84 Kant conceives of this as the subordination of the moral incentive to the incentive of self-love. See Kant, *Religion...*, pp. 31–2.

85 Kant, *Groundwork*, Ak. 421–2.

indulgence towards one's own desires. Suicide, it would seem, is far more typically motivated by a demeaning and disfiguring conception of one's own worth, and incidentally this seems to provide a far more convincing way of showing why the Kantian might deem it morally wrong. One might diagnose what in particular is pathological (or, on the Kantian view, morally deficient) in the suicide's self-conception by analyzing the judgments implicit in the feelings and desires that prompt him to take his life.[86]

To return to my main point, immoral impulses are not always so prudent as Kant would have them; they often arise from pure malice, unmoored from any independent self-interested end.[87] Human perversity is such that domination and manipulative deception can be direct sources of pleasure. If the physical domination of another human being were not itself a potential source of pleasure, rape would be merely one means among many for sexual release, and hardly the inexpungable human evil that it is. As I will now go on to argue, there is a morally important difference between maliciousness born of egoism and maliciousness born directly from malice, and this difference is obscured by the official Kantian view, under which they both count as a self-indulgent overestimation of the reason-giving force of one's own inclinations.[88] On Kant's view, the immorality of each can be traced to the fact that the agent implicitly grants to his/her inclinations a justificatory force that mere inclinations do not actually have. It

---

86 I am indebted to Christine Korsgaard for suggesting this way of viewing Kant's treatment of suicide.

87 I owe to Sanjay Tikku the point that malice must be considered an independent font of motivation, one that sometimes leads to actions which undermine or frustrate one's self-interest. After drafting this chapter, I discovered that Schopenhauer counted malice as one of the three fundamental incentives to action (the others being egoism and compassion). He suggested that the deepest form of moral depravity was malicious pleasure in the suffering of others, and that Kant's treatment of evil would have been more satisfactory if he had recognized this. See Arthur Schopenhauer, "The Foundation of Ethics," in *Philosophical Writings*, Wolfgang Schirmacher, editor (New York; The Continuum Publishing Company: 1994), pp. 201–251, esp. pp.205, 220, 226–7.

88 I think that this distinction is recognized in Dante's infernal circles. For instance, those who ruined themselves and misspent their fortunes through lack of self-control or overindulgence towards earthly desires are punished with the incontinent in the outer circles of hell. By contrast, those who dissipated their own fortunes out of self-hatred are punished with the violent in the inner circles of the damned.

seems to me that the particular immorality of malicious actions which are born directly from malice must be traced to the very fact that one is capable of gaining direct pleasure from the pains of others—in particular, by physically dominating or manipulating them, forcing them to submit to one's whims, or otherwise debasing them. Thus, on my view it is not only true that sometimes feelings are open to moral assessment, but also that we must know a good deal about the circumstances which give rise to them, and about the personal history of the agent in which they arise, before we are in a position to make such a moral assessment.

I said above that we could not imagine a full recognition of the equal worth of others in the absence of sympathy; here I would say, conversely, that we could not imagine a full recognition of the equal worth of others in the presence of malice. For those who are committed to nurturing a virtuous character, malicious inclinations and capacities to take pleasure in malicious actions will mark out a need and direction for self-reform. Such reform typically cannot be achieved simply by dwelling on the thought that such pleasures or inclinations are morally blameworthy. The heavy-handed verdict of guilt might lead only to the censorship of errant inclinations, or (following Nietzsche) to their redirection into masochistic activities. Progress is more likely to be made by deepening one's knowledge of the genesis of one's emotions and desires, either by exploring the idiosyncratic origins and contours of one's own affects (e.g. by journal writing or psychoanalysis), or by deepening one's knowledge of human affects more generally (e.g. by reading novels).[89]

This is a very different task of self-reform from the one set by overreaching egoism. I mentioned above that Kant traces all immoral action to the common human propensity to allot undue justificatory weight to one's inclinations simply because they are one's own. This form of wrongdoing stems from inclinations that need not be eliminated nor even overridden in all circumstances, but must merely be contained within their proper bounds. If this were the font of all evil, then virtuous character would be a matter of the strength of the will. The reform of inclinations would

---

89 Self-reform aside, I do not believe that we can understand what human values are at stake in—and potentially frustrated by—recurrent malicious inclinations unless we understand the critical role they play in determining our receptivity to the moral value of other persons. These desires frustrate us in our efforts to approximate an ideal of moral community with others.

have only a derivative role in our efforts to become virtuous. That is, insofar as we suspected that we lacked the strength of will to resist certain inclinations, we might seek to eliminate them. However, in so doing, our concern would be to quiet or perhaps to eliminate those inclinations that were strongest and most persistent. This would not necessarily call for any sort of investigation of the *prima-facie* evaluations of ourselves and others that are encoded in our inclinations.

It is worth stressing, at this point, that I do not wish to imply that people who have persistent malicious desires are unusually base or awful. To one degree or another, we are all such people— or so I think, from the limited indications I can gather from reading, conversation, observation and self-examination. What I *am* saying is that the moral assessment of goodness of character extends all the way to these inclinations, and not merely to their influence on deliberate action. Inclinations are not merely things that *happen* to us, with which we must try to *cope* or *manage* in our practical deliberations. They are revelations of our own semi-conscious beliefs and evaluative judgments. Our evaluative beliefs are not all clearly introspectible. Sometimes we find out about evaluations that we in fact make—that is, about values that are in some morally important sense our own—by attending to what we desire, and in particular to what we are *ashamed* to desire.[90]

---

90 It might seem that this moral concern with desires and inclinations will lead to an excessively rigoristic morality. One might object that it is not merely therapeutic but a positive mark of self-acceptance to refrain from applying 'oughts' to one's own desires and affections. This notion of self-acceptance seems to me to echo a theoretically unsound bifurcation of the self into mind and body, or reason and sensation, combined with a devaluation of the latter term. On the view that I will seek to develop in the course of this thesis, our sentiments and desires do not enter into morality as a further terrain that must be subjected to rational moral principles. Rather, when our desires and sentiments reveal to us something about the sort of person we are, this information is relevant in reassessing the commitments we have assumed. For instance, such information might prompt us to reconsider the fittingness of our political commitments, our marital commitments, our friendships, our group affiliations, and our career choices. In this way, our moral assessment of affections and desires can contribute to an ongoing self-reformation aimed at the harmonization of our character and our life commitments. This sort of self-reformation can be conceived of as a continual progress towards greater depth or integrity of evaluative commitments. So conceived, I do not think that it is objectionably rigoristic.

PART VI: KANT'S *SECOND CRITIQUE* THOUGHT EXPERIMENT

In Part II of the *Critique of Practical Reason*, Kant does take up the case of what seems to be a morally worthy observance of a perfect duty to another. However, the way in which he draws this case is importantly different from the formula he follows in the *Groundwork* cases. The result is a much more persuasive thought experiment, one which does not raise the sorts of objections that I have been pursuing. It is worth considering this case in order to see *why* it is so much more plausible than those of the *Groundwork*.

The case in question arises in Part II of the *Second Critique*, "Methodology of Pure Practical Reason," where Kant's concern is to describe the pedagogic methods best suited for teaching virtue— i.e. for securing a practical commitment to the moral law. Kant begins by asking what "pure morality" or "pure virtue" is.[91] By this, he explains, he means the "touchstone" by which "the moral import of each action must be tested."[92] This sounds very much like the moral worth that Kant sought to isolate in *Groundwork I*, so it comes as no surprise when Kant claims that the answer can be elicited, by means of an example, from our common understanding of morality. Indeed, Kant indicates that the answer could only be confused by philosophical obscurantism; and in a passage reminiscent of the teaching scene from Plato's *Meno*, Kant imagines that the example might be put before a ten-year-old boy in order to show that he could correctly identify the "touchstone" of morality without guidance from his teacher.[93] Kant suggests that it might then be pointed out to the boy, presumably in order to bring out what is implicit in his own understanding of morality, that the action is distinguished by the maxim from which it is done, and that it is precisely in virtue of its maxim that the action has moral worth.[94]

---

91 Kant, *Critique of Practical Reason*, Ak. 155.
92 *Ibid.*
93 *Ibid.* The reference to Plato's *Meno* is from pp. 82b–85e.
94 I infer that Kant intended the example to be used in this way from the fact that he introduces it as a central element of the "methodology of pure practical reason," through which subjective recognition of the authority of the moral law is to be fostered, and by the fact that he maintains that one of the two points which must be stressed to youths in bringing examples of morally exemplary actions before them is "whether the action also is done (subjectively) for the sake of the moral law, and thus not only is morally correct as a deed, but also has moral worth as a disposition because of the maxim from which it was done. See *Critique of Practical Reason*, Ak. 159.

The boy is to be told the story of an honest man who is offered great riches and high rank if only he will bear false witness against an innocent person. This innocent person lacks all power to retaliate, so from the standpoint of prudential self-interest there is nothing to lose by lying, and everything to gain. To tilt the balance of worldly motivations even further towards the immoral act, Kant imagines that the man has everything to lose by refusing to lie: friends and relatives have threatened to break off relations; powerful nobles threaten to torment, imprison, even to kill him if he does not yield. His wife and children beg him to save himself and to spare them the grief and suffering that will ensue if he refuses to yield.[95] The thought of causing pain to his loved ones make him rue his tragic predicament. But he does not doubt what he must do, and he does not waver in his decision.[96] He refuses to lie.

If I understand Kant's purposes correctly, this example is supposed to draw forth from the ordinary grasp of morality an attestation of our subjection to the moral law, irrespective of inclination (of the "fact of reason", at least under one interpretation of that protean fact). More particularly, it is supposed to elicit from us the respect we feel, whether we like it or not, whenever we are presented with the example of a righteous person.[97] This respect is only derivatively respect for a person; it is really respect for the law which his example holds before us.[98] And this respect just is the subjective operation of the moral incentive.[99] It produces in us an interest in obeying the law—that is, a moral interest.[100] In Kant's

---

95 One interesting feature of this case is that sympathetic feelings can be seen here to provide a guidance that is at best ambiguous, and perhaps favorable to the immoral action. On the view of the affects that I have been developing, the protagonist's sympathetic desire to spare his wife and children from suffering might be thought morally creditworthy, in that it marks the high worth he allots to their well-being.

96 This decisiveness, or resistance to real temptation, is not a feature (at least not an explicit feature) of the *Groundwork* cases, yet it seems relevant to our intuitive approval of this figure.

97 See Kant, *Critique of Practical Reason*, Ak. 77. Here Kant writes that: "Respect is a tribute we cannot refuse to pay to merit whether we will or not; we can indeed outwardly withhold it, but we cannot help feeling it inwardly." It is perhaps worth noting that the general notion of moral pedagogy found here is already discernible in the *Groundwork*, Ak. 410n.

98 *Ibid.*, Ak. 78.

99 *Ibid.*

100 *Ibid.*, Ak. 80.

view, moral pedagogy can only succeed by awakening this moral interest, and not by presenting us with valiant and heroic deeds as models for our imitation. "Certainly actions of others which have been done with great sacrifice and merely for the sake of duty may be praised as noble and sublime deeds, yet only in so far as there are clues which suggest that they were done wholly out of respect for duty and not from aroused feelings."[101]

Unlike the *Groundwork* cases, this case does make a very successful claim to our intuitive moral approval. However, I do not think that this approval shows that our assessments of moral worth abstract from all sensuous character elements. What makes this case work, I think, is that we are told a very particular story of *how* the inclinations have come to resist morality, and we do not morally condemn these inclinations once we see that they have their origin in tangible threats to the people and things that the story's hero cares most about, and once we see that these deep-seated cares— particularly his sympathetic desire to spare his wife and children suffering—are themselves laudable.[102] The inclinations that conflict with duty do reveal implicit evaluative judgments and beliefs, but we find nothing objectionable about these evaluations and beliefs. Kant, then, is perhaps right to claim that this case will arouse the approval and even the veneration of his imaginary ten-year-old. I am less persuaded by his *diagnosis* of this veneration. Kant holds that we admire the honest man because we see that his choice to remain dutiful is not driven by concern for anything that might be counted as a constituent part of his happiness.[103] On my view, our moral assessment of this person is at least partly colored by the fact that in these circumstances, we would not think it a mark of bad character if one were strongly tempted to lie; we might even think that the temptation felt by the protagonist is a mark of good character, since it manifests the properly high value that he allots to the well-being of his wife and children.

This can be seen by varying the case slightly and noting the consequent variation in our intuitions. I think that we would be far more tentative in our approval if we imagined the person as one

---

101 *Ibid.*, Ak. 85.
102 This point is prefigured by Philippa Foot in her insightful discussion of Kantian moral worth. See Foot, "Virtues and Vices," *Op. Cit.*, p. 11.
103 *Ibid.*, Ak. 156.

who finds it generally unpleasant to tell the truth and takes secret pleasure in telling lies, or alternatively as a person who would take great pleasure in seeing the innocent man punished and could never be happy so long as this innocent man's life goes well. Under these circumstances, duty would have a further cost in the metric of happiness. If Kant's diagnosis of the case were correct, then this would increase our admiration of the protagonist. This seems to me entirely counterintuitive. The trouble is that the extra cost in the metric of happiness stems from, hence manifests, character traits that we find morally objectionable. On my view, our objection here is best understood as a rejection of the evaluative judgments which are implicit in the inclinations and affections of the protagonist, so described. We object to the malicious pleasure he would take in the unwarranted punishment of an innocent man because this shows that at some level he takes this punishment to be good, or can't help seeing it as good.

PART VII: CONCLUSION

In this chapter, I have sought to argue that Kant's theory fails to account for our intuition that some desires are morally worse than others, and that this throws into doubt his twin accounts of moral worth and virtue. In general, it seems to me that if we are to make judgments about inclinations which are resistant to duty, we need to know a great deal about their origins. It is not enough to know whether they are accepted or rejected as reasons for action in the moment of deliberative judgment. Inclinations cannot be treated as one among many possible external circumstances that make compliance with morality difficult. I have followed Nagel in insisting that they cannot persuasively be assimilated to the category of bad moral luck. In order to judge inclinations that are resistant to duty, we require some knowledge of the beliefs and evaluations that are implicit in them. This typically requires us to know something about the circumstances in which they arise, about their persistence, and about their connection to other of the agent's desires, beliefs and aims.

Lawrence Hinman has suggested that the implausibility of some of Kant's claims about the emotions might be traced to a vacillation in Kant's understanding of his own "two worlds" doctrine. It is most plausible to conceive of the noumenal and phenomenal realms as determined by two mutually exclusive standpoints on the same entities. For instance, an action is viewed from the noumenal standpoint as originating in a spontaneous practical judgment, while from the phenomenal standpoint it is viewed as the causal consequence of prior circumstances and mental states (including beliefs and desires). Hinman argues that Kant sometimes interprets his own "two worlds" in a less plausible way, as demarcating two separate domains with entirely different contents. It may be that Kant did not include inclinations and desires within the scope of the morally assessable because he was tempted to think of all affects purely as mechanically caused phenomena. If I am right, however, the full import of emotions and desires cannot be grasped unless one attends to the judgments which are implicit in them. This suggests that like actions, so emotions and desires can be viewed from the noumenal standpoint, and can be assessed in terms of the practical judgments that they imply.

As we shall see in the next chapter, Kant has resources for incorporating many of the intuitions I have tweaked in this chapter in order to motivate my critique. However, his capacity for incorporating these sorts of intuitions is limited by his conception of moral worth, and by his closely related conceptions of virtue and autonomy. He is also restricted by his strict segregation of the faculties of practical judgment and desire, and by his related claim that we become responsible for our feelings and desires only to the extent that practical reason freely incorporates them into its maxims as reasons for action.[104]

Still, we have seen one rather slim indication that Kant recognizes that morality itself imposes certain requirements on the inclinations. The hint takes the form of a curious omission—particularly curious given the careful architectonics that Kant normally heeds and that structure the rest of the *Groundwork*. The omission is that he does not give us a case of the morally worthy performance of a perfect duty to others where the inclinations are in revolt. When he does formulate such a case in the *Second Critique*, its form is significantly different from the form followed in the

---

104 Tim Scanlon has pointed out to me that there are other ways that Kant might countenance a moral responsibility for inclinations. For instance, it might be possible to trace these inclinations to past voluntary choices, hence to see ourselves as their authors. I will explore these questions in greater detail in the next chapter.

Groundwork. This latter case cannot be used to draw the key conclusions that are supposed to follow from the *Groundwork* cases, though Kant seems to indicate that it can.

CHAPTER 2

Kantian Virtue, Affects and Rules

INTRODUCTION

In Chapter I, I argued that Kant's conception of moral worth and his closely related conception of virtue do not adequately represent our intuitive moral assessments of inclinations and desires. Kant traces all immoral actions to egoism, construed as excessive indulgence towards one's own inclinations and desires. As a result, his theory does not incorporate the common-sense notions that some desires are morally worse than others, and that otherwise similar actions are worse if they are born directly of malice than if they are born of self-centered insensitivity.

I made the further claim that certain desires ought to count as moral failings of the most direct sort under Kant's own understanding of morality. For Kant, the essence of morality is the recognition of the equal value of other human beings. I have suggested that certain desires themselves represent a failure to recognize, or a tendency to discount, the value of other human beings. They manifest *prima-facie* or proto-judgments which are in conflict with morality. The crux of the problem, as I see it, is that Kant does not adequately recognize the interconnectedness of judgment and desire. Kant assigns these two mental phenomena to two separate "faculties"—the faculties of judgment and desire. This philosophical distinction tends to obscure the fact that our inclinations and desires themselves sometimes indicate defects in judgment, and that one cannot really be said to be committed to principles—to have made these principles one's own—unless one characteristically experiences certain inclinations and desires. As I put it in the previous chapter, practical deliberation is already in "mid-stride" when certain desires arise. In my view, this calls for a reconsideration of the Kantian claim that moral assessment ought to be directed only at the principles implicit in the voluntary decisions of the will, and of the related claim that moral virtue can be exhaustively characterized as the strength of will necessary to overrule inclinations insofar as they conflict with the dictates of morality.

In the last chapter, I focused my attention on Kant's early critical moral writings—especially the *Groundwork* and the *Critique of Practical Reason*. A wave of recent literature has brought to light a more appealing picture of the place of the desires and emotions in Kant's moral theory.[1] This scholarly literature draws heavily from later works such as the *The Metaphysics of Morals, Anthropology from a Pragmatic Point of View and Religion Within the Limits of Reason Alone*. One of the objectives of this chapter is to assess the resources in these later works, and in the work of contemporary Kantian theorists, for resolving the difficulties I raised in Chapter I. My aim, in examining this literature, will not be primarily scholarly—that is, my principal concern will not be to determine what precisely Kant thought about these matters. My purpose, instead, will be to identify the most promising Kantian responses to the criticisms I have raised, in order to make these criticisms both more precise and more plausible. I will also attempt to specify what particular tenets of Kant's theory must be abandoned or modified in order to permit a resolution of the difficulties I have raised. My conclusion, in a nutshell, will be that the Kantian cannot adopt a defensible conception of the place of affects in practical judgment without

---

1 For a flavor of this interpretive literature, see: Barbara Herman, *The Practice of Moral Judgment, Op. Cit.*, especially chapters 1 and 4; Christine Korsgaard, "From Duty and for the Sake of the Noble: *Kant and Aristotle on Morally Good Action*," *Op. Cit.*; Paul Guyer, Kant and the Experience of Freedom, Op. Cit., especially Chapter 10; Henry E. Allison, *Kant's Theory of Freedom, Op. Cit.*; and Onora O'Neill, *Constructions of Reason: Explorations of Kant's Practical Philosophy* (Cambridge; Cambridge University Press: 1989), especially Chapter 8.

giving up the intuitively attractive idea that moral responsibility is always grounded in voluntary choice.

PART I: KANTIAN VIRTUE AND JOYFULNESS IN DUTIFUL ACTION

Throughout his writings on moral theory, Kant equates virtue with the strength of will needed to overcome any and all resistance to the dictates of duty which might arise from the inclinations.[2] On one natural interpretation of Kant, this strength of will amounts to a *reactive* capacity—exercisable only in moments of voluntary choice—to overrule whatever inclinations might happen to have arisen insofar as they conflict with morality. If this interpretation were correct, then it seems that one could be virtuous no matter what one's characteristic feelings and associated inclinations, provided at least that one had the strength of will needed to overcome these inclinations in the moment of deliberate choice. In the last chapter, I attempted to show that this reactive notion of virtue is implicit in key passages of the *Groundwork* and the *Second Critique*. It is also suggested by certain passages in Kant's later writings on ethical theory, as for instance when he characterizes virtue, in *The Metaphysics of Morals*, as "the force and herculean strength needed to subdue the vice-breeding inclinations,"[3]

There are, however, other passages in Kant's later writings which seem to reflect a somewhat different conception of virtue. For instance, Kant claims in *The Metaphysics of Morals* that we have a derivative duty to engage in social intercourse, and in so doing to display the social graces. Among the social manners or graces, Kant lists affability, sociability, courtesy, hospitality, and gentleness. Kant explains that these are not part of virtue itself, but are "only *externals* or by-products (*parerqa*), which give a beautiful illusion resembling virtue that is also not deceptive since everyone knows how it must be taken."[4] We are obliged not only to display the social graces, but to strive "to bring this illusion as near as possible to the truth."[5] This striving is a duty because it "pro-

---

2 See for example Kant, *The Metaphysics of Morals*, Ak. 376, 380, 394, 397 and 405.
3 *Ibid.*, Ak. 376.
4 *Ibid.*, Ak. 473.
5 *Ibid.*

motes the feeling for virtue itself"—presumably by altering one's feelings over time so as to make them conformable to virtue.[6]

My interest in these passages is not that they provide a way of explaining our moral concern with inclinations contrary to the dictates of morality. Kant here provides grounds for objecting only to the *appearance* of such conflicting sentiments, and not to their *occurrence*. This could not help us to illuminate the private, first-personal objection to these feelings which I have been attempting to highlight. My interest in this passage is rather that it suggests that the Kantian conception of virtue is more complex than the reactive conception of virtue described above.

Kant seems to understand the social graces as outward expressions of sentimental love and esteem for others.[7] Though these sentiments cannot themselves be commanded, and hence are no part of our duty, still they are highly moralized sentiments in that those who feel them will often be immediately inclined to perform actions which (as it happens) duty requires. Affability, for instance, is an outward display of neighborly love. To be affable is to present oneself as if one were eager to pursue the well-being of one's fellow humans, simply in virtue of one's affection for them. Furthering the happiness of others is in turn an imperfect duty of virtue. The other social graces can be given similar analyses. Hospitality is presumably a narrower version of affability, involving a display of eagerness to share one's home and possessions with another, and it indicates a felt readiness to fulfill particular imperfect duties towards others. Courtesy and gentleness are the outward displays of esteem for others. Those who are courteous and gentle present themselves as if they lack any inclination to violate the perfect duty to respect others—that is, as if they lack all inclination to be arrogant or contemptuous, to defame or ridicule others.[8] This helps to explain why

---

6 *Ibid.*
7 This interpretation fits well with Kant's description of the social graces as "merely manners" that we must "show" to others. (Ibid.) It also coheres with his claim that we are obliged to be gracious in social intercourse, since Kant argues elsewhere that it is incoherent to suppose that we are obligated to feel anything in particular. (See for example *Groundwork for the Metaphysics of Morals*, Ak 399, *The Metaphysics of Morals*, Ak. 401–2 and *Critique of Practical Reason*, Ak. 83)
8 On duties of virtue arising from the respect due to others, see The *Metaphysics of Morals*, Ak. 462–8.

Kant says that gentleness is shown in disagreeing without quarreling.[9]

If this reading of Kant's discussion of the social graces is correct, then it is mightily obscure how the social graces resemble virtue. It might seem that one could provide a more convincing show of virtue by doing one's duty in the presence of very obvious inclinations to violate it. And indeed, as I attempted to show in the last chapter, Kant gives us ample reason to suppose that this would provide ordinary human reason with the most convincing possible display of virtue.

Why, then, does Kant claim that the social graces provide an illusion of virtue? It is true that the social graces share a limited commonality with virtue conceived on the reactive model. Like this sort of virtue, so too the sentiments expressed in the social graces provide a kind of assurance that one will act in accordance with duty, at least in a wide range of circumstances. However, the assurance provided by the social graces does not stem from any indication of strength of will. It stems, instead, from an indication that one will generally be inclined to do that which duty demands, and hence that conformity with duty will generally require no particular strength of will.[10] This suggests that the reactive model is too simple to capture Kant's conception of virtue, and that Kant endorses the view, normally associated with Aristotelianism, that dissonance between inclinations and moral requirements can indicate a lack of virtue.

This is not the only textual indication that Kant's conception of virtue is more complex than the reactive model described above. Perhaps the clearest and most forceful statement of this point is

---

9 Kant, *The Metaphysics of Morals*, Ak. 473. Kant maintains that we have a perfect duty of virtue to avoid any manifestation of disrespect for others due to their logical blunders or poor reasoning, and that we must always suppose that there is some kernel of truth to be uncovered even in those judgments which seem most absurd and confused. On this, see *The Metaphysics of Morals*, Ak. 463–4.

10 In Kantian terms, what the social graces seem to resemble is not so much virtue as holiness—an ideal consummation of virtue that is beyond the reach of humans. Holiness, for Kant, is characterized by the absence of inward reluctance to do what the moral law dictates. The holy will does not experience the moral law as a constraint because it feels no temptation to violate the dictates of that law. (See *The Metaphysics of Morals*, Ak. 379 and 383; see also *Critique of Practical Reason*, Ak. 84.)

found in *Religion within the Limits of Reason Alone*, in a footnote
in which Kant responds to Schiller's charge that the Kantian ethical ideal amounts to a joyless asceticism:

> Now if one asks, What is the *aesthetic character*, the *tempera-*
> *ment*, so to speak, of virtue, whether courageous and hence
> *joyous* or fear-ridden and dejected, an answer is hardly neces-
> sary. This latter slavish frame of mind can never occur with-
> out a hidden *hatred* of the law. And a heart which is happy in
> the *performance* of its duty (not merely complacent in the
> *recognition* thereof) is a mark of genuineness in the virtuous
> disposition—of genuineness even in *piety*, which does not
> consist in the self-inflicted torment of a repentant sinner. . .
> but rather in the firm resolve to do better in the future. This
> resolve, then, encouraged by good progress, must needs beget
> a joyous frame of mind, without which man is never certain
> of having really *attained a love* for the good, *i.e.*, of having
> incorporated it into his maxim.[11]

This passage is puzzling for a number of reasons. First, it
seems to carry the suggestion that those who feel joy in the per-

---

11 Kant, *Religion*, p. 19n. Kant does not offer much explanation of this
point, nor to my knowledge does he elaborate on this point elsewhere.
He does write, in the *Metaphysics of Morals*, that "what is done not
with pleasure but as mere compulsory service has no inner worth for
him who so responds to his duty. Such action is not loved; on the contrary, one thus involved avoids, as much as possible, occasions for prac-
ticing virtue." (Ak. 484) He concludes this passage by claiming that
asceticism "makes virtue itself hateful and drives away its adherents,"
and that, "The discipline which man practices on himself can therefore
become meritorious and exemplary only through the cheer which
accompanies it." (Ibid., Ak. 485) It seems as if Kant's point here is not
that cheerlessness indicates a lack of virtue, but that cheerless self-disci-
pline tends to corrode the fragile human attachment to the moral law.
But Kant might have had something more fundamental in mind,
depending upon what he meant by "inner worth." In the *Groundwork*,
Kant writes that the care that people take to preserve their lives has no
"inner worth" to the extent that it arises from an immediate wish to
continue to live. (Ak 397–8) This is translated "intrinsic worth" by
Ellington, but the German phrase is *innern/inneren* Werth in all of these
cases. If intrinsic worth is the right translation, then the point is that the
person does not find dutiful action intrinsically worthwhile—and that
this can only mean that he does it because of some other inducement,
perhaps a fear of God's judgment, or a concern for reputation, or both.
Then Kant's claim here would echo the above-quoted claim from the
Religion. There is also a passage in Kant's *Anthropology from a*
Pragmatic Point of View (section 62) which might be interpreted as a
reiteration of the point under discussion.

formance of their duty *might* be certain of their virtue. However, Kant makes clear throughout his writings on ethical theory, and even within the confines of the same text, that there is *nothing* which could warrant perfect certainty of a virtuous disposition, so it seems best to deny that Kant intended to convey this suggestion.

A second, somewhat deeper puzzle is that Kant might seem to lack any ground for claiming even a probabilistic correlation between virtue and joyfulness. There is a real puzzle about what sort of claim this could be. It could hardly be an analytic truth, since it does not follow from Kant's abstract analysis of virtue as strength of will. At first blush, it might seem that it could not be an empirical generalization, since such a generalization would required repeated observation of a conjunction between action flowing from a genuinely virtuous disposition and joy, and Kant makes clear that we have no way of observing genuine virtue. This would seem to imply that Kant is forwarding this claim as a bit of synthetic *a priori* knowledge. Yet it is not at all clear what synthetic *a priori* grounding the claim could have.

As far as I can see, the only place in Kant's corpus where it might seem that we could find a synthetic *a priori* grounding for this claim is the second *Critique* discussion of the non-empirical feeling of respect. In that work, Kant believes himself to have established that our awareness of the moral law must itself be able to serve as a sufficient incentive to action.[12] When we act from inclination, some particular inclination is our incentive. When we act from duty, our incentive is our awareness of the unconditional authority of the moral law, and this awareness is what Kant calls respect. Now, virtuous agents are precisely those who are committed to acting on this incentive of respect whenever it conflicts with candidate incentives arising from the inclinations. For such agents, respect operates as an authoritative check on the inclinations, insofar as they come into conflict with duty. Since the inclinations are "based on feeling," Kant claims, the moral incentive's check on the inclinations can be known *a priori* to produce a painful feeling.[13] Kant says more specifically that the painful feeling arises from the striking down of self-conceit, where self-conceit is a propensity to

---

12 Kant uses the term 'incentive' to refer to the subjective determining ground of the will. See Kant means Kant, *Critique of Practical Reason*, Ak. 72.
13 *Ibid.*, Ak. 72–5.

take our subjective inclinations as unconditionally authoritative grounds for action.[14] Kant maintains, however, that the striking down of self-conceit "also contains something elevating," in that it makes us conscious of the sublimity of our personality—i.e. our "freedom and independence from the mechanism of nature..."[15] Consequently, the painful element of respect is leavened by a pleasurable feeling of self-worth or self-approbation.[16]

One might think, then, that Kant claims that the aesthetic character of virtuous action is joyful because such action is accompanied by a pleasurable awareness of the sublimity of our freedom. As I said, this is the only way I see of interpreting Kant's claim as a bit of putative synthetic *a priori* knowledge. However, this interpretation has a serious flaw. The problem is that some sort of pleasurable feeling would presumably accompany other dutiful actions which do not flow from a virtuous character, since they must be done from some inclination and the satisfaction of inclinations would presumably bring with it some pleasure. The mark of virtuous action, then, would be a very particular sort of joy, quite different from these ordinary pleasures, and known in part by the painful humiliation that necessarily accompanies it. Yet Kant says nothing to indicate that the joy which the virtuous take in dutiful action has this sort of phenomenological complexity. This leads me to think that Kant has some other reason for claiming that the virtuous are joyful in the performance of their duty.

At any rate, if the synthetic *a priori* interpretation elaborated above were correct, then the passage would not provide a way of incorporating my claim that there is something morally objectionable about feelings of malice, spite, and the like, even if we do not act on them. After all, there is no reason to suppose that one would cease to feel the sublimity of one's freedom if one were beset by persistent malicious inclinations yet overcame these in the moment of decision. My aim, then, will be to look at ways of understanding the passage which do provide responses to the problem I have raised. This will require either that we find an alternative *a priori* grounding for the importance of taking pleasure in doing one's duty, or that we find some consistent and plausible way of understanding Kant's claim as an empirical generalization.

---

14 *Ibid.*, Ak. 74.
15 *Ibid.*, Ak. 86–7.
16 *Ibid.*, Ak. 80–81.

PART II: EMPIRICAL AND INTELLIGIBLE VIRTUE

We need some way to make sense of Kant's response to Schiller and to square it with the numerous suggestions, even in the later works, that Kant holds what I have called a reactive model of virtue. This can be done, I think, by bringing in the Kantian distinction between empirical and intelligible virtue. The noumenal or intelligible conception of virtue is the strength of the will's attachment to the moral law, where this strength is understood as a capacity to resist the temptation posed by the inclinations. The empirical conception of virtue is that set of observable or introspectible features of our deliberation and action which give us grounds for hoping that we are virtuous from the noumenal point of view. Kant's position, I think, is that one such ground for hope is a rough harmony between duty and inclination. The actions of those with a virtuous disposition will conform with duty provided that they understand the situation in which they find themselves, and such understanding is common enough that conformity with duty is a sign of a virtuous disposition. This helps to explain why the social graces resemble virtue, and why those who feel no joy in the performance of their duty lack an important ground for hoping that they are genuinely virtuous—i.e. virtuous from the intelligible point of view, which is the point of view relevant to divine judgment.

The intelligible conception of virtue is derived *a priori*, by applying the notion of the good will to rational beings who are always subject to inclinations that might conflict with the requirements of duty. In the last chapter, I attempted to show that the good will, for Kant, is the will which has adopted the moral law as its supreme maxim, and that virtue is goodness of will in humans—or more generally, in rational beings with sensuous natures. In such beings, Kant maintains, evil originates in the erroneous judgment that a particular inclination is an independently conclusive reason for action, unconditioned on moral permissibility.[17] Given that *this* is the source of human evil, Kant concludes

---

17 Kant does not think of this as an empirical finding about the causal origins of evil actions. Rather, it is an *a priori* claim about how we would have to understand the deliberations of rational beings with sensuous natures, in order to think of those actions as immoral. I believe that Kant's reasoning, in its rough outlines, runs as follows: Given that we are rational beings with sensuous natures, our deliber

that virtue is the strength of will needed to act in accordance with the moral law even when presented with the most powerful inclinations to do otherwise. This abstract, reactive conception of virtue is found throughout Kant's writings on moral theory.[18]

Now, Kant makes clear both in the *Groundwork* and in his later writings on ethics that no set of empirical facts is criterial for virtue. Kant writes that we can observe actions which are unlawful, and we can sometimes observe in our own case that we choose such actions in full consciousness of their unlawfulness.[19] In such cases, we can know ourselves to be vicious. However, we cannot confidently conclude that another is either virtuous or vicious, since any observable stretch of behavior could be produced by the self-conscious adoption of unlawful maxims, just as it could be produced by a sincere determination to act only on permissible maxims. We also cannot know *ourselves* to be virtuous, since there is no private, introspectible feature of experience which could provide complete assurance that, in one's own highest-level maxim, one gives supremacy to moral incentives over all incentives derived from inclination.[20]

---

ation is always occasioned by inclination. Our task as deliberators is either to do what we are inclined to do, or to do otherwise on purely moral grounds. All immoral actions are actions we are inclined to do. However, if we think of these transgressions as bits of behavior caused by our inclination, then we cannot think of ourselves as agents who are morally assessable for what we have done, and hence we cannot think of them as immoral actions after all. In order to think of what we do as *immoral* (or, for that matter, as *action*), we must think of our actions as determined by our principled judgments about what we have most reason to do. This means that we must think of our immoral actions as occasioned by our having taken up our inclinations into our maxims as reasons for action, without conditioning our action on moral permissibility. Thus, we must think of virtue as steadfast adherence to maxims which do not do this—i.e. to maxims which always give priority to moral incentives in any conflict with incentives derived from inclination.

18 See for instance *The Metaphysics of Morals*, Ak. 376, 380, 394, 397 and 405; and Critique of Practical Reason, Ak. 118.

19 See Kant, *Religion*, p. 16.

20 See for instance *Metaphysics of Morals*, Ak. 392–3 and 447. One might wonder why Kant believes that we can sometimes know our maxims to be unlawful, yet can never know them to be moral. The most plausible explanation, I think, is that Kant supposes that we are not tempted to pass off moral maxims as immoral ones, hence we can be counted on not to deceive ourselves into the conclusion that we are vicious. This seems plausible, though it is a conclusion which Nietzsche might have disputed, given his diagnosis of morality as the flower of a positive will to find oneself unworthy.

However, while Kant maintains that we can never know ourselves or others to be virtuous, he also makes clear that certain
empirical facts do provide us with a defeasible indication of a virtuous disposition. Kant maintains that virtue in its *intelligible*
character (or *virtus noumenon*) is the actual ascendancy, in one's
highest-level maxim, of moral incentives over any and all incentives derived from inclination.[21] To say the same thing in another
way, it is the actual ascendancy of the moral law over the principle
of self-love.[22] By contrast, virtue in its *empirical* character (or *virtus phenomenon*) is reliable conformity with the outward dictates
of duty in one's actual conduct. While only a divinity could say
with confidence that we are virtuous, we can have grounds for
hope if our actions exhibit virtue in its empirical character. [23]

Now, there is no reason why this empirical conception of
virtue cannot be extended beyond the observed conformity of
actions to the requirements of duty. For example, when people
seem to have violated duties, those who have been harmed often
demand an explanation. The ability to meet this demand convincingly might be seen as an another element of our empirical conception of virtue. It provides us with a tentative and defeasible,
though by no means arbitrary way of distinguishing those apparent departures from the moral law which arise from vicious maxims from those which arise from excusable ignorance.

We might further extend our empirical conception of virtue by
observing correlations between characteristic sentiments and
desires, on the one hand, and outward conformity with the
requirements of duty on the other hand. For instance, we might
conclude that evident pleasure in the performance of one's duty is
a reliable empirical indication that one's past actions have been virtuous from the empirical point of view, or a reliable empirical indication that one's future actions will exhibit empirical virtue, or
both. We might come to such knowledge by observing that those

---

21 See Kant, *Religion*, p. 42.
22 The principle of self-love is the principle of doing what one is inclined
to do. This principle takes one's bare inclinations to be independently
conclusive reasons for action, rather than conditioning the satisfaction of inclinations on moral permissibility. Kant maintains that only
the maxim of self-love can rival the moral maxim for the position of
the will's supreme maxim, and that the general explanation of all
human evil is the subordination of the moral maxim to the maxim of
self-love. See Kant, *Religion...*, pp. 31–2, 37.
23 See Kant, *Religion...*, pp. 42 and 71.

who do not take pleasure in the performance of their duty often end up performing unlawful actions without convincing excuses, or by observing that those who routinely do their duty gradually begin to take pleasure in dutiful action. Kant suggests in various places that both of these empirical regularities obtain. For instance, he claims that those who are beneficent from duty will eventually come to have a direct inclination to help others, and he suggests that this provides a way of understanding the moral insight behind the Christian command to love one's neighbor.[24] He also claims that those who lack sympathetic feelings, and associated desires to help others, are less likely to do their duty than those who are generally sympathetic.[25]

If the empirical conception of virtue is extended in the way that I have suggested, it provides one possible way of understanding why Kant maintained that joyfulness in the performance of duty is a mark of virtuous character. A rough coordination between duty and immediate desire is an empirical indication that one has generally acted dutifully in the past and that one is likely to do so in the future. Indeed, this might be the soundest interpretation of Kant's claim.

Someone who interpreted Kant in this way might be tempted by the further thought that such empirical correlations, if indeed they obtain, provide an adequate response to the difficulties I raised in the last chapter. We have moral reservations about those who are strongly and persistently tempted to violate their duty because such strong and persistent temptations indicate that they have not done their duty in the past, and perhaps also that they are unlikely to do it in the future. While this might well be true, I do not think that it

---

24 Kant, *The Metaphysics of Morals*, Ak. 402. It is not strictly correct to call this an empirical regularity, since we can never simply observe, even in our own case, that a particular helping action is chosen from duty. I think that we can only make sense of Kant's claim if we understand him as saying that those who reliably help others, and hence evidence the empirical aspect of the virtue of benevolence, generally come to take pleasure in helping others. This at least is a regularity that Kant could possibly claim to know. See also *The Metaphysics of Morals*, Ak. 472–3, and *Anthropology from a Pragmatic Point of View*, Ak. 235 and 236.

25 Kant, *Anthropology from a Pragmatic Point of View*, section 75. In this passage, Kant claims that sympathy plays an important role in prompting us to do what duty requires, then adds that this role ends when reason has attained sufficient *strength* to do the job itself—thus suggesting that the role of sympathy is to reinforce subjectively weak moral incentives.

goes to the heart of the difficulties I have raised. The problem is that such empirical correlations do not give us any insight into the nature of the connection between characteristic affects and good maxims. Once we gain due insight into this matter, we will see that there is a *conceptual connection*—not merely an empirical connection— between having the right affects and acting on the right maxims. I will attempt to justify these claims in the next three sections.

PART III: AFFECTS AND PERCEPTUAL SALIENCE

It has become popular to claim that certain moral facts are obscured from view unless one has been socialized in such a way as to be appropriately sensitized to them. This claim, which seems to me a truism, can be used to shed light on why appropriate feelings and desires are essential elements of virtuous character. Sympathy, for instance, might be valued as a way—perhaps the only way—of ensuring that the needs of others are highlighted in one's immediate perception of the situations in which one must act. The sympathetic person notices the unfulfilled needs of others, and desires to help meet these needs. Since desires are spurs to practical deliberation, sympathy can be thought of as a reliable propensity to give deliberative weight to the needs of others—i.e. to assign to them the status of *prima-facie* reasons for action.[26] If one were abstractly committed to helping others but lacked a sympathetic constitution, one would not experience these highly particularized desires to help others, and one's abstract ratiocination might fail as a means of identifying all those occasions on which beneficence is morally required.

Now, this way of accounting for the moral importance of characteristic feelings and desires is very close to my own. There is, however, an important difference. I argued in the last chapter that practical judgment is already in "mid-stride"—that one has already provisionally mapped reasons onto the world—when one is in the grip of certain feelings and desires. The view at hand makes a more modest claim: that practical judgment is highly unlikely to track

---

26 The sympathetic person need not always judge at the endpoint of deliberation that she ought to help everyone in need. This is not just because no single person can help everyone, but also because there are some people whose projects are immoral and one ought not to help such people complete their projects.

the right unless one's feelings and desires are properly attuned to the space of practical reasons. On this view, feelings and desires are *instrumentally* valuable because they help us to make good judgments. Without *some* such pattern of variable salience, we would not know where to begin in determining what to do; practical judgment would be lost, so to speak, in a sea of extraneous detail. And with a *misleading* or *perverse* pattern of variable salience, practical judgment would be blind and very likely to wander astray.[27]

There are mixed indications as to whether Kant himself assigned a role of this sort to the affects. Some interpreters have found an expression of this view in the following passage from *The Metaphysics of Morals*:

> It is therefore a duty not to avoid the places where the poor
> who lack the most basic necessities are to be found but
> rather to seek them out, and not to shun sick-rooms or
> debtors' prisons and so forth in order to avoid sharing
> painful feelings one may not be able to resist. For this is still
> one of the impulses that nature has implanted in us to do
> what the representation of duty alone would not accom-
> plish.[28]

Paul Guyer, for instance, reads this passage as "suggesting that our natural inclination to sympathy can be used as an instrument for the discovery of what actions need to be taken in order to realize our general policy of benevolence." According to Guyer, Kant's idea is that "We are to visit places of suffering, bringing along our predisposition to sympathy as a pair of moral eyes, the painful sensations of which will alert us to the need for action."[29]

It seems to me, however, that Kant does not make clear in the quoted passage or in the surrounding context that he is recommending the cultivation of compassionate feelings as a way of heightening our awareness of occasions for helping others, and not

---

27 A *misleading* pattern of variable salience would highlight certain
   morally irrelevant features of the world and/or obscure certain moral
   reasons for action. A *perverse* one, by contrast, might highlight the
   fact that a certain action would cause another to suffer as an attractive feature of the action.
28 Kant, *The Metaphysics of Morals*, Ak. 457.
29 Paul Guyer, *Kant and the Experience of Freedom*, Op. Cit., p. 389.

merely as a way of reinforcing the distressingly weak attachment of humans to the moral law.[30] One reason to doubt Guyer's interpretation is that it fits poorly with Kant's efforts elsewhere to rehabilitate the Stoic virtue of apathy. In one telling passage in *Anthropology from a Pragmatic Point of View*, Kant argues for the superiority of apathy precisely on the ground that "an affect makes us (more or less) blind." Immediately thereafter Kant contrasts apathy with sympathy, and while he acknowledges that sympathy plays an important role in prompting us to do what duty requires, he claims that this role ends when reason has attained sufficient *strength* to do the job itself—thus suggesting that the role of sympathy is not to sensitize us but to reinforce subjectively weak moral incentives.[31]

While it is unclear what position we ought to assign to Kant, some contemporary theorists who count themselves Kantians have argued that one could not possibly be virtuous without having internalized certain characteristic forms of sensitivity, or patterns of awareness, since otherwise one could not reliably identify and respond to moral reasons for action. On this understanding of Kantianism—which is developed most convincingly in the groundbreaking work of Barbara Herman. In much of her work, however, Herman underestimates the degree to which Kantianism must be revised in order to accommodate her insights. I will argue that such insights require far-reaching and thoroughly welcome changes in the traditional Kantian understanding of maxims of action and virtues of character.

According to Herman, Kant's Categorical Imperative cannot provide a self-sufficient decision procedure, and was never intended to do so. It must be supplemented by an internalized moral sensitivity, typically acquired during socialization, which brings to our attention those features of the world which may be morally relevant, and flags these features for consideration in the course of

---

30 In her annotations to her translation of *The Metaphysics of Morals*, Mary Gregor seems to indicate that she reads the passage in this latter way. In this footnote, Gregor refers readers to Kant's comment in "The End of All Things" (Ak. 337–8) that Christian love of neighbors might be indispensable to human observance of the dictates of morality, since the incentive of duty is subjectively weak in many of us.

31 Kant, *Anthropology from a Pragmatic Point of View*, section 75. Kant also praises apathy in *The Metaphysics of Morals*, Ak. 408–9.

practical deliberation. Herman uses the term 'Rules of Moral Salience' (or 'RMS') to refer to such an internalized sensitivity to *prima-facie* moral reasons.[32]

Herman presents a number of different arguments for the importance of RMS to Kantian theory. First, Herman maintains that an agent must have moral knowledge independent of the Categorical Imperative in order to use the universalizability test at all. The test requires that we must formulate a maxim which includes all facts about our situation which seem to us to justify the action we are contemplating, and we could not discriminate which facts were relevant to the justification of our action unless we had some prior grasp of what counts as a moral reason.[33]

I find this argument unconvincing as it stands. To take up Herman's own example, we all are quite aware that the mere fact that an action takes place on a Tuesday is ordinarily irrelevant from the moral point of view.[34] There is no reason, however, to suppose that this sort of knowledge of moral relevance is independent of our knowledge of the Categorical Imperative. After all, those who grant that the Categorical Imperative is not entirely empty might well argue that we could substantiate the moral irrelevance of the fact that an action is done on a Tuesday by running tests on pairs of maxims which differ only in that one includes this as a condition for acting, while the other excludes it, and seeing for ourselves that this condition never alters the outcome of the test. Of course, it would be implausible to suppose that this is how we actually *learned* this bit of common sense—maybe we were just laughed at by our peers or parents when we pleaded for special rights or exemptions on the ground that it was after all Tuesday. Still, this might be the best *justification* we can supply for the moral irrelevance of the mere fact that something is done on Tuesday.

While Herman's argument does not show conclusively that the mature Kantian agent must have some moral knowledge which is *independent* of the Categorical Imperative, it does show that we cannot plausibly picture the virtuous agent as someone with a purely abstract commitment to veto any action whose maxim can-

---

32 *Ibid.*, p. 78.
33 *Ibid.*, p. 75.
34 *Ibid.*

not be universalized. As Herman points out, the virtuous agent must have a well-developed sense of which features of the world are morally relevant if her maxims are not to grow indefinitely in length, including reams and reams of irrelevant facts. Furthermore, as Herman also points out, fully virtuous agents must have a capacity to notice features of situations which indicate that there might be a duty in the offing. Such a capacity is necessary because it is implausible to think that morality requires us to consider, with each and every step we take, whether we are operating under acceptable maxims, or whether there might be some duty in the offing. If morality required this of us, it would be an onerous burden indeed: it would never be permissible to give our full attention to anything but the demands of morality. This would lend considerable plausibility to the complaints of that band of modern-day Romantics and Nietzscheans who find in morality a denial of life. Kantian theory can be made more attractive, and perhaps also more plausible, if it can be squared with the intuitive idea that we do not need to deliberate about morality ceaselessly, and that we can reserve moral deliberation for those occasions when there is some reason to suspect that there might be a duty in the offing.[35] But if this is right, then fully virtuous agents must have a capacity to notice features of situations which indicate that there might be a duty in the offing, and these features must trigger focused practical deliberation.

Herman's position is most convincing in the case of imperfect duties. Perhaps it is true, as Nietzsche argued, that a great deal of bloody and torturous "prehistoric labor" was required to burn into the human mind a capacity to remember one's promises, or to stop and think before pillaging, raping or killing. Still, with most members of each new generation we succeed in the ontogenetic recapitulation of this phylogenetic achievement, often without so much as a single spanking. It is a far rarer and more remarkable achievement to develop a capacity to take notice of what others need if they are to attain their own ends, and to help them to meet these needs—yet this is precisely what one must do if one is to fulfill the imperfect duty of beneficence. Ethical theorists sometimes have a way of simplifying the contours of this duty by focusing on cases where there is an obvious and dire need for some straight-

---

35 *Ibid.*, p. 75–6.

forward sort of material aid—e.g. where someone is drowning or
starving or in need of medication. There are, however, a variety of
other, more subtle obstacles to the attainment of ends—for example, lack of self-confidence, self-deprecation or self-loathing—and
those who are sensitized to the inarticulate debilities and sufferings
of others are in the best position to identify and help negotiate
these obstacles.[36]

I indicated above that I had doubts about Guyer's interpretation of Kant's treatment of sympathy. Kant's view aside, however,
it seems to me quite plausible to think of sympathy in the way
Guyer suggests, as a perceptual or quasi-perceptual sensitivity to
the needs and desires of others. We can bring out the importance
of sympathy as a form of moral sensitivity by considering other
ways that the frustrations and sufferings of others might be given
salience in one's conscious experience. These same features of the
world have great salience in the experience of the sadistic person.
Such a person notices and dwells on the sufferings of others as a
source of positive delight. Sadism draws one's attention to many of
the same morally relevant features of the world as does sympathy.
If sympathy is virtuous and sadistic feelings are not, this can only
be because of differences in the *initial valuation* they assign to
these morally relevant features of the world. The sadist characteristically takes suffering to be a good thing, and desires to produce
or heighten it, while the sympathetic person characteristically
takes suffering to be a bad thing, and desires to avoid or assuage
it.

We can also imagine someone who notices the same phenomena that are salient for the sympathetic person and the sadist, but
is entirely indifferent to them, taking them as neither good nor

---

36 I find it quite plausible to develop the duty of beneficence in this way,
as a perfectionist goal before which all of us will very likely fall short
to varying degrees, in part because we are not sufficiently sensitized
to the needs of others. This development of the duty of beneficence is
only plausible if we follow Kant in thinking of it as a duty of
virtue—that is, a set of requirements for which there are no corresponding rights to coerce performance of the duty. (See Kant, *The
Metaphysics of Morals*, Ak. 383) This permits us to say that we are
under a moral requirement to identify and help to meet the needs of
others, and that we ought properly to admonish ourselves to the
extent that we fail to do so, while permitting us to deny that particular others have a right to this sort of help and can demand it (or
even, if this were possible, extract it) as their due.

bad. Such a pattern of attentiveness would be quite unusual, but off-hand there seems to be no reason to think it impossible.[37] However, such a pattern of attentiveness would not serve as a prod to practical reasoning, since it does not present the suffering of another as a feature of the world which counts in favor of *doing* any thing in particular. While sadism would seem to be a perverse pattern of moral salience, this purely theoretical interest in suffering would seem to me not to count as a pattern of moral salience at all, because it does not flag suffering as something of practical import.

This brief discussion casts light on an important feature of moral sensitivity. Our initial experience of the practical salience of a feature of the world cannot plausibly be conceived as a neutral or non-evaluative prelude to practical judgment. We do not merely "flag" certain features of the world as things which ought to be considered in one way or another in deliberation; we notice them as features of the world that ordinarily have a very particular *kind* of weight in our deliberation. When we register the practical urgency of features of the world around, we already provisionally classify them as goods or evils, hence as reasons to do one thing or another.[38] This prompts us to engage in focused deliberation in order to determine, on reflection, whether these features of the world really do have the value or the reason-giving force that they

---

37 Here I believe I am in disagreement with Nancy Sherman, who claims that "any notion of attending or noticing presupposes some affective interest in the subject matter." I say that I *believe* I am in disagreement, because it is possible that Sherman would count abstract fascination or engrossment as a species of affective interest, whereas I am tempted to think of them as cases of affectless interest. See Nancy Sherman, "The Place of Emotions in Kantian Morality," in Owen Flanagan and Amelie Oksenberg Rorty, eds., *Identity, Character and Morality: Essays in Moral Psychology* (Cambridge; MIT Press, 1990), pp. 149–170, esp. p. 150.
38 Gestalt psychologists have tended to focus their attention on one particular mode of 'seeing as': foregrounding certain elements of the perceptual field while backgrounding others. This reflects an incomplete, uni-dimensional understanding of the ways in which our perceptions can carry what Wittgenstein calls "the echo of a thought in sight." (*Philosophical Investigations*, p. 212e) We can also see certain things as parts of some narrative, or as parts of some causal chain of events, or as answering to one or another concept. The "seeings as" which are most important to acuity in moral discernment are, I think, those which highlight some particular feature of the world as good or bad, and/or as a reason for action or inaction.

initially appear to us to have. When we picture what Herman calls "the structure of moral sensitivity" in this light, it is somewhat more obvious that it consists largely in characteristic feelings and desires, since these play precisely the role that Herman assigns to the RMS—they highlight features of the world and assign to them a provisional evaluation.

Developed along these lines, Herman's view of practical deliberation does suggest another possible Kantian resolution of the nest of problems I raised in Chapter One. In the first place, it provides a relatively convincing explanation of our intuition that there is something morally amiss about the unsympathetic benefactor presented by Kant in *Groundwork I*. It now appears that while the unsympathetic benefactor might occasionally act beneficently, he could not possibly fulfill the duty of beneficence in its entirety, since he lacks the characteristic feelings and desires which are needed to identify and respond appropriately to the needs of others. On these grounds, we might say that the unsympathetic benefactor is not fully virtuous. On the other hand, the unsympathetic benefactor might on isolated occasions manage to notice what others need and help them to secure it, and when he does his commitment to the *abstract* principle of beneficence shows through quite clearly. Kant wishes to draw our attention precisely to this sort of case, since it serves his purpose of isolating the motive of duty from all other possible motives. However, this does not commit Kant, or the Kantian, to the claim that the unsympathetic benefactor is virtuous. One clear sign that he lacks virtue is that despite his abstract commitment to the principle of beneficence, he will often fail to notice occasions on which he is morally bound to act beneficently, and as a result he will often fail to help even when he is duty-bound to do so.

If we were to interpret Kant in this way, then it might appear that I was wrong to argue in Chapter One that a morally worthy action could not be performed by someone who is not fully virtuous. I presented several arguments—both textual and more broadly philosophical—for this point. The key philosophical argument was that we could not make sense of the notion of a morally worthy action by a vicious person without presupposing the possibility of momentary commitment to a principle. Some commentators who argue for a clear separation between the notions of moral worth and virtue seem to presuppose that one could adopt a principle on an isolated occasion then immediately discard it. I argued that this possibility implies that we could have new principles with each passing action, and I claimed that this is absurd since the behavior of anyone whose standards were so fleeting and changeable would properly be called unprincipled. I believe that this criticism applies equally well to the Kantian position now under discussion, and I will attempt to substantiate this point below. On the surface, however, it would seem that the criticism does not apply. The constitutionally unsympathetic person described by Kant could be understood as someone who has a deep-seated and enduring commitment to the abstract principle of beneficence, and whose actions are morally worthy whenever he manages to act on this enduring principle, but who lacks the moral sensitivity to discern the concrete implications of this principle reliably.

There are textual grounds, which I reviewed in the previous chapter, for doubting that this is the most faithful interpretation of Kant. In the first instance, Kant presents his examples of morally worthy action as a way of illustrating the motivational structure of the good-willed person, and I supplied textual evidence in the last chapter to show that Kant equates virtue with goodness of will. There is also more direct textual evidence that Kant believed that virtue itself, and not merely moral worth, is displayed most clearly by cases of persons who act dutifully in the absence of any inclination to do so. This is clearest in Part II of the *Second Critique*—the "Methodology of Pure Practical Reason"—where Kant presents precisely this sort of case as an "exhibition of pure virtue."[39]

Still, even if this position cannot be attributed to Kant, one might present it as a compelling position which is broadly Kantian.[40] This might seem to provide a Kantian resolution of the problems I raised in Chapter One, since it provides us with a way of articulating our moral reservation about the unsympathetic benefactor. As just noted, we now have Kantian grounds for saying that he is not fully virtuous. Such a theory would also provide the seeds for a more illuminating explanation of the nature and source of human evil than is ordinarily attributed to Kant. I argued in the last chapter that Kant does not adequately distinguish

---

39 Kant, *Critique of Practical Reason*, Ak. 151–2.
40 This is the way Herman presents her position in *The Practice of Moral Judgment*, p. 73.

between moral wrongs arising from overindulgence towards unobjectionable desires and wrongs arising from sadistic desires. The Kantian position now under discussion has the resources for explaining the peculiar evil of sadistic desires. Such desires are objectionable, on this theory, because they distort our practical judgment by providing it with inappropriate or misleading starting points.

While this form of Kantianism does answer a number of the objections raised in the last chapter, it seems to me that it misses an important dimension of the problem. I noted above that one important distinction between my position and Herman's is that I claim that moral judgment is in mid-stride when certain feelings and desires arise. Herman, by contrast, draws a sharp demarcation between deliberation and moral judgment, and maintains that moral judgment is a discreet and occasional process, triggered only when our RMS prompt us to think about what we ought to do.[41] This distinction serves an important purpose for Herman, since she maintains that we can be blamed morally only for making and acting on judgments which are objectionable given the way that our particular patterns of moral salience have structured the choice situation for us. On Herman's view, we cannot ordinarily be blamed for defects in our moral sensitivity nor for mistakes in judgment arising from such defects.[42]

Herman's position has a certain intuitive appeal, since we do have the intuitive sense that there is something unfair about blaming people for the effects of a bad upbringing. However, I will try to show that Herman is mistaken in attempting to separate moral sensitivity from moral judgment, and in holding us responsible only for the latter. My argument will proceed in three stages. First, I will assume that we can make sense of the notion that we could always act on good maxims even if we had the wrong RMS, and I will try to show that Herman's view yields a distorted picture of the value of moral sensitivity. Second, I will try to show that

41 I believe that this is what Herman means when she writes that "Moral judgment is not the first step in moral deliberation." (*Ibid.*, p. 76)
42 As Herman writes, "Someone who fails to understand the nature or seriousness of another's need will fail to help without acting non-beneficently (he has no desire to refrain from helping acts)." (*Ibid.*, p. 89.) Herman goes on to compare this case to the case of someone who unknowingly deceives another because he does not know the truth. In such a case, the problem "lies at the level of the RMS [Rules of Moral Salience] and not in the agent's willing." (Ibid., p. 90)

Herman is wrong to assume that we could act on good maxims even if we had bad RMS, and I will suggest that this error arises from a distorted picture of the place of rules in moral deliberation. Finally, I will try to provide an alternative ground for distinguishing between those distortions of moral sensitivity which are morally blameworthy and those which are not.

PART IV: THE VALUE OF MORAL SENSIBILITY

Herman's view, in essence, is that the value of having the "right" sort of sensitivity is purely instrumental; the objection to defective RMS is that they lead us to make errors of moral judgment. When they do, we cannot ordinarily be held responsible for our errors. The first and perhaps most obvious problem with this claim is that it introduces an expansive new category of moral excuse, one which frees people of accountability for all actions whose maxims seem to be universalizable only because of a particular, idiosyncratic way of seeing (or overlooking) the reasons for action imposed by the circumstances. This might provide fodder for a telling criticism of Herman's position. However, I want to begin by challenging Herman from a different direction. If an internalized moral sensitivity had the purely instrumental sort of value that Herman assigns to it, there would in principle be nothing wrong with being sensitized to moral reasons in some other way. I will try to show that there would in fact be something wrong with this.

Suppose for a moment that we could enlist the services of some advanced pocket-sized computer (fitted with the functional equivalent of eyes and ears) to notify us of the morally relevant features of the world around us, and to feed us (perhaps via earphone) a first-blush approximation of their reason-giving force. We would then have no need for an internalized moral sensitivity of our own. (If the notion of so supple and intelligent a computer strains credulity, imagine that morally insensitive people could rent the services of other, more sensitive people as full-time advisors.) If moral sensitivity were valuable merely as a means of supplying accurate inputs to practical deliberation, then it would be no more a mark of a personal shortcoming to need a sensitivity computer than to need eyeglasses in order to insure an accurate perception of the world around us. Just as needing eyeglasses does not show a lack of good judgment about the way the world is, so needing a sensitivity computer (or personal advisor) would not manifest poor judgment about what is valuable or what ought to be done.

Well then, *would* it be disturbing to have need of a "sensitivity computer" in order to make good moral judgments? Consider the closely related case of sensitivity within friendships. A person who had not internalized the right "Rules of Friendship Salience" might be prone to annoying blunders. Suppose, for instance, that Bill's friend's mother has just died, and that Bill happens across this friend just prior to her departure for the funeral. Bill remembers that his friend is going away on a trip, but it simply does not register in Bill's mind that this particular trip will be a somber one. We might imagine that Bill has simply forgotten the trip's purpose, or better, that he remembers it in an abstract way (he would give the right answer if asked what the trip's purpose was) but does not properly attend to his knowledge prior to speaking. At any rate, this fact lacks salience for him. What this means is that rather than offering comfort and moral support, Bill says casually, "I hope you have a terrific get-away!"

This all-purpose send-off is obviously not tailored to the particular needs of Bill's friend, and this is disturbing. It seems implausible to say—as Herman would say in the moral case—that Bill cannot be faulted because, given his unfortunate way of perceiving the world, his intentions and actions are entirely praiseworthy. There is a certain betrayal, albeit a minor and forgivable one, in Bill's absence of sympathetic attention to the distress of his friend. What is critical to my case, though, is that this deficiency would hardly be removed if Bill had a computer in his pocket which reminded him that his friend was off to her mother's funeral, and that other things equal this counts in favor of offering words of comfort and moral support. We do not want our friends to have our needs and interests in mind simply because this will increase the odds of their saying and doing appropriate things; we want them to have our needs and interests in mind because we want them to care about our needs and interests, and having our needs and interests in mind is part and parcel of caring about them.

Now, it might be thought that the affects are important only in friendships and other intimate relationships, and that a moral responsiveness to persons in general does not require any such thing. I think this is mistaken. The reason that sympathetic feelings matter within friendships is that they manifest that one grants importance to the needs and interests of one's friend. Sympathetic feelings are important for precisely the same sort of reason in the context of impersonal relationships. There are differences, of course. We are not expected to give the same weight to the needs and interests of strangers as to those of our friends, so our sympathetic feelings need not be so extensive. Furthermore, there is no single stranger who is particularly hurt, or can claim to have been betrayed, if our feelings for humanity in general are not sufficiently lively. However, an important similarity between the two cases can be brought out by focusing on self-evaluation. If we find it difficult to attend to the needs and interests of our friends, but still avow a commitment to the friendship, this might well show that we do not actually allot to them the value that we take them to have in our considered judgments. From the first-personal point of view, the problem is not just that we might hurt our friend; it is that our considered assessment of the value of the friendship does not have the force of a conviction. Likewise, if we find it difficult to attend to the needs and interests of other persons in general, but still avow a commitment to the duty of beneficence, this might well show that we do not whole-heartedly allot to others the sort of value that we profess them to have. We profess a belief that they are valuable as ends in themselves, and this entails that we are to assign value to their ends and help them to further these ends. Our insensibility, however, shows that this professed belief does not have the force of a conviction. From the first-personal point of view, this is disturbing for some of the same reasons as an affective detachment from friendships.

Needing a "sensitivity computer" to fulfill the impersonal duty of beneficence is importantly different from needing eyeglasses to make accurate judgments about the way things are. This is because there is no reason to suppose that e.g. near-sightedness manifests a lack of conviction that the world has the sharp edges and well-defined contours that one takes it to have. By contrast, an insensitivity to the concrete markers of one's professed principles and values does sometimes manifest a lack of conviction in these principles and values. And this, I think, is why it can sometimes (though not always) make sense to blame oneself for one's own insensitivity, and perhaps to praise others for their sensitivity. I will attempt to develop and substantiate this point further in Part VI below, where I make a distinction between two kinds of perceptual illusions.

PART V: THE PLACE OF RULES IN MORAL SENSIBILITY

In arguing against Herman, I have been assuming that our maxim could be right even if our sensitivity were askew, and I claimed that a lack of sensitivity might show that we lack conviction in our own maxims or principles of action. I will now argue that Herman is mistaken to suggest that our maxims of our actions can be identified without reference to our patterns of sensitivity. As I suggested above, I think that Herman's mistake has its source in a mistaken conception of the place of rules in moral deliberation. Herman herself notes that it is potentially misleading to use the term 'rules' to refer to the patterns of sensitivity required for appropriate responsiveness to moral reasons. After all, she notes, these "rules" are not learned in the form of "bits of information about the world" nor in the form of "rules of guidance to use when engaged in particular sorts of activities."[43] We might develop this point by drawing a comparison between sensitization to moral reasons for action and sensitization to the feelings of others (indeed, as I hinted above, the latter sort of sensitization is quite often an instance of the former). We are never taught explicit rules which map facial appearances to feelings, nor could those of us who have become competent in doing this actually articulate a set of rules which capture our competency. As Wittgenstein quite plausibly maintains, we do not need to conclude that a face is sad. Before we develop an appropriate sensibility, we are blind to sadness, and once we have developed it we simply *see* the face as sad. This, I think, is what it is like to take on what Herman calls Rules of Moral Salience (RMS); it is to change one's way of perceiving the world.[44]

---

43 *Ibid.*

44 Wittgenstein revealingly writes, "Is there such a thing as 'expert judgment' about the genuineness of expressions of feeling?—Even here, there are those whose judgment is 'better' and those whose judgment is 'worse'. . . Can one learn this knowledge? Yes; some can. Not, however, by taking a course in it, but through '*experience*'. . . What one acquires here is not a technique; one learns correct judgments. There are also rules, but they do not form a system, and only experienced people can apply them rightly. Unlike calculating-rules." (Ludwig Wittgenstein, *Philosophical Investigations*, Op. Cit., p. 227e.)

I believe, however, that there is a further distortion involved in thinking of moral sensitivity as an application of rules. The problem is that if the RMS are conceived on the model of rules, they cannot play the distinctive role that Herman assigns to them. One of Herman's key arguments for introducing the RMS is that we cannot picture the practical reasoning of the virtuous moral agent as a simple matter of applying general maxims to ever-changing situations. The trouble, as noted above, is that on this model we could never permissibly cease from moral judgment. The RMS are supposed to solve this problem by bringing to our attention those features of situations which call for moral judgment. They cannot solve this problem, however, if RMS are conceived simply as another set of rules. Suppose that someone were to memorize a commendable set of RMS and commit herself to apply them diligently so as not to overlook a single occasion that calls for moral judgment. Such a person would still have to engage in continual deliberation, testing each new situation against the RMS in order to determine whether there were any morally relevant facts in the vicinity.

Herman recognizes and responds to this difficulty. She says that the rules of moral salience must be *internalized*, so as to become second nature. However, it seems to me that by speaking of *rules* which must be internalized, Herman runs the risk of missing the real philosophical importance of her own observations about moral sensitivity. In my view, her observations ought to alter our way of thinking about what it is to have and act on a maxim.

A maxim links a set of circumstances and/or purposes to a kind of action, and asserts that the circumstances and purposes justify the action in the sense that they constitute a sufficient reason to perform it. Maxims, then, are personal rules of action. If *having* a maxim were nothing more than being disposed to avow the maxim sincerely as an authoritative guide to action, then having the right maxims could not be all there is to virtuous character, since it is always possible to apply maxims clumsily or stupidly.[45] By way of comparison, having an aptitude for logical inference is not simply a matter of sincerely affirming correct rules of inference, since (as is revealed by Lewis Carroll's famous puzzle)

---

45 On this point, see Gilbert Ryle, "Knowing How and Knowing That," in Ryle, *Collected Papers Volume II: Collected Essays 1929–1968* (New York; Barnes and Noble: 1971), pp. 212–225, esp. pp. 215–16.

these rules might simply be added to the list of propositions that one is ready to take as premises, and a fresh question might arise about what follows from the new list of premises.[46] The importance of Carroll's paradox, as Gilbert Ryle points out, is that knowing how to make logical inferences is not fundamentally a matter of knowing that certain rules of logical inference are the correct ones, but is rather a matter of being able to move fluidly from certain classes of acknowledgments to others. The rules of inference describe the moves made by people with this know-how or ability, but a mere recognition of the correctness of these rules cannot by itself account for their making these moves.[47] Nor can this know-how be accounted for as a mere recognition of the correctness of some further set of rules—rules which, like Herman's RMS, alert us that a particular inference rule ought to be applied—since the mere affirmation of these rules would not itself guarantee that we would apply inference rules at appropriate times.[48]

As with logical inference, so too mastery in practical reasoning

---

46 Lewis Carroll, "What the Tortoise Said to Achilles," *Mind*, Volume 4, 1895, pp. 278–80; reprinted for centennial in *Mind*, Volume 104, Number 416, October 1995, pp. 691–3.

47 *Ibid.*, p. 216–17.

48 Kant himself seems to recognize this point, at least in the case of rules of logic. This is evident in the following passage:

> If it is sought to give general instructions how we are to subsume under these rules [of general logic], that is, to distinguish whether something does or does not come under them, that could only be by means of another rule. This in turn, for the very reason that it is a rule, again demands guidance from judgment. And thus it appears that, though understanding is capable of being instructed, and of being equipped with rules, judgment is a peculiar talent which can be practised only, and cannot be taught. It is the specific quality of so-called mother-wit, and its lack no school can make good. For although an abundance of rules borrowed from the insight of others may indeed be proffered to, and as it were grafted upon, a limited understanding, the power of rightly employing them must belong to the learner himself; and in the absence of such natural gift no rule that may be prescribed to him for this purpose can ensure against misuse. (Immanuel Kant, *Critique of Pure Reason*, translated by Norman Kemp Smith (New York; St. Martin's Press: 1929), A133; B172.)

is not just a matter of a purely intellectualist recognition of the authority of universalizable maxims, nor of the authority of some further set of rules which provide guidance in the application of universalizable maxims. What is needed, instead, is know-how— understood here as deftness in moving from certain classes of circumstances to certain classes of decisions about what to do.

It seems to me, then, that the temptation to introduce rules of moral salience arises from a misconception of what it means to have and to act on a maxim. This point can best be brought out by considering the various perspectives from which the demand to identify one's maxim can arise. This demand does not always arise during deliberation, as part of some formal or informal test of universalizability. The Kantian assigns maxims even to those actions performed whimsically and without forethought, since this is a condition of viewing them as actions rather than mechanical events. The demand for a maxim arises from a commitment to keep in sight the agency of ourselves and others, and it can arise retrospectively, as it does when one is asked by another to justify what one has done, or when one feels a sudden and unanticipated scruple about what one has done. When the demand to identify one's maxim arises in this retrospective way, it cannot be met by simply *recollecting* the maxim that we have already formulated and self-consciously accepted in the course of deliberation. In many cases there is no such maxim. Even if we did formulate a principle in the moment of decision, this alone would not settle the question what maxim we acted on, since we are all prone to self-deceptive exaggeration of the nobility of our motives. We can only meet the retrospective demand to identify our maxim by engaging in sincere scrutiny of our own deliberative processes, with an eye to determining which features of the situation gained our attention and prompted us to act as we did. Furthermore, we cannot limit our attention to the particular action under consideration, but must take into account the entire series of our actions. After all, it will not do to conclude that our maxim is to help others whenever they need it, if the only occasions on which the needs of others are salient for us are those on which we stand to benefit greatly by helping. The fact that this is what we are thinking when we help does not provide a reliable indication of true altruistic concern. When we identify a set of features of the world which reliably prompt us to perform actions of the kind we performed, and which were salient in our experience just prior to the action in question, then we have done all we can do to identify our maxim: it is the maxim which counts precisely those features of the world as sufficient reason for acting in the way we did.

In many actual cases, then, we will be unable to identify the maxims of our actions without reference to the actual patterns of salience that structure our experience of the world and that set the stage for our decisions.[49] Our maxims are not simply those general policies which we sincerely affirm, in calm moments of inaction, as authoritative for us. A maxim cannot be considered fully one's own—it cannot be considered one's standing policy—unless the features of the world which the maxim counts as sufficient reason for action are salient elements of one's experience, for only then can those features of the world determine one's actions.[50]

I am not suggesting that this is what we ordinarily do when someone asks us, perhaps with an air of indignation, why we did one thing or another. No doubt most of us, most of the time, respond to such requests by fishing for rationalizations—that is, reasons whose justificatory force is superior to our actual reasons. I am only claiming that we *must* engage in this sort of reconstruction of our actions if we are to isolate their *maxims*.

I suggested above that someone who accepted Herman's picture of deliberation and judgment might argue that the unsympathetic helper's maxim is morally commendable when he helps, but that he lacks virtue because he does not help reliably. I also sug-

---

49 The parallel between maxims and rules of inference holds at this level as well. We do not say that someone accepts or follows correct rules of inference unless they tend to notice occasions on which these rules apply and draw the inferences specified by these rules.

50 As I argued in the last chapter, the attribution of maxims must also be guided by diachronic considerations—i.e. by what has had salience for us, and what we have done, in other relevantly similar situations. Our actual incentives are not entirely transparent to us. Other things equal, we ought not to conclude that our reason for doing X was some feature of a situation that has never prompted us to do X before, or that did not prompt us to do X on several other occasions. Thus, if I kept a promise yesterday, when it was very convenient for me to do so, but have consistently broken promises in situations differing only in that promise-keeping would have been inconvenient, this counts against the claim that my maxim was moral—even if the mere fact that I had promised had a kind of phenomenological salience for me yesterday, when I kept my promise.

gested that one might hold this without presupposing the absurdity of momentary commitment to a principle. The idea was that the constitutionally unsympathetic person described by Kant could be understood as someone who has a deep-seated and enduring commitment to a universalizable principle of beneficence, but who lacks the moral sensitivity to discern the concrete implications of this principle reliably. I am now in a position to bring out the incoherence of this picture of the unsympathetic helper. In order to identify the maxim of the unsympathetic helper, we would have to survey a long stretch of his biography with an eye to determining what circumstances generally prompt him to help. His maxim will be one of helping when those circumstances obtain. If sympathy is indeed essential to noticing and responding dutifully to the unmet needs and interests of others, then his maxim will be immoral. It will not do, then, to see the constitutionally unsympathetic person in *Groundwork I* as someone whose maxim is to help others when they need it, since there are persuasive grounds for supposing that his lack of sympathy would make it impossible for him to notice and act respond reliably to the needs of others. We could only make sense of Kant's claim that his action is morally worthy by thinking of him as adopting, in this action, a maxim which he does not ordinarily have, and then discarding this maxim in the moment of his next failure to provide morally required help.

Herman's position, as best as I can reconstruct it, is that the unsympathetic person's failures to help are not morally blameworthy because, given the patterns of moral salience that he happens to have, he is under no obligation to help. Hence even when he does not help, his maxim is above reproach. I think that this picture gets its appeal from a misconstrual of our capacity for self-direction in accordance with maxims of action that we accept. Kant insists that we have to see our actions as following from maxims we accept in order to make sense of ourselves as agents. If this is taken to mean that we have to see each of our actions as following in fact from the conscious practical recognition of the authority of a maxim, then it requires that we take a thoroughly inhuman and hence implausible view of ourselves. It seems to me much more plausible to suppose that in order to keep our agency in view, we are required to *reconstruct* our behavior by interposing an implicit maxim-structured judgment between our immediate perceptual organization of the world and our response to the world so organized. If we think of maxims in this light, then we will not be tempted to conclude that the unsympathetic helper's maxims are beyond reproach on those occasions when he fails to provide morally required help (nor in fact on those occasions when he does manage to provide such help). His lack of sympathy means that he often fails to notice the needs of others as prima-facie reasons for action, and presumably on those occasions he gives undue priority to his own needs and interests.

Perhaps we would lose sight of his agency if we thought of the needs and desires that structured his perception of the world as the *cause* of his action. However, we can keep his agency in view while thinking of that view of the world as a clue to the reconstruction of his *reasons* for thinking it worthwhile to act as he did. We sometimes do things in thrall to considerations which we would not consciously and reflectively affirm as sufficient grounds for acting as we did. We neglect a promise because we are bewitched by the beauty of the weather. When we do, we can only take responsibility for what we have done by attributing to ourselves a practical judgment which in hindsight we renounce—e.g. the judgment that enjoying beautiful weather is sufficient reason to break a promise.

I noted above that Kant distinguishes between intelligible virtue, which is given by one's actual maxims and which we cannot verify with certainty, and empirical grounds for hope that one has intelligible virtue. I suggested that Kant assigns importance to sympathetic feelings, and in general to affective traits which bring desire and duty into a rough harmony, because they are empirical signs that one's actual maxims are moral. It should now be clear why I find this position unsatisfactory. There is a conceptual connection between our affects and our actual maxims. And this means that we cannot prise apart the intelligible character of virtue, which concerns the actual maxims of our actions, from the affective character traits which are ordinarily praised as virtuous.

Herman is quite right to insist that good deliberation requires not merely that we acknowledge the authority of correct maxims, but also that we internalize a capacity to notice the features of the world which these maxims pick out as reasons for action. Without such a capacity, we would be blind to many moral reasons for action. I believe, however, that like Kant, so too Herman is mistaken in claiming that there is a sharp boundary between the faculty of judgment and the various quasi-perceptual sensitivity which sets the stage and determines the occasions for judgment. A sensitivity to moral reasons is valuable not merely because it makes it possible to take these reasons into account when making the practical judgments that determine our voluntary actions, but also because such a sensitivity is sometimes constitutive of real commitment to moral maxims. Once this point is recognized, it forces us to give up the notion that we can commit ourselves to maxims at any time, by a spontaneous exercise of practical judgment, no matter what our characteristic feelings and desires. My own view, as is perhaps by now obvious, is that we ought to reject this claim.

If we do away with this implausible bit of moral psychology, but retain the Kantian claim that we are morally assessable for the maxims of our actions, this points the way towards an attractive theory of the virtues of character. The virtue theorist is centrally concerned with the pruning and shaping of our characteristic emotions and desires. If my main conclusions are correct, then the Kantian ought not to think of this process merely as the graceful adornment of a will that has adopted correct maxims, nor merely as an instrument for correctly applying antecedently adopted maxims. The appropriate shaping of emotions and desires is the way in which sensuously affected rational agents—i.e. humans—come to have praiseworthy maxims.

As I see it, this revisionist Kantianism can incorporate certain insights of the virtue theorists without inheriting their most notorious vices. I do not wish to follow Aristotle in saying that the standard of right action is given by the discerning judgments of fully virtuous agents, while leaving it unclear how we are to identify such agents. I leave open the possibility that considered moral judgments might be guided by the Categorical Imperative. When these judgments come into conflict with the maxims actually manifest in one's willings, this provides a clear signpost for reason-driven reform.

My conjecture is that Herman and Kant reject the position I have sketched, and insist upon a clear distinction between the *activity* of practical judgment and the purely *passive* psychological forces which set the stage for it, partly because they wish to deny the existence of constituve moral luck—i.e. variations in moral praiseworthiness or blameworthiness stemming from unchosen features of character. There is after all a powerful tendency to reject any moral theory which implies that our moral worth is captive to history, in the twin sense that we are assessable for character traits which result from unchosen events in our biographies, and that there may be nothing we now can do that would render our current actions morally irreproachable. However, I side with Thomas Nagel in thinking that our intuitive rejection of moral luck leads not to a clear starting place for moral theory-building, but rather to a deep paradox. As Nagel persuasively argues, a consistent rejection of moral luck reduces the self to an extensionless point, hence undermines the very possibility of moral assessment that it might be thought to rescue.[51] The implausibility of Herman's familiarly Kantian moral psychology, with its strict distinction between practical judgment and passive perception, provides us with one more reason to renounce the initially attractive pictures of responsibility and continuous redeemability which inspire it.

In the next two sections, I will sketch an alternative picture of the extent of our responsibility for character. For now, I should note that this re-conception of responsibility for character must be accompanied by corresponding revisions to the prevailing blame-centered language of moral assessment. I will not here discuss this topic in detail, but will limit myself to three programmatic points. First, the language within which we conceive of our moral short-comings ought to be expanded so that it distinguishes particular kinds of blindness to moral reasons. But, one might say, it already does. Just here is the place for the "thick" language of moral assessment advocated virtue theorists. After all, avarice, cowardice, rashness, pride, hard-heartedness—to name just a few vices—often grip us in the form of distortions in our attentiveness to reasons, and need not (perhaps typically do not) show up in the principles we sincerely avow on reflection or consciously apply in deliberation. Second, this form of moral assessment ought to be understood along perfectionist lines, so that no one seriously entertains the possibility of remaining beyond moral reproach, and each limits his realistic hopes to steady improvement in responsiveness to moral reasons, together with consistent adherence to a few simple "thou-shalt-nots." Third, this "thick" assessment of our patterns of attentiveness and responsiveness ought to be used only for the purposes to which it is best suited—the orientation of our efforts to reform our character over time—and not for frivolous fault-finding. This implies that it ought to be taken up only by

---

51 Nagel, "Moral Luck," in *Mortal Questions* (Cambridge; Cambridge University Press: 1979), pp. 24–38 (especially pp. 35–7)

those who are committed to such reform and who have the intimate knowledge needed to help it along. Assessments of strangers ought generally to be focused on their conformity with the few simple "thou-shalt-nots" mentioned above. Indeed, there are few morally untainted motives for engaging in a more ample assessment.

PART VI: TWO KINDS OF ILLUSIONS

Let's consider cases in which our moral sensibility and our reflective judgments conflict. This might happen because we tend to see certain features of the world as having *prima-facie* reason-giving force even when we make the all-things-considered judgment that they do not, or because we fail to notice features of the world that we do judge to have such force. That is, we might tend to see reasons where we judge them to be absent or fail to see them where we judge them to be present. Either sort of wayward sensibility structures one's perception of the world so as to make (what one takes to be) an erroneous practical judgment seem right. Given this, it seems appropriate for us to think of such perceptions as "practical illusions." I hope to show that like more ordinary illusions, so too these practical illusions can have two importantly different origins, and that we cannot assess those who are subject to them until we have diagnosed the origin.

In developing this line of thought, I will attempt to retain the guiding Kantian idea that we are assessable only for our practical judgments, while articulating a more ample conception of the sphere of practical judgment than Kantians ordinarily embrace. Along the way, I hope to generate fresh insights into the value of *enkratic* action—that is, dutiful actions performed in the face of contrary desires. I think it is wrong to claim, with Kant, that such actions provide uniquely clear manifestations of the will's goodness or moral worth, just as it is wrong to claim, with Aristotle, that such actions always reveal the incompleteness of one's virtue. I will attempt to carve out an intermediate position by attending to a little-noticed distinction amongst illusions, then showing how the same distinction can be used to categorize and evaluate errant desires.

Consider, to begin with, the familiar illusion which scientists have labeled the Mach band: the band of brightness which appears to surround dark objects when they are seen against light back-grounds. This band of brightness is illusory, in that it does not cor-respond to the actual intensity of light striking the corresponding portion of the retina. Now, a student of the neurology of vision might have a clear scientific understanding of the genesis of Mach bands, and be perfectly convinced that they are distortions of real-ity, yet still *see* them. Like most others, she too could not help but see the portions of the evening sky just next to a distant mountain as brighter than adjacent areas of the sky. However, the persistence of the illusion would not in any way indicate that she is uncon-vinced by the scientific evidence that Mach bands are illusory. It would not indicate any lack of confidence in her own considered judgments. The reason is that the best explanation of the illusion's occurrence does not assign to her the belief or suspicion—whether conscious or unconscious—that the evening sky really is brighter just next to distant mountains than in immediately adjacent areas. The best explanation of her subjection to the illusion is that the human perceptual apparatus has been shaped by evolution to dis-tort reality in this way, since this heightens our capacity to discern the boundaries of objects, thus providing us with extremely useful information which would not be salient if our visual rendering of the world were more accurate.

The case is entirely different with other, more idiosyncratic illusions. As popular history would have it, Christopher Columbus sailed west across the ocean partly to prove that the world was spherical. (In fact this was already well-established by Columbus's time, but I will make use of the apocryphal Columbus to elaborate a little thought experiment.) In order to take this step, Columbus must have been rather certain that the world was in fact spherical. Imagine, however, that each evening as Columbus looks out at the line where sea and sky meet, he cannot help seeing the horizon's bright band as the opening of a chasm at the end of the earth's sur-face, rather than as a receding arch of buoyant water. He sails forth each night haunted by what he thinks he has seen, and in dread of falling off the earth. My claim is that the persistence of this illusion is best explained by Columbus's lack of conviction in his own calmly considered judgments. The persistence of the illu-sion, in this particular case, does indicate that Columbus's avowed belief that the world is spherical has not yet gained the force of a conviction. It remains a somewhat tentative hypothesis, even though his actions show that he puts more credence in it than most of his contemporaries. This diagnosis is plausible because the illusion is not endemic to all humans no matter what their actual beliefs; it is not shared by those who truly are convinced that the world is spherical. The diagnosis would be even more certain if Columbus found that a great deal of his thought and behavior made clearer sense on the supposition that he was not entirely convinced that the world was spherical. The diagnosis would be all but confirmed if, on a second trip across the ocean, the illusion disappeared.

Now, one might conjecture that Columbus's case is not really a matter of perceptual illusion, but rather a matter of erroneous *interpretation* of perceptions. This, one might think, is why Columbus is in a sense responsible for his illusion, while no one is responsible for the illusory appearance of Mach bands. I do not think that this hypothesis correctly specifies what it is that can make us "responsible" for an illusion. This can be seen in the fact that mirages clearly involve an illusory interpretation of the visual field, yet our proneness to this class of illusions does not indicate any half-heartedness in our considered judgments. When we see a mirage, we do not merely see a bright and highly reflective patch of light in the distance; we see a pool of water. This would seem to be an erroneous *interpretation* of the visual field. Yet the fact that a driver on a long, flat stretch of sunlit road cannot help but see puddles of water ahead does not tell against the driver's conviction that the road ahead is perfectly dry. We can draw this inference even without a scientific explanation of our proneness to this illusion, from the mere fact that the illusion occurs predictably in a very wide variety of people who have no reason to think, or to fear, that their car is soon to be engulfed in water. This inference is bolstered by the fact that attributing a secret suspicion that there is water ahead to all those who see mirages would not help to make sense of their other thoughts and actions. It is all but confirmed by the fact that one would continue to see mirages ahead even if one shifted into reverse and backed up over the same stretch of road, yet after a couple of minutes these mirages would appear in spots which one knows very well to be dry. We are not responsible for seeing mirages, then, because the best explanation of our proneness to this illusion does not assign to us a belief or suspicion that the world really is the way the illusion presents it.

One might also object that my imaginary Columbus is not really subject to anything which could properly be called an *illusion* at all, but is rather experiencing a *projection* of his own fears. The temptation to say this can perhaps be traced to our difficulty in seeing any feature of Columbus's visual field as truly suggestive of a yawning abyss. My imaginary Columbus's distortion of the visual field is particularly egregious, and this might be thought to convince us that it manifests his fears and suspicions. Again, this hypothesis seems to me mistaken. It seems to me that Columbus's case is fundamentally no different from the case of a fearful insomniac who cannot help hearing the creaks and groans of an old house late at night as the fumblings of would-be murderers, and who perhaps also sees dim shadows in the room as outlines of malevolent intruders. In the light of day, such a person might well avow with sincerity and apparent confidence that these noises and shadows are not caused by humans. He might even assert this in the middle of the night, after turning on the light and investigating. However, if the illusions often return with the darkness, this indicates that his professed belief in his own safety lacks the status of a conviction.[52] We can easily imagine him silently rehearsing his reasons for believing that there are no intruders, as if he were arguing with someone he had not quite won over. We can't segregate projections from illusions, and absolve the faculty of judgment of any complicity in the latter, simply by attending to the severity of the distortion. In general, we will need a great deal of idiosyncratic information about a given case before we can say whether the faculty of judgment is complicit in the production of a distorted perception.

In the theoretical use of reason, then, the mere fact that one is subject to certain illusions can evidence a lack of conviction in one's professed beliefs. To be sure, this is not *always* the case. Quite the contrary, one might even demonstrate the depth of one's conviction in the uniformity of the brightness of the evening sky adjacent to a mountain, or in the dryness of the road ahead, by continuing to insist upon the belief even when seeing Mach bands or mirages. However, there are other cases where our subjection to

---

52 Such a person would not be like the driver who sees a mirage as a lake but knows perfectly well that he will not drive into water; he is more like a driver who believes that what he sees is a mere mirage but still cannot help seeing it as fearful, as threatening to engulf him.

a persistent illusion is best explained by our suspicion that the world really answers to the illusory appearance. In such cases, the very fact that we are subject to the illusion gives us first-personal evidence that our avowed beliefs lack the status of convictions, and might well point towards a need to rehearse the reasons for our avowed beliefs in order to *convince* ourselves of it. Such illusions indicate that we are in the sway of false beliefs, and have not rid ourselves of the suspicion that they are true.

In the domain of practical reason, one kind of illusion is a strong and persistent inclination to do that which, on reflection, one takes oneself to have good reason not to do.[53] Such an inclination is a species of "practical illusion" because it structures one's perception of the world in such a way as to make an erroneous judgment seem right. In the same way that we can sometimes show the strength of our theoretical beliefs by professing them in the face of illusions, so we can sometimes show the depth of our commitment to the moral law by overcoming strong inclinations to act immorally. On the other hand, just as there are illusions which indicate that one lacks conviction in one's theoretical beliefs, so there are strong inclinations whose very occurrence indicates that one lacks conviction in the values encoded in one's highest-level maxims.

Here again, the etiology of the inclination is all-important. Consider, for instance, a small group of shipwreck survivors who are running out of food. If one of these survivors persistently desired to take more than his ration of the remaining supply, yet overcame this desire and did not do so, this would not indicate any shortcoming in the depth of his conviction that his fellow survivors' lives are just as valuable as his own. Indeed, his conviction could hardly be more clearly manifested than in his capacity to act

---

53 There are different degrees of illusion which are covered over by this general formulation. For instance, one might have a purely irrational fear where there is absolutely no danger at hand, and be gripped by an inclination to flee even though, on considered reflection, one believes that one has no reason at all to flee. This would be a thoroughgoing illusion. Alternatively, one might have a strong desire to eat something which would be pleasurable if eaten, but which would be very bad for one's health. Unlike the desire to flee, this desire does track a real value, since eating the thing would be pleasurable, so this desire would be illusory only if it had a certain kind of strength and persistence which tempted one to think that eating the thing would be an all-things-considered good.

justly in the face of the wrenching prod to action associated with slow starvation. We can explain the strength and persistence of the desire for more food without imputing to him the judgment that it would be a good thing for him to have more food than others. In the first instance, this is because we have a perfectly good evolutionary explanation of the strength and persistence of the desire. Just as we have evolved so that we cannot help seeing Mach bands even when we are certain that they are not there, so we have evolved so that we cannot help experiencing extreme food deprivation as a decisive reason to eat, even in situations when we are certain that it is not. There is a perfectly good physiological explanation for the great salience of the cravings for food that accompany starvation. The case would be entirely different if one ordinarily had very strong urges to eat the food of others. As Barbara Herman convincingly argues, even primitive desires like hunger and thirst are ordinarily transformed as we mature, slowly coming to reflect the evaluative concepts and moral limitations that structure the social world. If our socialization goes well, our desire for food and drink is not ordinarily directed at food and drink possessed by others.[54] We do not have to overrule desires to take such food; it never occurs to us to take it. If it did, this might well indicate a shortcoming in one's commitment to widely accepted norms of justice. As Herman notes, the point is even more evident in the case of more complex desires such as the desire to have a child.[55] Absent some very particular story, if one continually had strong urges to kidnap the children of others, yet overruled these urges, this would hardly provide a convincing show of commitment to moral restrictions.[56]

---

54 Barbara Herman, "Making Room for Character," in Stephen Engstrom and Jenniger Whiting, eds., *Aristotle, Kant and the Stoics: Rethinking Happiness and Virtue* (Cambridge; Cambridge University Press: 1996), pp. 36–60; see especially p. 46.
55 *Ibid.*
56 Why, then, does it indicate a problem when one's desire for children is directed at children one cannot justly have, but does not indicate a problem when one hungers for food one cannot justly have? I think that the best answer lies in the physiological intensity of hunger. Extreme life-threatening hunger is akin to certain forms of torture, in that it presents the most horrible sort of challenge to one's practical convictions, and even threatens to short-circuit one's capacity to make and act on practical judgments. Something would be amiss if one's desire for sufficient food were ordinarily directed at the food of others, even when not hungry.

This discussion of "practical illusion" can also help to explain some of the features of our assessments of character which I brought out in the last chapter by introducing some variations on Kant's examples of morally worthy action. My immediate aim there was to critique Kant's claim in the "Methodology of Pure Practical Reason" that the higher the cost in happiness of a dutiful action, the more clearly it displays virtuous character. Kant offered the case of a man who is unwilling to bear false witness even though the political authorities have promised him great rewards if he does so, and have threatened to imprison him and to harm his wife and children if he refuses. Under these circumstances, an inclination to bear false witness would in no way tell against the man's commitment to truth-telling, since it could be explained entirely in terms of the value that he does allot, and indeed ought to allot, to his own freedom and to his family's safety and well-being. Indeed we might have doubts about this man's character if he felt absolutely no temptation to bear false witness.[57] On the other hand, if we increased the cost in the metric of happiness by imagining him as someone who is strongly inclined to make innocent people suffer, and who in fact would take great pleasure in doing so, this would not help to display his virtue more clearly. The reason is that even if he managed to deny himself these pleasures in practice, his proneness to such inclinations is most plausibly explained by a lack of whole-heartedness in his commitment to the moral values which make it wrong to lie in the first place—i.e. the dignity of self and others considered simply as rational beings.

In these cases and others like them, we cannot describe our moral shortcomings in familiar Kantian terms, as over-estimations of the reason-giving force of our desires. The problem lies in our desires and not in the judgments we make at the moment of deci-

---

57 This brings to mind the doubts which the nation's voters developed about the character of presidential candidate Michael Dukakis when, challenged publicly about his resistance to the death penalty and asked if he would not wish for the death of a man who raped and killed his wife, he answered dispassionately that he would not. This was not taken as a sign of the strength of Dukakis's conviction that capital punishment was wrong, but as an indication either that he was overly technocratic and had not really grasped the human dimensions of the question, or that he was incapable of passionate loyalty to intimates. The voting public might have been kinder to Dukakis if his response had shown that such circumstances would sorely try but not overturn his commitment to his principles.

sion concerning what these desires give us reason to do. These desires already provisionally map values onto the world, in the same way that a projected illusion provisionally maps facts onto the world, and the problem at hand is that these provisional mappings are misleading.

Finally, the discussion of "practical illusion" puts us in a better position to understand what precisely is wrong with Barbara Herman's insistence on a sharp division between the activity of practical judgment and the capacity to notice moral reasons for action. As noted above, Herman claims that one cannot generally be criticized morally for deficiencies in one's "Rules of Moral Salience," nor by extension for mistakes in judgment arising from such defects. Recall that one's "Rules of Moral Salience" serve to pick out occasions for moral judgment and to specify what features of the world must be considered in formulating a judgment. Herman's position seems to imply that we cannot be blamed morally for failing to act beneficently towards others if this failure derives from a background inattentiveness to the needs of others. What I am trying to bring out is that the judgments we make are partly encoded in our patterns of attentiveness. Such attentiveness is not merely an instrumental aide to keen moral judgment; it is quite often a mark of the depth of one's commitment to the very general moral judgments that one professes. Thus, inattentiveness to the needs of others can manifest a failure to make and/or fully to accept the judgment that the needs of others provide us with reasons for action. Likewise, an inability to *see* certain gender relations *as* coercive can manifest a failure to make and/or fully to accept the judgment that men and women have equal worth.

It is sometimes perfectly appropriate to blame ourselves for the sort of moral obliviousness or mindlessness that results from deficient "Rules of Moral Salience." Herman's refusal to recognize this seems to me to spring from an unsustainable distinction between the *activity* of practical judgment and the purely *passive* psychological forces which set the occasions and the contours of practical judgment. I believe that Herman is drawn to make such a distinction partly in order to rule out the possibility of constitutive moral luck—i.e., variations in moral praiseworthiness or blameworthiness stemming from unchosen features of one's constitution or

---

58 Nagel, "Moral Luck," in *Mortal Questions*, Op. Cit., pp. 32–3.

character.[58] As I see it, however, the implausibility of Herman's familiarly Kantian moral psychology, with its strict distinction between practical judgment and passive perception, ought to prompt us to reject the initially attractive picture of responsibility that inspires it. That is, it gives us another reason to accept constitutive moral luck.

In the domain of theoretical reason, our interest in having true beliefs outstrips our concern with the public justifiability of our assertions, and encompasses an interest in freeing ourselves from groundless suspicions and the illusions they generate. We are interested not merely in describing the world aright but also, quite literally, in *seeing* the world aright.[59] In the same way, and for parallel reasons, our interest in the moral goodness of our will outstrips our concern with the public justifiability of our voluntary actions, and encompasses an interest in freeing ourselves from the grip of illusions about the justificatory force of features of the world highlighted by our feelings and desires. We may not be the authors of these feelings and desires, but this fact alone does not make it inappropriate to appraise them as morally praiseworthy or blameworthy.

In a certain respect, being committed to moral values is like having religious faith. In both cases, deficiencies in one's belief can make their appearance in immediate, apparently unreflective reactions to the world. It seems to me nonsensical to attribute a powerful belief in e.g. the Christian God to someone who persists in the "illusion" of seeing the world as unstructured by any higher meaning, absurd; someone who persists, that is, in what theologians call despair. To say that someone despairs in this sense is just to say that their belief is not strong; it does not amount to conviction. I have been urging that the same can be said of moral belief.[60]

PART VII: DESIRES AS CONSEQUENCES OF PAST CHOICES

---

59 This point might be pressed too far. For instance, we do have an interest in preserving our illusory perception of Mach bands, since these are useful illusions. There may be other sorts of illusions which are good for us in one way or another.

60 This comparison might be used to highlight the possible role of morality in enlivening one's world with value, and also to bring out the reason for the impotence of mere argument in making people moral.

One disturbing aspect of my claims about virtue is that it implies that we are sometimes properly held responsible for feelings and desires, yet it does not seem that we choose our feelings and desires, and we are strongly inclined to think that we are morally assessable only for our voluntary choices and their effects. Those who find my arguments convincing, but feel the grip of this common intuition, might be tempted to claim that we are responsible for our desire only to the extent that they are the causal consequences of our past voluntary choices. This approach also holds the promise of incorporating the common intuition that it is inappropriate to criticize people morally for pathological or phobic desires. On this approach, such desires are beyond the scope of moral assessment provided that they are not the assignable consequences of the past voluntary choices of the agent whom they afflict.

Kant holds that we have "strict liability" for the unforeseen consequences of morally impermissible actions.[61] This might explain some cases of morally assessable desires, but it seems overly convenient to suppose that every such desire is the effect of some past immoral action. In order to account for the scope of desires for which people actually do assess themselves, it seems to me that we would have to introduce a standard of strict liability for the causal consequences not only of impermissible actions but also of permissible-but-not-required actions. The trouble with this strategy is that a mere causal link between our past actions and our current character traits lends little support to the intuition that we are responsible for those character traits. This is because these causal links are generally opaque to us in the moment of action. It is one thing to show that an agent's voluntary actions brought something about, and quite another thing to show that the agent brought it about voluntarily. Only the latter showing lends support to the conclusion that the agent is responsible for the outcome in question. However, the latter showing requires a demonstration that

---

61 Kant maintains that if we lie to a would-be murderer in order to prevent him from killing someone, yet our lie inadvertently makes it possible for him to carry out the murder, we make ourselves responsible for the death. See Immanuel Kant, "On a Supposed Right to Tell Lies from Benevolent Motives," in *Kant's Critique of Practical Reason and Other Works on the Theory of Ethics*, translated by Thomas Kingsmill Abbott (London; Longmans, Green and Co. Ltd.: 1873), p. 363.

the agent intended to bring about the thing in question.

It is a well-rehearsed point that the propositions which are the objects of intentional states are opaque contexts in which truth is not preserved when we make identity substitutions. Just because I believe that John F. Kennedy was shot in Dallas does not mean that I believe that the youngest president of the United States was shot in Dallas, even though Kennedy is the nation's youngest president. Similarly, just because I intended to trip up the woman running around the corner does not mean that I intended to trip up a plainclothes police officer in hot pursuit of a bank robber, even if the woman running around the corner was a plainclothes police officer in hot pursuit of a bank robber. I might have intended to trip up a criminal assailant in pursuit of her victim.[62] In this sort of case, the mere fact that my voluntary action caused a lamentable outcome (the thief's escape) does not mean that I can appropriately be held responsible for the outcome. And on strictly parallel lines, it does not follow from the fact that I intended to read certain books in my youth that I *intended* to read materials which would cause me to develop a callousness towards the poor, even if the books were such materials.

If this is right, then we cannot show ourselves to be responsible for our characteristic desires simply by showing that they are the causal consequences of our past voluntary actions. It must also be true that we acted with the intention of making these our characteristic desires. We do sometimes act with an eye towards sculpting our own future desires. We might, for instance, choose to meditate on the inappropriateness of untoward desires, or we might choose to engage in certain highly disciplined patterns of action, with hopes of preventing them from blossoming in us. Still, as I noted above, I do not believe that it is plausible that we pass moral judgments only on those of our desires which we ourselves brought about intentionally.

I realize, however, that there is nothing decisive about my own sense of the *scope* of the desires for which one might appropriately criticize oneself morally. No convincing argument could turn on so

---

62 We might still *say* that I intentionally tripped the police officer, but not in a sense that would lend support to the further claim that we are responsible for tripping up a police officer in pursuit of a criminal, unless we also think that we should have known, or should have been able to tell, that the person we were tripping up was a police officer.

hazy an intuition. The truly convincing reason for rejecting the Kantian strategy under discussion is that it does not accurately reflect our *reason* for distinguishing between those desires which are morally assessable and those which are not. In practice, we simply do not make this distinction by determining whether the desire in question is the causal consequence, foreseeable or otherwise, of past voluntary actions. This is not to say that we *never* look in the direction of the history of a desire when attempting to determine whether it is open to moral assessment. We sometimes do. However, if my theoretical approach is correct, we will find that when we do look at a desire's etiology, we are not primarily concerned with whether it is the effect—foreseeable or otherwise—of past voluntary actions, but with whether its origins contravene the claim that the desire manifests our evaluative judgments or proto-judgments. I think that this is precisely where our interest lies.

To illustrate, let us take the case of a man who feels a powerful disinclination to save a child who is drowning in relatively unthreatening surf. If he is conscientious, then however things turn out—e.g. whether he manages to drag himself into the water and save the child, or he hesitates and someone else saves the child, or he makes a half-hearted attempt to reach the child and the child drowns—this man will be keenly interested in scrutinizing his inclination to stay ashore. It would distort matters to think of this interest as purely instrumental. There is no reason to think that his interest ought to be limited to re-sculpting his characteristic inclinations so as to avoid (further) failures to help others in danger. It is not hard to imagine that a conscientious person would be interested in understanding and assessing his reluctance to help the child even on his deathbed, in the grip of complete certainty that he will never have another like opportunity.

If my theoretical approach is correct, the question that we would expect to be foremost on the person's mind is whether his own inclination to remain safely ashore manifested a tendency to overvalue his own safety, and/or to undervalue the needs and interests—and even the lives—of others. In an effort to answer this question, he might investigate the etiology of his inclination to stay ashore, but not in order to determine whether it is the causal upshot of past voluntary actions. He will be interested in the etiology of his inclination because this might help him to determine whether it manifests objectionable evaluations or proto-evaluations.

For example, if he were to conclude that his inclination arose from a general hydrophobia, induced by a near-drowning experience in his infancy, he would have little reason to reproach himself morally for having been inclined to remain ashore. This particular etiology suggests that his inclination does not manifest a morally blameworthy tendency to inflate the value of his own well-being in relation to the value of the lives of others; rather, it manifests a morally innocent tendency to overestimate the danger posed by water. On the other hand, if he were to conclude that his strong desire to remain ashore and avoid any risk to life and limb is the causal upshot of having been raised by parents who coddled and overprotected him, conveying to him the message that his safety and well-being was more important than that of all others, he might well feel that the pattern of his desires is itself a reason for moral self-reproach. This is not because his characteristically cautious and self-protective inclinations are the causal consequences of his own voluntary actions; one no more chooses to be coddled than one chooses to be subjected to near-drowning experiences in infancy. It is rather because this particular etiology suggests that his inclinations carry the residue of his parents' inflated evaluation of his own needs and interests. Such judgments, which are perhaps unobjectionable in parents, ought not to be taken up and endorsed by the children who are their objects. Yet his desires indicate that these values do have a hold on him. Even if, in calm moments and on due consideration, he professes a perfectly egalitarian assessment of his own value, this egalitarian judgment still has not restructured his immediate, felt reactions to the world around him, and thus it has not attained the status of an egalitarian *conviction*.

The root difficulty with the suggested Kantian position that I am criticizing is that it assumes that we are responsible for our characteristic inclinations and desires only because (and to the extent that) these inclinations and desires are our *doing*. Our responsibility, on this theory, is the responsibility of *authorship*. This is a natural thing to say if one is committed to the Kantian notion that all responsibility derives from voluntary exercises of will. Still, I think it is fundamentally mistaken. When we assess our own inclinations and desires, we are not assessing ourselves for what we *did* long ago, but for who we *are* today. We are answerable for our characteristic inclinations and desires not because we author them, which we rarely do, but because they reveal something important about the evaluative judgments which determine our deliberate willings. Where our desires are at odds with our considered judgments about what we have most reason to do, this often indicates that our considered judgments are half-hearted and lack the status of true convictions, or commitments.

This seems to me to specify precisely what the agent in question might conclude about himself. While he has the considered belief that saving the child is overwhelmingly important and far outweighs the modest personal risk it will involve, this belief is not whole-hearted. It has not penetrated into his affects, which give shape to his initial conception of the situations in which he must act. What this means is that contrary inclinations frequently arise in the moment of deliberation, lending *prima-facie* attractiveness to the alternative of insuring his own safety. This bare fact—that these contrary inclinations arise and must be overruled in the course of deliberation—itself indicates that the egalitarian evaluations of self and others which the agent endorses in his considered judgments have not attained the status of whole-hearted convictions.

This notion of whole-hearted commitment is perhaps best illustrated in the domain of intimate interpersonal relationships. Barring some extraordinary circumstance, to learn that one's friend or lover has to overcome persistent contrary inclinations in determining his will to spend time with one, is simply to discover that the friend or lover lacks whole-hearted commitment to the value of continued relationship. This is not merely a disappointment or harm to the putative friend or lover of the reluctant person in question. If we disentangle the various strands of objection that one might naturally have to one's own lack of whole-hearted-ness in one's *own* adult friendships and intimate relationships, we might well find among them a self-condemnation of one's own capacity fully to *register* or *appreciate* the value that one attributes to one's friends or intimates in one's own avowed judgments.

One might think that the case of impersonal relationships with others in general is entirely different. The most salient difference is that in the case of impersonal relationships, it is far less clear that any particular person is substantially harmed by one's errant affects, so there may be no one who is in a position to complain of them. As I have just indicated, however, errant inclinations are distressing from the first-person point of view, partly because they manifest an incapacity fully to register the values that one acknowledges on due reflection. Thus, for instance, someone who had a sexist upbringing yet has reflectively rejected the sexist beliefs of his parents, might still find that he is immediately inclined to dismiss the contributions of women in discussions of corporate strategy, and to doubt the suitability of female candidates for upper management jobs. These inclinations, I think, are best understood as the residue of a system of valuation that he rejects in his all-things-considered judgments.[63] Likewise, if a reformed racist were to feel a lingering disinclination to converse with or develop friendships with blacks, these inclinations might best be understood as the residue of his own rejected system of valuation.

Now, there is some question as to whether one could possibly correct for these sorts of inclinations in the course of deliberation, so as to achieve perfect even-handedness in one's actions. Indeed, as I will argue in later chapters, it seems to me that the correct description of certain collective actions is sensitive to the presence or absence of contrary inclinations in group members, and that this sometimes provides grounds for moral complaint against those who engage in such actions in the face of strongly conflicting inclinations. However, the more pressing question for my current purposes is whether there would be something objectionable about such inclinations even if they did not alter one's actions in the slightest. I believe that there would be. Even if no one else were in a position to object morally to such desires, still these inclinations might reasonably be thought morally objectionable by those in whom they arise. As in the case of personal relationships, so here the objection I wish to highlight is that these inclinations manifest that one's own considered evaluative beliefs lack the status of whole-hearted convictions.

PART VIII: KANT'S *REDUCTIO* OF VOLUNTARIST ACCOUNTS OF RESPONSIBILITY?

I have just considered and rejected one way in which one

---

63 His is the condition of the Aristotelian incontinent agent (*enkrates*). There is some sense in which the incontinent person knows what is good—if asked, he can identify it reliably. However, he cannot help seeing other things as good, and he must continually correct his errant impressions or perceptions of things. Thus, when he chooses and pursues what he believes to be good, he is in conflict with his own immediate desires. See Aristotle, *Nichomachean Ethics*, Book VII.

might attempt to take on board some of my arguments about the
place of affects in virtuous character, while holding on to the claim
that we are morally responsible only for those character traits
which we can be seen as having chosen voluntarily. In *Religion
within the Limits of Reason Alone*, Kant follows another strategy
for showing how our moral responsibility can coherently be
thought to be grounded in our choices. It seems to me that Kant's
strategy is not only implausible, but that it provides a convincing
reductio ad absurdum of the very powerful pre-theoretical intuition that moral responsibility is grounded in our choices.

Kant maintains that we have to view ourselves and others as
having chosen our fundamental disposition[64]—understood as the
hierarchical ordering of our highest-level maxims—since otherwise
we could not view ourselves as morally responsible for the actions
specified by these maxims. However, Kant continues, it would not
help to conceive of this choice as occurring in time, since it would
then be specified by temporally prior maxims which we would
have to be shown to have chosen. This leads Kant to conclude that
we must view our choice of fundamental disposition as a singular
and atemporal action which unfolds, or takes on a phenomenal
character, in the temporal succession of our actions.[65]

The lives of humans who are virtuous from the intelligible
point of view are marked by an overcoming of corruption, and a
progressive approach to the purity and strength of will character-

---

64 By 'fundamental disposition,' I mean to refer to what Kant calls
   Gesinnung. While the term is standardly translated with the English
   'disposition,' this seems to me inexact. This translation fails to make
   perspicuous that one's *Gesinnung* is determined by the *highest-level*
   principles which govern one's voluntary decisions. It fails in the first
   instance because a disposition might be quite superficial, nearly inci-
   dental to one's character, while one's *Gesinnung* is the very heart of
   one's character, and the sole determinant of one's real virtue or vice.
   It fails in the second instance because 'disposition' connotes something altogether passive—a mere mode of reactivity—while one's
   Gesinnung is operative precisely in determining one's will.
   I continue to use the English term 'disposition' because Kant scholars
   will readily associate this with *Gesinnung*. However, I suspect that a
   better alternative would be 'fundamental convictions.' According to
   the *Harper Collins German-English English-German Dictionary*,
   Second Edition (New York; Harper-Collins: 1991), this is a standard
   translation of '*Gesinnung*.' Thus, 'his fundamental moral convictions'
   can be translated 'seine moralische *Gesinnung*.' (English-German, p.
   140)
65 See Kant, *Religion*, pp. 17 and 17n, 20–21, 45n.

istic of perfect virtue. This progressive reform of character, in which one gradually gains control of one's propensity to evil, just *is* the temporal unfolding of the timeless choice of a virtuous character. In the eyes of God, the halting steps of humans towards self-reform can be grasped in a unity as an unending series which advances continually towards perfect virtue. This, Kant explains, is because God can grasp the fundamental disposition of each person's character—i.e. the actual supreme maxim of their will and the strength of their attachment to it. This fundamental disposition contains the basis for an omniscient divinity to extrapolate a continuous series of actions, which might or might not have the morally praiseworthy form of an unending advance towards virtue.[66]

However, while only God can know that we are virtuous, Kant maintains that we might find empirical grounds for hope in the actual history of our conduct. According to Kant, we have grounds for hope that we have in fact acknowledged the supreme authority of the moral law, and that we would be found virtuous by a divine judge, if we see that over our lifetime our actions have demonstrated an increasingly reliable conformity with the requirements of morality, even in the face of temptations. To put matters another way, we can think of ourselves as virtuous if our actions manifest a continual rapprochement to what Kant calls the *empirical* character of virtue.[67]

There is something quite persuasive about Kant's claim that we cannot conclusively verify the purity of our own maxims or the maxims of others. One could only know one's maxims to be perfect in their purity and strength by knowing that one would act dutifully in the face of all possible temptations. Since no particular

---

66 Kant, *Religion*, pp. 43 and 68–72. This claim that only a supreme being could discern the true worth of our character is also implicit in *The Metaphysics of Morals*, where Kant argues that we must represent the self-monitoring function of our own conscience as a court of judgment presided over by a "scrutinizer of hearts," and condemn ourselves in the name of that judge. We must conceive of the judge and the accused as different persons since otherwise acquittal would be guaranteed; we must think of the judge as a "scrutinizer of hearts" since the judgments of conscience concern our deepest motives. For these and other reasons, Kant concludes that "conscience must be thought of as the subjective principle of being accountable to God for one's deeds." See Kant, *The Metaphysics of Morals*, Ak. 438–9.

67 See *Religion...*, pp. 42 and 71.

person could possibly face all possible temptations, this implies that we cannot know anyone to be virtuous.

It might seem that in this respect, virtue is no different from ordinary dispositional properties which range over a variety of circumstances too wide to be reproduced experimentally one-by-one. Such a comparison, however, obscures a vital dimension of the unknowability of virtue. To explain, when we claim that a particular lump of sugar is soluble in water, we claim that it would dissolve in every sample of H_2O in the universe (*modulo* certain temperature specifications, etc.). We can make headway here because we are entitled to assume that other things with observable resemblances to this lump of sugar can go proxy for this lump, while a few samples of water at different pressures and temperatures can go proxy for all the water in the universe. We cannot do this in the case of virtue. If we presumed that other people with observable resemblances to us would respond identically to changes in circumstances, then we would be thinking of our actions as causally determined by laws linking observable personality traits and circumstances to kinds of behavior. This would be to lose sight of our agency, hence of our virtuousness or viciousness. This helps to illuminate the common-sense insight that we cannot conclusively be deemed vicious just because other people with similar upbringings or other empirical likenesses to us have shown an incapacity to resist temptations to which we have not (yet) been exposed.[68]

While Kant's position is persuasive to this point, it seems to me that there is a serious flaw in Kant's grounds for positing a timeless choice of fundamental character behind all rational agency. As noted above, Kant maintains that we must posit such a choice if we are to see our character and the actions which manifest that character as morally assessable. However, if Kant were right to maintain that we could not ground our responsibility for our fundamental disposition on a choice determined by an antecedently held maxim, then I do not see how we could ground it on a choice determined by a timeless maxim. The threatened regress seems equally damning, since we would have to be shown to have chosen the timeless maxim which determined our choice of fundamental disposition, and the maxim which determined this further choice, and so on. To assign a maxim to the choice of highest-level

---

68 Perhaps this gives a certain, modest ground for affirming, with Kant, that real virtue must be understood as an intelligible property.

maxim is self-contradictory, since the maxim governing the choice would then have to be considered our highest-level maxim. Nor will it help Kant to think of the choice of our highest-level maxim as ungoverned by any maxim, since he would be compelled to understand such a choice as an arbitrary and unreasoned exercise of will. It is true that we ordinarily hold people accountable for seemingly whimsical or arbitrary exercises of will, on the presumption that they could and perhaps should have been responsive to reasons for acting otherwise than they did. However, this presumption would fail in the case of a choice which is *necessarily* divorced from practical judgment. This choice *could not in principle* manifest that very capacity for rational agency which alone makes us responsible for what we do. Thus, it is not at all clear why we ought to be held accountable for it.

It seems to me, then, that there is a fatal flaw in the very notion of a voluntarist vindication of responsibility for fundamental disposition. I do not mean to imply that we are not responsible for the most fundamental elements of our identity as practical reasoners. Rather, I wish to contest the claim that we are responsible for these fundamental elements of our character because we have voluntarily chosen them. We are ordinarily held responsible for our voluntary choices because it can ordinarily be presumed that they manifest our practical judgments. This is the nugget of truth in the voluntarist account of responsibility. However, it would be misguided to extrapolate a general voluntarist theory of responsibility from this commonplace truth, and to claim that we must have chosen all of our evaluative judgments in order to be viewed as responsible for them.[69] This would get things precisely backwards, taking moral judgments to be assessable on the condition that they

---

69 At the risk of "illuminating" the dimly understood with the hopelessly obscure, a comparison might be made here with accountability for what we say. When we make an assertion, others can demand that we justify our assertion by revealing our grounds for believing it to be true. This demand for a justification does not itself stand in need of a voluntarist justification to the effect that we have chosen or otherwise meaningfully authored all of the beliefs that we might rely upon to justify what we have said. The demand is appropriate wherever it can be presumed that our words manifest our judgments, and it is defeated in cases where no link between word and judgment can be presumed (e.g. in cases of senility or feverish delirium, or when acting in a play, or when conveying the demands of a group of terrorists, etc.).

are chosen, rather than acknowledging that choices are assessable on the condition that they manifest our judgments. I think that Kant does get things backwards in this way, and that his posit of the timeless choice of *Gesinnung* provides a *reductio ad absurdum* of the voluntarist thesis of responsibility to which he subscribes.[70] I have tried to show that traces of this same picture of responsibility appear in Herman's otherwise commendable work, and prevent her from striking upon the real implications of her own insights into the nature of practical reasoning. I think that my criticisms show that if a plausible Kantian theory can be developed and defended, it must jettison this initially attractive picture of responsibility, and the untenable picture of the separation between affect and judgment which it supports. Such a Kantianism would acknowledge that our maxims cannot be specified without reference to our affects, and that our upbringing will play an important part in determining whether our maxims are morally acceptable.

---

70 For the clearest statements of this voluntarist thesis, see *Religion* pp. 20 and 40.

CHAPTER 3

Two Conceptions of Commitment

INTRODUCTION: UNDERTAKING COMMITMENTS

What I say, and what I do, sometimes *commits* me to saying or doing further things. This is obvious when what I say is "I promise" followed by some suitably precise specification of what I am promising; it is similarly obvious when what I do is to sign a contract in which my legal obligations are specified. These are accepted ways of making clear that I am undertaking a commitment, and of making explicit just what commitment I am undertaking. However, we can commit ourselves by what might seem a motley array of other utterances and actions whose workings are considerably less clear and explicit. For instance, we often commit ourselves by announcing our intentions, professing our love, kindling a friendship, publicly affirming our ideals or values, assuming a professional role or participating actively in a civic group. My aim is to shed light on how such performances commit us. Along the way, I hope to isolate two different kinds of commitments and to distinguish two fundamentally different kinds of social groups which are held together by these different sorts of commitments.

The diversity in the modes of undertaking commitments presents a challenge for anyone who would offer a unified theory of commitments. Any such account must identify what it is that gives to commitments their normative force, or bindingness, then show

how this normative force could be carried by all of the diverse acts and utterances by which we commit ourselves. One familiar theoretical strategy is to take promises and contracts (or more generally, voluntary agreements) as paradigms for the undertaking of commitments, and to treat other modes of undertaking commitments as *implicit* or *tacit* promises or contracts. I hope to show that this strategy is fundamentally misguided. However, it is an extremely tempting strategy, and it is worth dwelling a moment on why.

There are at least two features of promises and contracts which seem to make them fit paradigms for all undertakings of commitments. First, promises and contracts have a relatively uncontroversial normative force: we are bound to their terms by our voluntary agreement. If we could convincingly interpret other modes of undertaking commitments as implicit promises, this would lend similar clarity to their normative force. This hope, I think, is in vain. The predictable result of following this strategy is either to constrict the domain of commitments to an implausible degree, or to stretch the notion of free consent beyond the bounds within which it provides a plausible grounding for commitments. If the appeal of this analytical strategy persists, I believe that this owes to the bare voluntarist thesis (or dogma) that nothing but our free agreement could possibly give rise to a new commitment.[1]

The second feature of promises and contracts which seems to make them paradigm cases of undertaking commitments is that as socio-linguistic transactions go, their workings are unusually clear and transparent. When we promise or contract, we make it clear to others that we are undertaking a commitment, and that we know ourselves to be doing so. We also specify, and make clear that we acknowledge, exactly what we are committing ourselves to

---

1 My point here parallels a point made by Michael Hardimon in his interesting discussion of non-contractual role obligations. Hardimon criticizes the flawed deliverance of common sense that "the only way in which we can acquire role obligations—or in any case, role obligations with genuine moral force—is by signing on for the roles to which they are attached." He calls this mistaken common-sense notion the "volunteer principle." I differ from Hardimon in that he seems to believe that the volunteer principle governs relations within civil society—"the domain of private association distinct from the family and the state." I believe, and will argue below, that the principle cannot plausibly be applied so widely. See Hardimon, "Role Obligations" in *The Journal of Philosophy*, Volume XCI, No. 7 (July, 1994), pp. 333–363, esp. 343, 352–3.

do. These features make promissory and contractual commitments relatively easy to specify and hard to dispute or deny. These same features also help to make it possible to think of promises and contracts as voluntary agreements, since we cannot voluntarily agree to something unless we know what it is that we are agreeing to, and know that we are agreeing to it.

It might be thought that anything which could really play the social role played by commitments would have to have a similar transparency and undeniability. However, this point can be turned around to cast doubt on the notion that promises or contracts could possibly be appropriate paradigms for all undertakings of commitments. The trouble is that many other commissive utterances and actions do not exhibit this sort of transparency. We ourselves are likely to be uncertain to what degree, and in what particulars, we are implicitly committing ourselves when we announce our intentions, profess our love, publicly affirm our ideals or values, assume a professional role, or say or do a host of other things that can commit us. In these moments we take on vaguely defined and open-ended commitments—commitments which we have not yet formulated, even under a very general description, and hence are not yet in a position to agree to. This casts doubt on the tidy thesis that all new commitments must originate in express voluntary agreements.

As I see it, the fundamental problem with the analytical strategy I have been criticizing is that it ignores an important facet of our ordinary, admirably complex concept of commitment. The strategy tends to highlight one facet of committed action—remaining true to one's past word—while obscuring another important facet—remaining true to one's own core ideals and values. By focusing on the independent importance of this second sense of 'commitment,' I hope to develop a more nuanced and defensible account of the different ways in which we might commit ourselves, and of the different kinds of commissive force at work in each.

Essentially, my strategy is to divide and conquer—that is, to acknowledge that different commitments bind us for different reasons, and to attempt to illuminate these reasons. I should mention, at the outset, that one way of "dividing and conquering" which will *not* do is to reserve the honorific title 'obligations' for those commitments arising from promises, contracts and the like, and deny this title to commitments arising in other ways. Despite their varying parentage, these latter commitments can be every bit as morally weighty as those born of promises or contracts—or so I will argue.

I can describe the purpose of the essay from a different angle by connecting it to an ambiguity in the ordinary conception of integrity. There is a wide consensus that integrity is the virtue of those who remain true to their commitments.[2] This seems right as far as it goes. However, if I am right in believing that 'commitment' has two importantly different senses, then we might wonder whether 'integrity' is similarly ambiguous. I believe that while 'integrity' always refers to a sort of unity of character and action, this unity can have two importantly different dimensions: a synchronic and a diachronic one. The basic idea is that we might think it a breach of integrity (in its synchronic dimension) to fail to act on ideals or principles whose bindingness one recognizes in the moment in which one is acting, and we might also think it a breach of integrity (in its diachronic dimension) to break with the values to which we have professed allegiance in the past. Those theorists who take promising to be the paradigmatic mode of undertaking commitments, and who analyze other modes of undertaking commitments as if they were implicit promises, tend to overemphasize the diachronic dimension of integrity while overlooking the synchronic dimension altogether. In this chapter and the next, I hope to develop an alternative paradigm for understanding commitments which gives due importance to both the synchronic and the diachronic dimensions of integrity, and which brings out the connections between them.

Before launching into the argument, I should make a few comments about my view of what I have called the "bare voluntarist thesis"—i.e. that nothing but our voluntary agreement could commit us. While I think that this thesis is mistaken, it seems to me that there is an element of truth in it: it is true that we cannot be coerced into taking on particularistic commitments. This alone, however, does not imply the bare voluntarist thesis that commitments must have their origins in a free and conscious act of will. To think that it does is to embrace a false

---

2   See for example Gabriele Taylor, "Integrity" in *Proceedings of the Aristotelian Society*, Supplementary Volume LV (July, 1981), pp. 143–159, esp. p. 144. See also John Kekes, *Moral Tradition and Individuality* (Princeton; Princeton University Press: 1989), p. 219.

dichotomy, since there is conceptual space for a class of commitments that we have neither voluntarily chosen to undertake nor been forced to assume. Further, we have phenomenological grounds for doubting that this class of commitments is empty. When we honor many commitments, we do so out of an acknowledgment of values or personal attachments which we feel compelled to recognize. It seems to us that these commitments are discovered and not chosen, since we identify them by deliberating about what attachments are truly our own, or what is truly valuable. For example, we do not take our commitments to friends and lovers to arise *simply* from the fact that we have made a voluntary choice to be friends or lovers. Perhaps this fact alone is enough to establish *a* commitment to a friend or a lover, but it is not all that is at work in establishing *the* commitment which many of us take ourselves to have to our intimates. Likewise, members of civic associations do not take their commitments to each other to arise *simply* from the fact that they have *chosen* to join a group. If the group is vital and if their attachment is genuine, they take their commitment to arise from and to be justified by the ideals and values which they affirm in common with other group members, and which prompted them to join the group in the first place.

These sorts of commitments cannot be coercively forced upon us because of the sort of things they are. As I will go on to argue, these commitments are the practical dictates of certain of our core ideals and values. It is futile to try to force anyone to undertake *these* sorts of commitments. Coercion does not reach all the way to our convictions; it extends only to our actions. Furthermore, as will become clear in the last section of the paper, we have reason to care about these sorts of commitments, and to hold ourselves and others to them, only if they are the product of free deliberation about what there is reason to value. Thus, there is little reason to *want* to force them upon others.

PART I: THE WORDS THAT COMMIT US

I do not claim novelty for my contention that not just promises and contracts, but a broad assortment of other utterances and actions, can give rise to commitments. In his lectures series *How to Do Things with Words*, J.L. Austin provides a list of thirty-three "commissives."[3] Austin chooses this name to register the fact that when uttered in their first-person indicative form, these verbs sometimes *commit* us to future performances. For my purposes, Austin's list is interesting because of a particular continuum of variation amongst the verbs—one to which Austin pays insufficient attention. I have arranged locutions featuring some of Austin's verbs (and some additions of my own, in brackets) into five groups which stand at successive points along the continuum that interests me:

Group One: 'I promise...', 'I swear...', 'I guarantee...', 'I vow...'

Group Two: 'I declare my intention...'

Group Three: 'I consent...', 'I agree...', 'I adopt...'

Group Four: 'I intend...', 'I am determined to...', 'I mean to...' ['I stand by...', 'I aim to...', 'I aspire to...', 'I adhere to...']

Group Five: 'I side with...', 'I embrace...', 'I favor...', 'I oppose...'
              ['I value...', 'I esteem...', 'I care about...', 'I deplore...', 'I protest...', 'I challenge...', 'I commend...', 'I applaud...', 'I approve...'[4]]

---

3 J.L. Austin, *How to Do Things with Words* (Cambridge; Harvard University Press: 1962), pp. 157–8. It is worth clarifying the connection between commissive verbs and the category of "performatives" for which Austin is more widely remembered. Austin begins the lecture series *How to Do Things with Words* by focusing on a dichotomy between performatives like "I promise"—which are not used to describe the world and which cannot be straightforwardly assessed as true or false—and constatives like "I have eleven fingers" which are used to describe the world, and which do so either truly or falsely. By the end of the book he acknowledges—correctly, I think—that there is no sharp distinction here but only a continuum. Austin then replaces his talk of performatives with a more general theory of speech acts, in which various kinds of illocutionary force must be distinguished and assigned not merely to locutions but to particular utterances in particular contexts. He introduces the category of commissives in order to mark a kind of illocutionary force carried by some utterances in some contexts. The differentiation that I wish to explore within the category of commissives is just the performative/constative distinction, displayed not as a clear dichotomy but as a continuum. In other words, I wish to examine performative-constative hybrids of just the sort that indicate the truth of Austin's own conclusion that the dichotomy ultimately breaks down.

4 The last six verbs are taken from a list provided by Austin of what he calls "behabatives"—verbs that register our reactions to the behavior or plight of others. Austin himself notes that these verbs can function as commissives. See Austin, *How to Do Things with Words* (*Op. Cit.*), pp. 160–61.

Let me make a first rough attempt to characterize the key variables of the continuum marked out by these groups of verb phrases. The locutions in Groups One and Two are not descriptions of states of affairs, and it would be odd at best to appraise them as true or false. These sorts of utterances do not so much *say* something as *do* something: they bring about a normative change in the world, giving rise to a commitment where previously there was none. When I say, "I promise to ø," I do not ordinarily think of myself as *describing* what I am doing; when I say this, I thereby promise to ø. By contrast, the locutions in Groups Four and Five (and perhaps also in Group Three) can be used to make assertions, and hence can be appraised straightforwardly as true or false. Further, when I say such things as "I intend to ø" or "I favor øing," I do not thereby make it the case that I intend to ø or that I favor øing. What I say might well be false.

I believe it is true, as Austin claims, that utterances such as "I intend to ø" and "I oppose øing" can have commissive force. My point here is that this does not exhaust their semantic analysis. They also function as assertions. Indeed, they often function simultaneously as assertions and as commissives—or so I will argue.

How sharp a differentiation is there between the verbs at the extreme ends of this continuum? We might try to soften the difference by associating a descriptive meaning with utterances like 'I promise...' along the following lines: 'I promise to ø' is true just in case I promise to ø. This is tempting because a moment after I say "I promise," I can (given suitable background conditions) truly say "I promised," and this seems to be an assertion. Since the latter utterance differs from the former only in tense, it seems odd to think that the former asserts nothing. However, there are at least two difficulties with this strategy. The first is that in normal cases, when speakers sincerely say "I promise," they simply do not *mean* to be describing what they are doing; they mean to commit themselves. The second and, I think, more telling difficulty is that even if we were to assign a descriptive meaning to "I promise..." this locution would still be markedly different from those in groups four and five, since it would ordinarily make itself true in the moment it is spoken. Thus, it could not be construed as a description of some antecedently identified state of affairs, and the speaker could not coherently be thought to use the words to communicate his or her belief that this state of affairs obtains. In particular, the utterance could not be construed as an assertion of the existence of some as-yet-unarticulated mental state of the speaker—e.g. the speaker's *intention* or *determination* to do that which she promises to do—because however we try to specify the relevant mental state, it will be true that the speaker promises whether or not the mental state obtains.[5]

The case is subtly different with the locution 'I declare my intention...'—the sole member of Group Two. Like promises, so declarations of intent are not naturally understood as assertions, nor straightforwardly assessed as true or false. Still, declarations of intent often *imply* that one has an antecedently formulated and firmly held intention which one is making known to another. This points towards a subtle distinction between promises and declarations of intent. There is nothing untoward about promising to do that which one has no prior intention of doing, provided that in the moment of promising one takes on the relevant intention. Of course, it might be untoward to promise to do anything at all, if not does not have a standing commitment to do whatever one promises to do. But one can quite properly promise to do something while believing that apart from the promise, one would have no reason in the world to do that particular thing. By contrast, there are many circumstances in which it would be inappropriate to declare an intention to do that which one has no prior intention of doing, or that which one recognizes no pressing reason to do.

These observations might give rise to some doubt as to whether declarations of intent *establish* commitments or *reveal* them. In some instances they seem to do both at once. In such instances, we reveal to another a substantive commitment which we have antecedently, and also at the same time commit ourselves to the other by giving the other license to hold us to our commitment.

This has a paradoxical air. How could we establish a commitment by revealing it to others? If we are in a position to reveal it, wouldn't it be redundant to establish it? I will have a good deal to

---

5 There is a familiar but derivative sense in which a promise might be false: a promise is false if made with no intention to fulfill it. When I make a false promise, however, it remains true that I promise, else I could not be held responsible for doing what I have promised to do. The falsity does not lie in some failure of correspondence between what I say I am doing and what I am doing. It lies instead in the fact that I am using my words to deceive my interlocutor about what I will do in the future.

say about this below. At this point, I want to begin to take the sting out of the paradox by drawing attention to the above-noted ambiguity in the ordinary notion of commitment. In ordinary speech, we use the noun 'commitment' and the various forms of the verb 'to commit' in two importantly different senses: we say that P is committed to øing (or has a commitment to ø) if others can legitimately demand that P ø, and we also say that P is committed to øing (or has a commitment to ø) if his own deeply rooted values, or life projects, give him reason to ø. These two senses often come apart. For instance, a courtroom witness can take an oath, thus *committing herself* to telling nothing but the truth, yet she can remain secretly *committed* all the while to lying. If such a witness were to claim, upon being unveiled as a perjurer, that she never really committed herself to telling the truth, one would not know quite what to say. On the one hand, the claim might be thought a cynical rationalization, for there is an externalist sense of 'commitment' in which one truly commits oneself by oaths and other acts which give rise to legitimate public expectations about one's future actions, no matter what one actually cares about or is actually motivated to do. On the other hand, the claim might be thought an evident truth, for there is an internalist sense of 'commitment' which is more closely connected to the principles, goals and values that we affirm and characteristically act on.[6] We have the internalist sense of commitment in mind when we say of Martin Luther King that he was *committed* to the struggle for racial equality. What we mean to say by these words could not possibly be captured by saying that King *promised* to further the struggle, even if this were true.

It is not easy to make precise just what internalist commitments are. As a first approximation, one might say that one is committed, in the internalist sense, to do that which one firmly

---

6 This distinction can be found in the *Oxford English Dictionary* (Second Edition), where the following two meanings of 'commitment' are noted: (6b) "An engagement; a liability; pl pecuniary obligations..."; and (6c) "An absolute moral choice of a course of action; hence, the state of being involved in political or social questions, or in furthering a particular doctrine or cause, esp. in one's literary or artistic expression..." The distinction is perhaps more clearly noted in *Second College Edition—The American Heritage Dictionary*, where 'commitment' is said to mean (among other things): (2a) "A pledge to do something" and (3) "The state of being bound emotionally or intellectually to a course of action."

intends to do, or that which is dictated by the principles, ideals or values which one professes on reflection. This leaves out one thing. The intentions, principles, ideals or values must not merely be ones that one avows on reflection; they also must be efficacious—that is, they must ordinarily be manifest in one's actions. One might have a firm intention to do something, or to act in accordance with some principle or ideal, yet be unable to fulfill this intention. This is the plight of the self-conscious *akratic*, and of the many of us who silently and somewhat desperately repeat the same New Year's resolutions, year after year. Such intentions might be firm at the time when we avow them, but that alone does not make them commitments.[7] One must generally be able to act in the future as one now firmly intends in order for one's intentions to count as internalist commitments. We would not have said of King that he was committed in the internalist sense to the egalitarian reform of race relations if he greatly insisted upon his intentions to reform race relations, or professed an attachment to the ideal of equality, yet did not characteristically act on these intentions or ideals. An internalist commitment penetrates more deeply into one's actual perceptions and motivations than a mere intention, and it provides greater protection against *akrasia*. This is why we say that the road to hell is paved with good intentions, not good commitments.

As I see it, when we speak in the internalist sense of a person's commitments, we often mean to refer to the person's *convictions*— that is, to the ideals, values, goals or principles which the person stably and reflectively judges to be worthy of allegiance, stands prepared to act on, and generally does act on. This, I think, is what we mean when we say that Martin Luther King was committed to racial justice. However, 'conviction' is not an exact synonym for the internalist sense of 'commitment.' We sometimes speak in the internalist sense of what we have a commitment to *do*, as when we say that King had a commitment to march on Birmingham, yet we would not say that King had a conviction to march on Birmingham. We would say, instead, that King's convictions gave him reason to march on Birmingham. This indicates that when we

---

7 Perhaps we could stipulate a definition of the adjective "firm" such that *akratics* could not have firm intentions. However, the interesting work would lie in figuring out what this curious notion of firmness amounts to.

speak of (internalist) commitments, we refer either to convictions or to the practical dictates of convictions.[8]

I can now say, in a rough and provisional sense, how it can be that a commitment is established by being revealed. In these sorts of cases, a declaration of intention can reveal an internalist commitment and in the same breath create an externalist commitment, in the sense that it licenses others to form legitimate expectations—and perhaps also to make legitimate demands—concerning one's future actions. As noted above, this marks a critical difference between a declaration of intent and a promise. This difference can sometimes be all-important, both from the first-person viewpoint and from the viewpoint of the person to whom the commitment is made. Some commitments are only properly undertaken by public utterance if they are already there in the internalist sense, waiting to be revealed. To take a particularly dramatic example, it is ordinarily improper to declare one's intentions to marry another if one has no prior intention of marrying the other, or if one does not take oneself to have good reason to marry the other. By dwelling on this, we begin to see why we normally speak of proposals of marriage as involving declarations of intent and not promises, and why we modern romantics might think there is ordinarily something shabby—perhaps even subtly offensive—about *promising* to marry another. Promises are most naturally invoked when the promiser requires some extra inducement to do what he promises to do (or alternatively, they are extracted when the promisee believes that the promiser needs an extra inducement). We are tempted to think that couples in need of such inducements and assurances are not yet committed enough to utter marital vows. We can begin to make sense of this thought if we understand marital vows not as promises but as public expressions of internalist commitments—though we still must explain why publicizing one's internalist commitments changes one's normative relations to others.

To continue our exploration of the continuum of commissives, recall what it is that promises (Group One) and declarations of

---

8 The relationship between convictions and commitments is analogous to the relationship between beliefs and commitments: our beliefs are commitments and we are committed to whatever propositions follow from our beliefs.

intent (Group Two) have in common: they cannot plausibly be understood as assertions nor assessed as true or false. This sets them off from the locutions in Groups Four and Five, at the far end of the continuum. We can misrepresent our own intentions (Group Four) and evaluations (Group Five). When we do, it seems that we make a false assertion, though this may not be all we do. [9]

This same contrast can be further illuminated by considering that while I can promise insincerely, I cannot insincerely intend nor insincerely value. This reflects the fact that given suitable background conditions, when I insincerely utter the words "I promise," I really do promise; saying it makes it so. By contrast, my intentions and evaluations are not whatever I say they are. I can *represent* them insincerely, but there is no obvious sense in which my intentions and evaluations *themselves* might be insincere.[10]

Given these observations, we might be tempted to think that the verbs listed in Groups Four and Five are really descriptive phrases and not commissives at all. Austin provides a condensed argument for regarding these verbs as commissives: "'I declare my intention' [Group Two] undoubtedly does commit me; and to say 'I intend' [Group Four] is generally to declare or announce."[11]

This seems quite right. When an integral, strong-willed person speaks sincerely about her own values and intentions, she gives *to all listeners* good grounds for making *predictions* about what she will do. If such locutions were merely descriptive, then this is all her words would do. It is not. Her words often give something additional *to those whom she addresses*, especially if their lives are inter-

9 More controversially, there may be a sense of 'I consent' or 'I agree' (group 3) in which what I say can be false, and this not because of some external circumstance which nullifies the commissive force of the proceedings (for instance, not because I have been coerced), but because I am mistaken about my own beliefs and/or attitudes. I will return to this question below.
10 Declarations of intent are an intermediate case here. There is a sense in which I can insincerely declare my intentions. When I do so, we might not know whether to say that I have declared my intentions. It depends upon where our real interest lies. On the one hand, it is true that I have *declared* my intentions—that is, I have declared intentions which I have passed off as my own. On the other hand, I have not really declared *my* intentions—the intentions I declared were not really mine at all.
11 Austin, *Op. Cit.*, pp. 157–8.

twined with her own in ways I will describe below. She often gives to these persons good grounds for making *legitimate demands* on her future actions, and for *rebuking* her if she fails to meet these demands. Put another way, her words often commit her.[12]

These legitimate demands are different in kind from predictions. This is best seen in cases where the two come apart. For example, if John says to his wife, "I intend to stop gambling," she may know enough about him to make the well-founded prediction that his next paycheck will end up in a slot machine. Nevertheless, these same words give her grounds for legitimately demanding that he not gamble, and for rebuking him if he does. If John says this— perhaps in the context of a dispute over control of finances—and then proceeds to gamble away his paycheck, I think it is quite natural to say that he has broken a commitment to his wife. Further, it is not at all clear to me that this commitment, or others originating in similar ways, must always be weaker or less binding than those originating in promises.

Austin thinks that a similar point can be made for such locutions as 'I dedicate my life to...', as well as for evaluative utterances like 'I favor...' and 'I oppose...' (Group Five).[13] Again, this seems true. When we say what it is that we value, we do not merely describe our values; we also and at the same time affirm our values, and announce where we are ready to take our stand. In some circumstances, we can justly be said to fail in our commitments if we fail to act on the values we have affirmed in the presence of others. This is perhaps clearest in cases where we are conversing with others whose activities and projects are bound up with our own, and where our aim is to articulate the values that we take to guide, and to give importance to, these activities or projects. To illustrate, if the members of a civil rights protest organization come together to decide how to respond to a proposed piece of legislation, and if Peter says that he favors civil disobedience if the legislation is

---

12 I believe that there is a sense in which purely descriptive assertions are also commissive: they commit the speaker to justify his implicit claim to knowledge should any question arise as to the truth of his assertion. Here I follow Robert Brandom, who lays out these and other normative implications of assertion in Robert Brandom, *Making It Explicit: Reasoning, Representing and Discursive Commitment* (Cambridge; Harvard University Press: 1994), especially Chapter Four, pp. 199–271.

13 *Ibid.*

passed, his utterance sets the terms under which he is committed to joining fellow members in civil disobedience. Again, it is not generally true that commitments arising in this way carry less normative weight than promises.

PART II: THE PECULIAR CASE OF CONSENT

I have said very little about the commissives in Group Three: 'consent', 'agree', and 'adopt'. In part this is because they fit uneasily into their assigned spot in my continuum. I noted above that the verbs in Groups One and Two, in their spoken first-person present indicative use, cannot be understood as describing a state of affairs, nor as making any sort of claim that can straightforwardly be appraised as true or false. By contrast, the verbs in Group Three are often used in the first-person indicative to describe the speaker's mental attitudes. For instance, I might sometimes say "I agree..." in order to register the fact that my considered beliefs are the same as those of the person I am addressing; likewise, I might sometimes say "I consent..." in order to make known my attitudes of approval or acceptance. It is because these phrases have a descriptive use that I have placed these commissives below "declare my intention" (Group Two) in my continuum. However, there are competing considerations which indicate that these verbs ought to be included in Group One, with 'promise', 'guarantee', etc. Unlike "I declare my intention," such locutions as "I consent" and "I agree" are sometimes quite appropriately used to commit oneself to do that which one has no antecedent intention of doing. When used in this way, they function quite like the locutions "I promise" and "I guarantee," and distinctly unlike the locutions "I intend" or "I favor."

Given this, one might object that the locutions I have placed in Group Three have two different uses, and that their descriptive use in the first-person indicative is irrelevant to their analysis as commissives. When used as commissives, the objection might proceed, these locutions are not intended as descriptions at all, any more than promises are so intended. Thus, when these verbs are used as commissives, they are in all relevant respects just like promises and not at all like the hybrid descriptive-commissive verbs in Groups Four and Five.

This is roughly the position taken by A. John Simmons in his discussion of consent theories of political obligation. Simmons distinguishes between two senses of 'consent': an "attitudinal" sense and an "occurrence" sense. In Simmons' view, the attitudinal sense (which corresponds to the descriptive sense I have been discussing) is "quite irrelevant" to the discussion of the role of consent in the genesis of obligations.[14] In fact, not only is it irrelevant, it must be assiduously distinguished from the morally relevant sense of 'consent' when considering consensual obligations, on pain of philosophical error. "It is my view," writes Simmons, "that confusions about this attitudinal-occurrence distinction, conjoined with similar failures to distinguish signs of consent from consent-implying acts, are responsible for most of the mistakes made in discussions of consent theory from Locke down to contemporary writers."[15] One might extend Simmons' view to all of the commissive utterances listed above, claiming that it is simply a semantic accident that some locutions can both describe and commit us, and that we never commit ourselves when we use such locutions descriptively, but only when their use amounts to an implicit promise.

I believe that the ambiguity in 'consent' which Simmons rightly identifies is not merely a potential source of confusion, but also a potential source of *insight* into the *point* of our belief that consent can generate commitments. In my view, one can understand the normative force neither of implicit nor of explicit consent if one ignores what Simmons calls the attitudinal meaning of 'consent.' My full argument for this conclusion will be given in the last chapter of this dissertation. For now, I will restrict myself to a short and hardly more than suggestive discussion of the relationship between the commissive and descriptive uses (i.e. what Simmons calls the occurrence and attitudinal senses) of the utterance 'I consent'.

In many but not all cases, when one gives one's consent, one thinks of oneself *both* as reporting one's standing normative convictions *and* as undertaking a commitment to act on these convictions. Further, in these cases one typically thinks that the norma-

---

14 A. John Simmons, *Moral Principles and Political Obligations* (Princeton; Princeton University Press: 1979), p. 93.
15 *Ibid.*

tive force of the commitment one undertakes is borrowed, so to speak, from the normative force of one's standing convictions. This means that when one is called upon to fulfill one's commitment, one's *reason* for fulfilling it is not simply that one said one would do so, but more fundamentally that one's own standing convictions give one good reason to do so. As I will argue, this point is most salient when one confronts extraordinarily costly obligations, such as the obligation to risk one's life for one's country. Any convincing reason to fulfill such an obligation would make ineliminable reference to one's reflective affirmation of the substantive goods for which one's country stands. The bare fact that one has consented seems too insubstantial to support so grave and costly an obligation.

This suggests one way of illuminating *why* it is that we think consent is only binding if given freely, after the "age of consent", and in conditions where no one has rigged the ceremony by making certain that withholding consent will have catastrophic consequences. These conditions all play a recognizably important role in making it the case that the commitments one undertakes by consenting actually do reflect one's own standing convictions. To put it in the terms I used above, these conditions serve to ensure that in undertaking (externalist) commitments one is also at the same time revealing internalist ones.

One way to put my disagreement with Simmons is to note that he thinks the consent theory of obligation owes a great deal of its plausibility to what I call the bare voluntarist intuition, to the effect that each person can legitimately be held only to those obligations which he or she has voluntarily undertaken.[16] On the view I have been pressing, this bare voluntarist thesis owes its attractiveness in part to a more fundamental concern, which we take to be operative in many socio-political contexts, that no one be required to act on grounds which have not actually gained their conviction. Consent must be voluntary because otherwise it provides no indication of one's actual convictions. Since I do not take the bare voluntarist thesis to be fundamental, I leave open the possibility that one's commitments might change with changes in one's fundamental convictions. I will argue in the next chapter that this possibility ought to be left open by any ade-

---

16 *Ibid.*, pp. 62–5 and 70.

quate theory of the obligations that govern an important class of social relations.[17]

One might ask whether what I have said about consent-giving does not also apply to many cases of swearing, vowing, promising or guaranteeing. As noted above, promises and guarantees are to my ear most appropriately used to enter into commitments in situations where there is some ground for doubt as to whether one already has the commitment in the internalist sense. Promises and guarantees are conventional means of increasing the assurance of others that one will act in particular ways in the future. In order to perform this function, they must be seen as binding no matter what one's actual convictions might be. Swearing seems to me to have the same connotation (though it has become so rare these days, at least in my social circles, that I distrust my intuitions about it). Vows and oaths, I think, are often quite different. For example, it seems to me that we think of marital vows, or oaths of citizenship, as inappropriate or even deceptive when taken by someone who is not already committed, in the internalist sense, to meeting their terms.

This might raise questions about whether I ought to have categorized vows and oaths with promises and guarantees. I did so because locutions of the form 'I vow...' do not have a straightforward descriptive use, and given suitable background conditions, vowing makes it true that one vows. However, my central aim is not to present the best possible architectonic of commissives; it is

---

17 Here I disagree with Simmons, who maintains that "When a man consents, he has consented and may be bound accordingly, regardless of how he feels about what he has consented to." (Simmons, *Op. Cit.*, p. 93) I will discuss my reasons for disagreeing with Simmons in the next chapter. For now, suffice it to point out that Simmons' way of putting the matter is already slightly tendentious, in that it might not be a matter of what one "feels" at some later stage but also and more importantly a question of what one sincerely judges to be the right thing to do. To take the example of the soldier who is asked to risk his life for the state, it seems to me that there is a morally relevant distinction between a fear-driven refusal, which evidences a failure to act on conviction, and a refusal stemming from a newfound commitment to pacifism, which might well evidence a real courage of conviction. The fact that third-person observers are hard-pressed to make this distinction in practice, and tend to suspect that apparent instances of pacifist conversion are really instances of fear-driven refusal, does not vitiate the moral importance of the distinction. Far from it. A refusal born of fear does not display any recognizable sort of integrity, while a refusal born of a pacifist commitment does.

rather to illuminate the importance that we invest in our commitments by considering ways of undertaking commitments which differ markedly from the ordinary philosophical paradigms of promises and contracts. As will emerge in the latter portion of this chapter, I do not think that these alternative commitments can reliably be identified simply by attending to the locution used to undertake them, though this can be a significant clue. The pragmatics of the utterances under discussion can only be determined conclusively by attending to the kind of social group in which the conversation is embedded. The general points I have made about the differences amongst commissive locutions are intended as a way of raising the question why our linguistic practices might have evolved so as to offer us a way of simultaneously making our internal commitments known and entering into external commitments. The theory of social groups that I offer in the last section of the paper represents my answer to this question.

PART III: COMMISSIVE FORCE AND DESCRIPTIVE TRUTH

I argued above that declarations of intent are subtly different from promises in that they function as revelations or public confirmations of existing commitments. One can sincerely and appropriately promise to do something that one has no antecedent intention of doing. By contrast, it is quite often insincere and inappropriate to declare an intention to do that which one has no antecedent intention of doing. Utterances such as "I intend", "I mean to", and "I am determined to" are in this particular like "I declare my intention" and unlike "I promise." However, they are unlike "I declare my intention" in that they *have* a descriptive meaning, and their appropriateness (taken as commissives) often depends upon their truth (taken as descriptions). Thus, it is often inappropriate to say "I am determined to ø" if I am not antecedently determined to ø, and often inappropriate to say "I mean to ø" if I do not antecedently mean to ø. A similar point can be made with respect to the commissives in Group Five. It is inappropriate, because untrue, to say "I favor øing" when in fact I favor not øing, or to say "I side with candidate P" when in fact I side with P's opponent, candidate Q.

What is the nature and source of our admittedly vague intuition that such utterances are inappropriate? In order to shed light on this question, we will have to explore a feature of the semantics of these utterances to which Austin did not attend: the *connection* between their descriptive and commissive uses. I hope to show that even when such utterances are clearly commissive, they retain a descriptive meaning which is far from irrelevant. It is often a matter of considerable importance to those whom the speaker addresses that the utterance is true when taken as an assertion. I will also seek to show that at least in certain cases, it will be quite proper for the speaker herself to attend to the descriptive sense of her words, taking care that they accurately represent the way things are with her.

Along the way, I hope to shed some light on what it is that we are doing when we make our internalist commitments public, beyond merely revealing existing commitments to others. That is, I will try to specify the normative change that we effect when we say what we intend to do, what we value, and the like (i.e. when we use the verbs from Groups Four and Five commissively).

IIIA. Moran on the Irresponsibility of Mere Self-Description

In ordinary cases, when we say what it is that we intend or value, we do not *think* of ourselves as offering descriptions of our own mental states. This point can be brought home by dwelling on those cases where we speak sincerely but mistakenly about what we intend or value. In these cases, there is a mismatch between our careful and sincere reports, and the evaluations or intentions which must be attributed to us in order best to account for our thoughts and actions. It is tempting to think that the mismatch can be traced to the fact that we lack clear insight into our own evaluations and intentions. This, however, is a potentially misleading way of putting matters. It is potentially misleading because it suggests that before we announce our intentions or evaluations, what we do is to look inwards, examining our own behavior and mental states to identify our intentions or evaluations. In most cases, this is not and ought not to be what we do.

Richard Moran points out that even though utterances of the form 'I believe that p' seem to be assertions about our mental states, we do not prepare ourselves to utter them by attending to our mental states, nor by determining which beliefs ought to be attributed to us in order to make most sense of our behavior. We attend instead to the world, and in particular to whether p. To think that we attend to ourselves, Moran says, is to mistake the "direction of gaze" most appropriate for the sort of reflection which prepares us to say what we believe.[18] Moran argues quite persuasively that if we were to direct our attention at ourselves, and to seek in a purely theoretical spirit to describe the beliefs at work in shaping our thoughts and behavior, we would exhibit a particular kind of irresponsibility: we would fail to acknowledge our own status as "practical and theoretical deliberator[s]."[19] Moran's point is that if we are to think of ourselves as rational agents who seek to commit ourselves to the truth of propositions (i.e. to have beliefs), then we must enunciate beliefs by deliberating about what we have most reason to affirm as true, and not by interpreting our own behavior.

I believe that Moran's claim is substantially correct, and that it can be extended quite naturally to evaluations, to declared intentions, and in general to the commissive locutions in Groups Four and Five above.[20] When we utter these commissives, we ordinarily do not and ought not to examine ourselves at all. If we did, we would fail to acknowledge our status as practical agents who act on what we judge to be good reasons. Intentions ordinarily are and ought to be formulated by attending to the situations in which we must act, and to the nature, significance and likely consequences of alternative actions. In this way we determine what we have most reason to do. Similarly, evaluative beliefs ordinarily are and ought to be formulated by attending to the states of affairs we wish to evaluate evaluate (e.g. to pleasures and pains, or satisfactions and dissatisfactions, or unfairnesses, etc.). In this way we determine what we have most reason to value. While it may be true that our spoken evaluations *express* our subjective reactions to the world that confronts us, still we do not forward evaluations as *descriptions* of our subjective reactions.

The comparison between Group Four and Five commissive locutions and avowals of belief is fruitful for another reason: these utterances commit us for the same reason that expressions of belief

18 See Richard Moran, "Self-Knowledge: Discovery, Resolution and Undoing" (unpublished manuscript), esp. p. 30.
19 Moran likens this irresponsibility to Sartrean bad faith. See *Ibid.*, pp. 16–18.
20 Moran explicitly extends his claims to the case of resolutions, which are in certain relevant respects similar to declared intentions. See *Ibid.*, pp. 16–19.

commit us. They do not commit us because they accurately describe us. An accurate self-description of our dispositions to say and do certain things would provide others with a useful tool for predicting what we will say or do, but it would give these others no basis for rebuking us if we frustrated their predictions. These utterances commit us because when we say them, we imply that we affirm ourselves under the description that our words might be thought to proffer. The commitment stems from the presupposition that we judge ourselves to have good reason to stand where we say we do.

There are at least two kinds of cases which strain the analogy between avowals of beliefs and avowals of intentions and evaluations. In these sorts of cases, it does seem appropriate to attend to ourselves—i.e. to try to divine what it is that we intend or value. However, in neither case does the speaker have a merely theoretical interest in her intentions or evaluations. Thus, these cases do no impugn the main point I am drawing from Moran, which is that there would be something amiss about taking a merely theoretical interest in those of our own mental states which ought to be responsive to reasons.

The first sort of cases are those in which we have already engaged in world-directed reflection and have already formulated stable intentions or evaluations. In these cases, we need not direct our attention at the world in order to make up our minds afresh; our minds are made up and we need only reveal them. As indicated above, I believe that many kinds of commitments are only appropriately undertaken when they are already there in a settled form, waiting to be expressed or revealed to others. I do not think that these kinds of cases present a serious challenge to Moran's view, but it is instructive to see why not. The reason, I believe, is that even in these cases we are not *merely* describing our mental states but also in the same breath *affirming* (or reaffirming) them.[21] It seems reasonable to trace the commissiveness of these

---

21 What we are doing, in effect, is affirming the adequacy or reliability of the past reflections (or the non-reflective means—e.g. the socialization) by which we have come to have the intentions or evaluations whose existence we are asserting. This is in essence no different from what minimally competent adults do when they assert that the earth revolves around the sun: though they are making an assertion about the world, they need not engage afresh in world-directed reflection to determine whether what they say is true. Their minds too are already made up and need only be revealed publicly.

utterance to the implication that we affirm ourselves under the description they proffer.

There is a second and more interesting set of cases in which it seems appropriate to turn our gaze inwards in preparing to declare our evaluations (and perhaps also our intentions insofar as they are properly responsive to our evaluative judgments). These are the cases in which we are introspectively aware of an inchoate evaluation but cannot yet bring it into focus. To borrow Charles Taylor's terms, we cannot yet "formulate" or "articulate" it. As is suggested by Taylor's terminology, we proceed by trying to put the evaluation into words. When we do so, we "can now get an articulated view of the matter, and thus focus on it properly."[22] I believe this is a phenomenologically accurate description of how we sometimes make up our minds about our values. Furthermore, it seems to me misleading to think that as we seek the proper words, our attention is always directed outwards. Sometimes we consult our immediate impulses, or our unreflective reactions of admiration or shame, in order to make sense of them. We do not seek to describe them. Rather, we seek to formulate a clarifying interpretation of them—to give them articulate verbal content so that we can express them to others.

Now, it seems to me that this sort of self-clarifying interpretation is far from rare. In the first instance, we often engage in such interpretation when we announce intentions or evaluations of the sort that can give rise to bonds of love and friendship. We think it proper that such commitments be tailored to personal facts about us—our likes, pleasures, cares and concerns. When we speak commissively of what we care about, or whom we value, we might well attempt to diagnose the cares and values implicit in our past and present thought and behavior. Our gaze is directed at ourselves, or at our own ongoing life. We must attempt to articulate the values that drive us in a way that simultaneously gives coherence to our ongoing life story and gives direction to that story. This means that our self-interpretations must gain our current endorsement. When we say what we value or intend in this spirit, we enunciate guidelines for our current and future actions. Here again, if such utterances are commis-

---

22 Charles Taylor, "Theories of Meaning," in *Human Agency and Language: Philosophical Papers I* (Cambridge; Cambridge University Press: 1985), pp. 248–292; see esp. p. 258.

sive, this is because they imply that we affirm ourselves—or at least do not disown ourselves—under the self-description that they can be understood to offer.

In other instances, we might think that we ought to ignore all idiosyncratic facts about ourselves and act in light of a considered evaluation of the options before us. However, we might lack articulate evaluations of the options before us. In these sorts of cases, it seems to me that we often make up our minds by imagining ourselves acting in one way or another. If we then feel a vague uneasiness about acting in a certain way, we might attend to our felt uneasiness and try to bring it into words. That is, we might regard our felt uneasiness as an inchoate judgment which must be given articulation before its adequacy can be assessed.[23] It seems to me that this sort of reflection is particularly important when we are attempting to articulate the values that we take to govern the activities we share with other members of certain social groups. I will have more to say about this topic below. For now, I will restrict myself to observing that in these very interesting sorts of cases, it is very hard to say whether our gaze is directed out towards the world or back towards ourselves. It might be most accurate to say that the metaphor of "direction of gaze" is here stretched beyond the limits of its coherent application.

As noted above, even if I am right that we sometimes must engage in this sort of self-interpretive articulation before we can say what we value, this does not impugn the central point I am borrowing from Moran's discussion of belief avowal. The claim is this: although the utterances under investigation appear, in terms of their surface semantics, to be assertions about one's mental states, they cannot be voiced in a fully responsible way if the speaker thinks of them *merely* as self-descriptive assertions. Even when our evaluations require articulation before they can be

---

23 In an intriguing early paper, Alasdair MacIntyre argues that the resolution of moral conflicts or perplexities often takes this form. Such decisions, he says, can only be illuminated by the sort of phenomenology supplied by the novelist. MacIntyre draws upon the example of Huck Finn, who draws guidance from "an only half-articulate sympathy," and not from any articulable moral rule, in deciding to help Jim escape from enslavement. See MacIntyre, "What Morality is Not," in *Against the Self-Image of the Age: Essays on Ideology and Philosophy* (Notre Dame; University of Notre Dame Press: 1978), pp. 96–108, esp. pp. 106–7.

uttered, still when we voice them publicly we are ordinarily understood to affirm or endorse ourselves under the proffered description.[24] This, as I have been insisting, is the origin of the commissive force of these utterances.

IIIB. The "Confessional" Use of Commissive Verbs

In order to highlight the source of commissiveness, I turn now to the special social settings in which the utterances under investigation do *not* function as commissives. One clear example is psychoanalysis.[25] In the course of psychoanalysis, the analysand is bound by but one rule: she must say whatever it is that comes to her mind.[26] The analysand essentially agrees to give up mental privacy by announcing all introspectible thoughts without discrimination or censorship. This is tenable for the analysand precisely because she is otherwise entirely relieved of responsibility for her utterances; both parties to the conversation understand that the analysand is neither committed *to* what she says nor committed *by* what she says. Psychoanalysis, then, provides a special, well-demarcated social setting for what might be called "confessional" speech—that is, speech aimed at self-revelation yet freed from the ordinary burden of commissiveness. The point of such speech is to provide the data, and otherwise to prepare the way, for analysis.

There is also a stage of psychoanalysis in which the patient is encouraged to formulate, or to accept, an analysis of her own behavior. At this stage, the analysand is free to *identify* evaluations or intentions which she actually holds, in the sense that they actually have shaped and continue to shape her thoughts and actions, without implying that she *endorses* herself under these self-interpretations. When we engage in this sort of self-interpretation, our words do not implicitly set down terms under which we might

---

24 Here I follow Moran, who observes that avowals of belief imply that the believer endorses the belief as true, or is reflectively committed to the truth of the belief, while third-person attributions of belief do not necessarily carry these implications. (*Op. Cit.*, pp. 28, 30)

25 This example is also explored by Moran (*Op. Cit.*, pp. 22–27.)

26 Freud calls it "the fundamental rule of psychoanalysis" that the patient must relate whatever it is that crosses his/her mind, whether dishonorable, embarrassing, unpleasant, nonsensical, or seemingly irrelevant. See Sigmund Freud, "Further Recommendations in the Technique of Psychoanalysis: On Beginning the Treatment..." in Philip Rieff, editor, *Therapy and Technique* (New York; Collier Books: 1963), pp. 147–8 (quote from footnote 4, p. 147).

later be criticized for abandoning our announced intentions or undermining the values to which we have professed attachment. Indeed, the point of this sort of self-analytical speech is to make it possible for the analysand to change herself, ridding herself of those aims and values which she cannot endorse upon full reflection.

In the course of this sort of self-interpretation, we effectively adopt a third-personal stance towards ourselves. We bracket the practical project of directing ourselves and focus simply on *understanding* or *interpreting* ourselves. This sort of self-interpretation differs from the interpretation of others only in that we must account for an unusually wide array of phenomena. We must make sense not only of our overt behavior but also of our introspectible impulses, sentiments, fantasies, thoughts, patterns of deliberation and the like—all of which we are to reveal, via stream of consciousness, to the analyst.[27]

Confessional speech is critical to our efforts to know ourselves and to reform ourselves in line with our own considered judgments of how we ought to be. We adopt the confessional voice whenever we identify mismatches between the intentions, goals, ideals, and evaluations which must be attributed to us in order best to make sense of our actual patterns of thought and action, and those we are ready to avow upon due reflection.[28] While it is obscure just how we might go about correcting such mismatches, it would seem at least that becoming aware of them is a necessary first step. Such awareness prepares the way for a kind of self-unification which is valuable both to oneself and to those whose lives are intertwined with one's own. It is valuable to oneself because the harmonization of characteristic thought and action with settled evaluative judgment increases the wholeheartedness of action and the reach of one's reflective

---

27 On the other hand, there are some indications of our mental states which are more readily accessible to others than to oneself—facial expressions, for instance, or gestures, tones of voice, speech hesitations, obsessive behaviors, characteristic self-deceptions and distortions of fact, etc.

28 Confessional speech, then, can help us to identify instances of what Michael Stocker calls "moral schizophrenia"—i.e. dissonance between the *motives* that give shape to our deliberation and action, and the *reasons* for action that we endorse in our considered judgments. See Michael Stocker, "The Schizophrenia of Modern Ethical Theories," in *The Journal of Philosophy*, vol. LXXIII, no. 14 (August 12, 1976), pp. 453–466, especially p. 454.

self-control. To use the terminology introduced above, those who achieve this sort of self-unification come to have settled internalist commitments. It is valuable to those whose lives are intertwined with one's own because it ensures that one's words reliably indicate where one actually stands. That is, the intentions and values one professes are actually manifest in one's actions. This not only makes one more reliable; it also permits one responsibly to assume commitments of the type I am exploring—that is, commitments which can only appropriately be undertaken by being revealed.

Given the importance of the confessional use of language, it would be surprising if the elitist setting of psychoanalysis were the only social space in which such speech is accommodated. It is not. There are impromptu means of carving space for confessional speech in the course of everyday conversation, and by availing ourselves of these means we can describe the intentions and evaluations that actually shape our behavior without using our words commissively.[29] We carve out such spaces by prefacing otherwise commissive phrases with some indication that we wish to distance ourselves from the intentions or evaluations we are announcing. One might say, for instance, "Judging from the way I act, I can only conclude that I intend to help you to carry out this nasty scheme of yours," without committing oneself to helping one's interlocutor in any way. Likewise, one can say to a friend, "It's mystifying to me, but I favor stability in friendships even at the cost of genuine mutual understanding," then go on to seek genuine understanding at the cost of stability without giving one's friend any ground for complaint.

To summarize, our self-descriptive claims are ordinarily taken to be commissive. We can relieve ourselves of this ordinary burden of commissiveness by signaling a purely confessional intent. We signal confessional intent by making clear that we do not affirm or endorse the intentions and evaluations we are attributing to our-

---

29 It is instructive to compare these special conversational spaces to the "bull sessions" which Harry Frankfurt attends to in his amusing essay "On Bullshit." Frankfurt suggests that the value of a bull session lies in the suspension of the responsibility which conversants ordinarily undertake to represent their considered beliefs accurately, and to the associated commitment to substantiate that which they assert. "The main point," he writes, "is to make possible a high level of candor and an experimental or adventuresome approach to the subjects under discussion." See Harry G. Frankfurt, "On Bullshit," in *The Importance of What We Care About* (Cambridge; Cambridge, University Press: 1988), pp. 117–133, quote from p. 126.

selves. This indicates that commissive uses of these utterances are distinguished from non-commissive uses of the same utterances at least in part because they carry the implication that the speaker affirms or endorses herself under the self-description proffered by the utterance.

PART IV: COMMITMENTS AND SOCIAL GROUPS

I have argued that the commissive force of the utterances under investigation can be traced to the self-endorsement they ordinarily imply. This, however, is not the whole story. The commissiveness of these utterances also depends upon the context in which they are spoken, and in particular on the audience's relationship to the speaker. To illustrate, I do not ordinarily commit myself when I say what I value about family life to a stranger on a train, but these same words might well be commissive when said to my spouse. Likewise, I do not ordinarily commit myself when I say to a stranger on a train that I favor going on strike over unsafe conditions at my workplace, but these same words might well be commissive when uttered at the meeting of a union to which I belong.[30] Such utterances may reveal my internalist commitments in any of these contexts; however, they establish commitments *to* someone else only if they are addressed to people who have the right sort of stake in what I do and why I do it.

This point might seem to fit awkwardly into the theoretical

---

30 This suggests that the therapeutic setting is particularly well-suited to its task because the parties to the conversation are not engaged in any shared projects or activities beyond the therapy itself. This is so for two reasons. First, it seems that the absence of shared projects is a necessary condition for observing the "fundamental rule of psychoanalysis," since it is unclear how such projects could possibly be sustained without commissive speech. Second, the absence of shared projects reduces the risk of confessional speech. Such speech is riskiest between intimates, since ongoing cooperative relationships are extremely vulnerable to revelations of mismatches between internalist and externalist commitments.

These points seem to me to shed light on the common dramatic device of confessional exchanges between strangers thrown together by fate (e.g. strangers on trains). Such exchanges are believable because the absence of ongoing commissive relations presents an enticing free space for self-revelation. It is also striking how frequently this dramatic device is used in ways that point towards another familiar phenomenon: the near inevitability with which thoroughgoing self-revelation draws strangers into committed relationship.

structure I have been building. I have argued that a range of commissive utterances establish commitments by making it known that the speaker is already committed in the internalist sense, and by implying that the speaker affirms this internalist commitment on due reflection. Further, I have argued that the bindingness of these commitments is most convincingly traced to the substantive values which prompt the speaker to affirm the commitment. Given this picture, it might seem unclear why the commissive force of the utterances under investigation should depend upon the audience's relationship with the speaker. It would seem to be enough if the audience had reliable insight into the reflectively affirmed internalist commitments of the speaker. Yet someone might gain this insight without ever being addressed by the speaker (think here of a private investigator, or perhaps a field anthropologist, who has observed the speaker carefully and interviewed all of the speaker's friends), and I take it to be intuitively obvious that we would not thereby undertake any commitment to the person in question. Such insight might put another person in a position to speak truly about what we take ourselves to have most reason to do, and to identify cases in which we fail to do it; however, it would not necessarily give that person the standing to demand that we do what we take ourselves to have most reason to do, or to rebuke us if we fail to do it. The difficulty is to say why this is so.

One of the attractions of analyzing all commissive speech as implicit promises is that it provides a straightforward answer to this difficulty. On this theoretical approach, one could argue that an utterance which reveals an internalist commitment only commits the speaker to another if the utterance is reasonably understood to imply a promise to act in line with the internalist commitment in the future. Since promises are most naturally used to provide assurance to others, one might argue that a promise is implied only when two conditions are met: (1) the speaker's audience has reason to value an assurance that the speaker will act in line with her internalist commitment in the future; and (2) the speaker can reasonably be expected to be aware that (1) obtains. The utterances under investigation, then, would only be commissive when addressed to people who are evidently likely to take the speaker's self-revelatory utterances as the basis for forming expectations about the speaker's future actions, and who might be exposed to harm if these expectations are ill-founded. They establish obligations because it is wrong to manipulate people's expectations for one's own ends, particularly when one thereby exposes these others to significant harm.[31]

I believe that this promissory analysis of Group Four and Group Five commissives is correct in one kind of social setting—the setting provided by a class of social groups that I will call *aggregations*. However, it seems to me that the analysis fails to illuminate the workings of these forms of commissive speech in a wide range of other social settings—the settings provided by groups and relationships that I will call *associations*. My views on this matter will be discussed fully in the next section. The main idea is that the curious linguistic devices under investigation—i.e. devices by which we can simultaneously describe and commit ourselves—play a critical role in establishing and maintaining a distinctive and extremely important form of social relationship. These linguistic devices are necessary if we are to have social groups that seek to coordinate their actions in line with evaluative judgments that each member affirms as true.

To prepare the way for my discussion of associations, I will discuss the analysis offered by Margaret Gilbert of the mutual obligations that bind together the members of all social groups. While I disagree sharply with Gilbert, her position has the great virtue of clarity in a domain where clarity is exceedingly hard to come by. By beginning with Gilbert's position and saying as clearly as possible where I disagree and why, I hope to attain a similar clarity for my own position.

IVA. Margaret Gilbert on "Walking Together"

Gilbert argues that the nature of the obligations which bind together members of a wide range of social groups can be grasped by focusing on the simplest sorts of shared activities.[32] She takes her

---

31 This is a rough statement of Thomas Scanlon's view of the nature and source of promissory obligations, about which I will have more to say below. See Thomas M. Scanlon, "Promises and Practices," in *Philosophy and Public Affairs* (Summer 1990), pp. 199–226.

32 Margaret Gilbert, "Walking Together" in Peter A. French, Theodore E. Uehling, Jr., and Howard K. Wettstein, editors, *Midwest Studies in Philosophy, Volume XV: The Philosophy of the Human Sciences* (Notre Dame, Indiana; University of Notre Dame Press: 1990), pp. 1–14.

bearings from the case of two persons who take a walk together. Gilbert rightly observes that such persons are mutually obligated to each other simply because they are taking a walk together.[33] For instance, each has an obligation to regulate his/her speed in order to remain together. Neither may walk heedlessly ahead and abandon the other just because the other's walking pace proves frustratingly slow.

It might seem that Gilbert's view is orthogonal to mine since she is interested in *obligations* and I in *commitments*. However, as Gilbert herself notes, she is using the word obligation in a deflationary sense, and does not mean to refer to moral obligations, which she takes to be more objective.[34] As I understand Gilbert, to say that a person P has an obligation to act in a particular way means nothing more than that P's failure so to act would give some other person a *prima-facie* reason for rebuking P. I believe that a failure by a person P to fulfill the sort of commitment with which I have been centrally concerned—that is, the sort that can be undertaken by the first-person singular use of the commissive verbs listed above—also gives some other person a *prima-facie* reason for rebuking P. Thus, I will take the liberty of interpreting Gilbert's analysis of obligations as an analysis of commitments of the sort I have been discussing. If I differ with Gilbert here, it is because I believe (and will argue in the next chapter) that many moral obligations can be analyzed in terms of such commitments.

Gilbert's project, then, is to account for the commitments incurred by participants in such simple shared acts as taking a walk together. She maintains that such commitments cannot be grounded simply in the fact that each walker has the intention or the goal of walking together with the other, and that each has announced that intention or goal to the other.[35] This might lead them to walk together, and it might give each grounds for questioning the other's prudential reasoning if the other were to walk ahead heedlessly. However, according to Gilbert, it does not provide grounds for rebuking the other if the other does walk ahead heedlessly, and she takes this to mean that neither is committed to regulating his/her behavior so as to walk with the other. If either fails to do so, the other cannot complain of a broken commitment. This complaint, or rebuke, is only justified if "each party has made it clear to the other that he is willing to join forces with the other

---

33 *Ibid.*, p. 4.
34 *Ibid.*, pp. 4 and 6.\
35 *Ibid.*, pp. 5–6.

in accepting the goal that they walk in one another's company."[36] This is done when each registers a conditional willingness to take a walk together if the other is similarly willing.[37]

I believe Gilbert to be mistaken here, since I maintain that one sometimes undertakes commitments simply by declaring one's intentions, values or goals. However, there is something persuasive about Gilbert's elaboration of her case: we do feel some temptation to judge that those who have nothing more in common than a mutually recognized overlap of intentions do not thereby incur commitments to each other. What, then, accounts for the appeal of Gilbert's claim? I will begin by saying what seems to me to be right about Gilbert's claim, and why it has the appeal it does, then I will say how and why I differ with her.

I agree with Gilbert that two strangers who begin walking beside one another without exchanging a word do not thereby commit themselves to walking together.[38] However, I do not agree with Gilbert's claim that this is because they have not each signaled a conditional willingness to walk together if the other is similarly willing. I argued above that what makes confessional speech non-commissive is that the listener is not entitled to the presupposition that the speaker affirms or endorses the intentional states which her words pick out. This same observation helps to explain why two walkers who find themselves silently walking alongside each other do not thereby commit themselves to walking together. After a few hundred yards, they might have good grounds for attributing to each other the intention to walk together, but neither has good grounds for claiming that the other *affirms* or endorses this intention, and hence neither is entitled to claim that the other is

---

36 *Ibid.*, p. 7.
37 Gilbert makes the intriguing claim that under such conditions, the two walkers form a "plural subject", and that their relationship to each other becomes analogous to the relations of the parts of an organism to the whole. (Gilbert, *Op. Cit.*, p. 8) I have some doubts as to whether this analogy really helps to illuminate the normative force of the relationship between persons engaged in shared projects, since it is not clear to me that the parts of an organic whole are *obligated* to do their respective parts to realize the purposes of the whole. However, the analogy does seem to me to be illuminating in that it offers a persuasive account of the precise content of their mutual obligations: each must attend to what the other does, and adjust his/her actions in response to what the other does, so as to make it the case that they move together in their walk as one coordinated body.
38 *Ibid.*, p. 2.

committed to walking together. Something more must happen before they are committed to walking together.

I also agree with Gilbert that the something more which is needed here will typically take the form of a brief conversational exchange.[39] However, I do not think that the conversational exchange which grounds mutual commitments must always have a quasi-contractualist structure, as Gilbert thinks it must. As suggested above, I believe that in order to speak commissively of one's intentions, values and the like, one must reveal them in such a way that it is understood that one also affirms them.[40] As will now be obvious, I think that this is quite easily done, since the same phrases which we commonly use to describe our intentions and evaluative beliefs are also generally understood as affirmations of them. There are cases in which one's affirmation of the intention or evaluation is understood as conditioned on an affirmation of the same intention or evaluation by those whom one addressed. I will have more to say about these sorts of cases below. However, I do not believe that all commissive speech is conditional in this sense.

To return to the case of the walkers, I believe that Gilbert simply gets our intuitions wrong when she maintains that two persons who say to each other that they intend to walk together, or that they would value a walk together, do not thereby undertake any commitments to each other. These declarations are not ordinarily understood in the confessional voice, as descriptions of intentions and values; rather, they ordinarily carry the implication that each speaker affirms the relevant intention or evaluation.[41] If two persons said that they each intended to walk with the other, then

---

39 *Ibid.*, p. 5.
40 This same standard also provides us with insight into how one might commit oneself silently, through public actions. A commissive action is one which does not merely provide evidence of the values one holds (all actions do this), but also stands as a clear signal that one holds these values self-consciously and affirms them as compelling grounds for action. This, I take it, is what makes it commissive to burn a draft card, join a vigil, stand in a picket line, raise one's hand in support of a proposed group action, etc.
41 Gilbert evidences an awareness of this point, and she responds by stipulating for her purposes that we must think of the two walkers as extreme literalists who understand each other's words purely as descriptive claims. This, I think, is a misleading strategy. The burden of the present essay is to show that the commissive force of our words is intimately tied to the descriptive use of our words: it is because our words say who we are, and imply that we approve of ourselves thus, that they engage us in commitments.

began walking next to each other, it seems to me that their case would be different from the case of the silent strangers, and that each would have grounds for rebuking the other if summarily deserted. If such a rebuke were registered, it would not be an adequate response to say, "I only said that I *intended* to take a walk with you, not that I *would* do so." Such a response, I believe, would rightly be received as an unsavory literalism, and as a refusal to take responsibility for one's own words.

This leaves open the possibility that Gilbert is right about the fundamental structure of commitments, and mistaken only about the conversational implicature of assertions about one's own intentions and values. I think that Gilbert's mistake runs deeper. Gilbert takes herself to be arguing from our ordinary intuitions about simple cases of shared activity to a general theory of social groups and the mutual commitments that bind their members together. I believe that Gilbert ties the commissive force of group membership too closely to past declarations of conditional readiness to engage in shared activities, and disassociates it too thoroughly from the substantive convictions of group members. As will emerge in the next section, I think that some social groups might have the quasi-contractualist normative structure that Gilbert outlines, but it seems to me that many groups do not.

This objection requires a bit of elaboration. Gilbert maintains that social groups can be constituted not just around shared goals, but also around shared principles and shared beliefs. In all of these cases, what is necessary is that each party to the nascent group express a readiness to jointly adopt some goal, principle or belief. Once all have expressed their like readiness, the parties have joined together as a "plural subject"—a "we" to which the goal, principle or belief can correctly be attributed. Each party is simultaneously obligated to further the goals, adhere to the principles, and/or profess the beliefs around which the group has been formed.[42] This, Gilbert asserts, is quite like the ceremonies of consent which political contractarians like Hobbes and Rousseau took to be necessary to the founding of a legitimate state. [43] (It seems to me, by the way, that the problem with Gilbert's position is already visible in her implausible conflation of Hobbesian and Rousseauvian ceremonies of consent. I think her picture errs precisely in being too thorough-

---

42 *Ibid.*, p. 7.
43 *Ibid.*, p. 11.

ly Hobbesian, and in ignoring the possibility of an alternative, broadly Rousseauvian founding ceremony.)

I believe that this provides an implausible picture of how members of many actual groups understand the commissive force of the shared goals and principles which bind them together. The members of many groups—including religious congregations, fraternal associations, political activist organizations and revolutionary cells—view the commitments springing from their shared principles and ideals as unconditional, often because they view these commitments as rooted in moral truths or in religious revelations. Gilbert's picture is least compelling as a general account of how we might come to share *beliefs*. There are *some* circumstances in which we can make sense of a conditional willingness to profess a belief provided that others do likewise. The members of a group might have instrumental reasons for professing common beliefs, either to avoid intra-group conflicts over relatively unimportant issues or to present a strategically united front to non-members. In more rarefied cases, we might even make sense of a willingness to have a belief—that is, to take something to be true—provided that others are similarly willing. The cases that come to mind involve beliefs about social conventions (e.g. the belief that ten pennies are worth one dime, or that shaking one's head from side to side means no.)

Still, it seems to me implausible to think that we *generally* come to share beliefs by announcing a readiness to hold and/or profess some belief if all other group members announce a like readiness. Gilbert's own example—in which she envisions her two walkers coming to share the belief that the weather is great—is a case in point.[44] It is quite implausible to imagine anyone saying, "The weather's fine if you say so"—except perhaps out of an unwillingness to argue about trivialities or an obsequious concern to be agreeable.[45] We arrive at shared beliefs by deliberating

---

44 *Ibid.*, pp. 9–10. Not surprisingly, Gilbert's own presentation deviates from the usual pattern here, and she speaks of the shared belief as having its genesis in individual assertions, absent anything like a contractualist ceremony. It seems to me that shared beliefs can be generated in this way; they require only that each has the belief and knows the other to have it.

45 Gilbert thinks that group beliefs about even the most important of subjects rest on expressions of conditional willingness to believe something as a group, provided that other group members do as well. In her article "Modelling Collective Belief" (*Synthese*, volume 73, no. 1, October 1987, pp. 185–204), Gilbert argues that group members

together about what propositions warrant our assent. We do this by saying what we believe and why. No special account is needed to show how our participation in such conversations can obligate us. It seems to me—and here I follow Robert Brandom, among others—that assertions of belief are quite generally commissive, whether or not others are disposed to agree with them. Indeed, as

are obligated not to contradict beliefs which are arrived at through this sort of quasi-contractualist ceremony, and that they can be rebuked for having done something wrong if they do contradict such beliefs without explicitly noting that they are speaking strictly for themselves. I suppose there could be highly authoritarian groups in which such norms are generally acknowledged. There might also be non-authoritarian groups which hold their members to this standard out of a strategic interest in presenting a united front to outsiders. However, I believe that Gilbert is wrong to suggest that such norms are always in place whenever we can sensibly attribute beliefs to a group.

The general problem here is that two of Gilbert's central claims about collective belief are in tension with each other. First, Gilbert takes it that group beliefs are identified procedurally: they are whatever the group ends up deciding in accordance with its usual deliberative procedures. This leads Gilbert towards a radical separation of group belief and individual belief. Indeed, she claims that a group might hold a belief that no member holds. Second, Gilbert maintains that group beliefs are binding on the members of the group that endorses them, in the sense that members are properly rebuked for contradicting group beliefs.

These two claims come into sharpest tension in the case of groups which are themselves devoted to participatory deliberation. The deliberative ideal accepted by these sorts of groups is not easily captured in any actual procedure for arriving at group beliefs. This is what makes it odd to think that group members might rebuke each other for openly voicing opposition to the results of past deliberations. The oddness here is the implication that after a certain point, the group's beliefs must remain as they are even if further deliberation exposes inadequacies in them. This might be a sensible expedient in a group that must come to certain practically important decisions under significant time pressures. However, it seems out of place in a participatory group whose primary aim is to have true or cognitively unassailable beliefs—for instance, in a scientific association, or a philosophical society, or a non-hierarchical Protestant sect, or (to take Gilbert's own example) a poetry reading group. It would be extremely odd to view the members of these sorts of groups as bound to mouth the beliefs of the group, regardless what they personally take to be true. If the members of such groups are bound by the shared beliefs of the group, their commitments run deeper than a mere surface deference to these beliefs.

Gilbert's view also seems to raise general puzzles about how a change in the beliefs of any group might ever take place without individual violations of obligations, since all members are obligated not to voice dissent.

Brandom argues quite convincingly, it is precisely when the truth of one's assertion is challenged that one must fulfill one's implicit commitment to show that one had good grounds for believing that which one asserted.[46]

It is here, in the domain of what Brandom calls assertional or doxastic commitment,[47] that we see most vividly the fundamental flaw in Gilbert's understanding of the commitments which bind groups together. Gilbert is under the sway of the idea that all commitments must ultimately be tied to expressions of readiness to act in particular ways in the future, provided that others express a like readiness. Like promises, so expressions of willingness are all-purpose tools for taking on commitments, and in particular can be used to undertake commitments to do or say that which one believes to be misguided, debased, valueless or false.[48] On Gilbert's picture of group-formation, then, anyone could form or enter any group, simply by uttering the right words. What this pic-

---

46 Brandom argues that assertions are implicit knowledge claims, and that they commit the speaker to substantiate the assertion if it is challenged. As with the utterances discussed in this essay, so with assertions some clear signal (e.g. an expression of uncertainty) is required if one is to be relieved of the ordinary burden of commissiveness. See Robert Brandon, Making It Explicit: Reasoning, Representing and Discursive Commitment, Op. Cit., Chapter Four, pp. 199–271; especially pp. 203–5 and 228–9.

47 *Ibid.*, p. 201.

48 While Gilbert takes her view to accord with, and to capture the essential truth of, the Hobbesian and Rousseauvian accounts of the social contract, she does not think that the formation of plural subjects can be accomplished by an exchange of conditional promises. She argues that the mutual obligations that structure a plural subject are established *simultaneously*, and that they are *interdependent* in the sense that each member ceases to be bound by them if other members cease to acknowledge their force. See Margaret Gilbert, "Agreements, Coercion and Obligation" in *Ethics*, Vol. 103, No. 4 (July 1993), pp. 679–706, esp. pp. 690 and 690n.
   I am not entirely certain that I understand Gilbert's argument here, but it does not seem to me to be convincing. Suppose that each of two parties were to utter the following conditional promise: "On condition that you make the same conditional promise (i.e. a conditional promise to plow my field), I promise this: I will plow your field." It would seem that they would both have simultaneously undertaken promissory obligations to plow each other's fields. I take it that Gilbert might object that these promises are not properly interdependent, in that party X would not be let off the hook if party Y refused to fulfill his promise. I think that this is beside the point, since party Y would not be let off the hook, morally speaking, by his own refusal to fulfill his promise.

ture of commitment obscures is that many of the shared goals and values which bind people together in groups are such that one cannot undertake them merely by willing to do so. This helps to illuminate why Gilbert's model serves up a distorted picture of the establishment of shared beliefs. It is extremely hard to make sense of an expression of willingness to believe something, since in most cases what we believe is not, and ought not to be, determined by what we *will* to believe. Rather, we are *compelled* to believe some proposition because it seems to us to be true.

The same can be said of our evaluative convictions. It is true that obligations often arise directly from the evaluative convictions which are self-consciously shared by the members of social groups, and which shape the identity and purposes of those groups. However, when members express these convictions, they do not typically think of themselves as expressing a conditional willingness to act on certain values provided that others do. They take themselves to be compelled to act on those values because such action is good or right.

PART V: TWO KINDS OF SOCIAL GROUPS

It is no accident, I think, that Gilbert fails in her attempt to specify the common normative structure of all social groups. Her attempt was bound to fail because there is no single normative structure common to all social groups. There are many kinds of social groups, and while perhaps all provide settings in which Group Four and Group Five utterances can function as commissives, they do so in different ways and for different reasons.

For my particular purposes, I will distinguish two broad categories of social groups. In the first sort of social group, which (following Rousseau) I will call "aggregations," members are bound together by overlapping self-interests, which give to each an instrumental reason for engaging in a common cooperative scheme. In the second sort of group, which (again following Rousseau) I will call "associations," members are bound together by self-consciously shared convictions about the good, in light of which they assign intrinsic value to some mode of cooperative activity. I do not take these categories to exhaust the possible modes of group formation. I am interested in these two categories of groups because of the different ways that commissive speech functions within them. In aggregations, the utterances under investigation have an almost purely commissive use, and their normative force is quite like that of promises. In associations, the same utterances play the hybrid commissive-descriptive role in which I am most interested.

This critical distinction between aggregations and associations is normally overlooked even by those who reject the promissory account of obligations. Aggregations and associations are ordinarily lumped together under the Hegelian sphere of civil society, and it is often taken to be particularly obvious that the commitments we undertake in this social sphere must arise from our voluntary agreements, even if familial obligations or political obligations do not.[49] I believe that a finer-toothed typology of social groups is needed if we are to illuminate the kinds of commitment we actually take ourselves to have.

VA. Aggregations

Aggregations are rule-bound groups organized around a cooperative activity that serves the pre-existing individual interests of members. There is reason for aggregation only when two conditions are met: (1) some scheme of cooperation could meet the pre-existing individual interests of prospective members better than non-cooperation; and (2) this form of cooperation is subject to free rider problems. If (1) did not hold, there would be no reason to cooperate. If (2) did not hold, there would be no needs for partic-

---

49 Michael Hardimon, for example, rejects the contractual account of obligations, since he denies that "role obligations" such as the obligations we have to parents and siblings can be traced to our past voluntary agreements. However, Hardimon believes that what he calls the "volunteer principle"—the principle that we can only undertake obligations by freely agreeing to them—does have a natural "home" within which it is valid. That home is civil society—a sphere that he takes to include business partnerships, unions, private clubs, social movements and neighborhoods. I do not deny that this sphere is voluntary in the sense that we cannot properly be forced to join the groups that make it up. However, this does not mean that the volunteer principle governs the sphere. It need not be the case that the normative authority of the obligations of membership arising in this sphere can invariably be traced to past voluntary agreements.

For Hardimon's account of these matters, see Hardimon, "Role Obligations" (*Op. Cit.*), pp. 343 and 352–3.

ipants to make commitments to each other.[50] Aggregations need rules because they require for their survival that most members make sacrifices which each would prefer not to make, provided that he could continue to enjoy the full benefits of membership. These required sacrifices are the commitments of membership.

What is most important about aggregations, for my purposes, is that they serve interests that each members holds in an articulate form prior to entering the group, or would hold in an articulate form even if the group did not exist. The value of these groups is instrumental: members would not value such a group if it did not help them to achieve their individual ends. The group directs its actions by attempting to determine the best way of bringing about its defining ends. This sort of deliberation does not raise substantive questions about the goods which ought to guide group actions.

I do not think that there are many pure cases of aggregations. Some business partnerships might have this form, though no doubt many do not. One might argue that some American unions are like this today, since they tend to pursue ends such as higher pay and safer working conditions which are already held in an articulate form by almost all workers, while they no longer pursue the political education or socio-economic transformation of workers. I will indicate below that this classification would likely be misleading. However, while it might be difficult to find a pure case of an aggre-

---

50 This is a bit too simple. A free rider is one who benefits from a cooperative scheme without making the sacrifices or bearing the burdens that make the cooperation possible. An otherwise mutually beneficial scheme of cooperation might be impossible to get going because of the malice of some potential cooperators. They might have to forego random killings, etc., in order to make the cooperation possible. If one thinks of this as a burden of cooperation, then my claim is correct. However, malicious desires to kill others are not easily assimilated to the class of self-interested excesses that are ordinarily thought to pose free-rider problems, and restraints on arbitrary killings are not easily assimilated to the class of restraints on self-interested activity that are ordinarily considered to be solutions to free-rider problems.

What these complications indicate, I think, is that pure cases of aggregation are exceedingly rare. This is because humans do have a variety of immoral and anti-social urgings that must be overcome in order to make enduring cooperation possible. Thus, any successful form of cooperation will require an ongoing effort to reform characteristic inclinations and desires, and to inculcate an internalist commitment to certain standards of moral behavior, together with a moralized view of the value of one's collaborators.

gation, the idea that this is the fundamental form of social cooperation, and the fundamental source of interpersonal obligations,
has bedeviled moral and political philosophy at least since Hobbes,
and continues to exert a powerful influence on the field.[51]

Aggregations have two important characteristics for my purposes. First, when I say that group members hold the goals which
define the group in an *articulate* form quite apart from their membership in the group, I mean to point out that these instrumental
groups are not what might be called the "stewards" of a particular evaluative language, or of particular evaluative standards,
whose use must be mastered in order to grasp the group's defining
goals, ideals, values, or principles. One thing this means is that
becoming a member of an aggregation does not require any distinctive transformation in what it is that one values, or in how it is
that one thinks and talks about one's values. Second, since members place only an instrumental value on the group, it would seem
that members could have only instrumental reasons for placing a
distinctive value on the *depth* of other members' commitments to
shared ends, or on the *sincerity* of other members' avowals of commitment.[52] Members have a distinctive concern with the commitment of other members only to the extent that this commitment
affects their own chances of securing individual ends.

As I see it, it is in the evaluative arena of aggregations that
Gilbert's quasi-contractualist picture of mutual commitment has
its clearest application. In the context of a union which is a mere
aggregation of persons (supposing there were such a thing), utterances such as "I favor striking" would seem to function, *a la*
Gilbert, as expressions of willingness to strike provided that all
others do likewise. In such a union, it would be futile and senseless
for any member to strike if few others did likewise, since this
would likely lead to nothing but summary dismissal. In this context, then, the utterance "I favor striking" would not reveal the
speaker's antecedent personal conviction about what she ought to
do, given that she herself has internalized the defining goals and

---

51 See, for instance: David Gauthier, *Morals by Agreement* (Oxford;
   Oxford University Press: 1986) and James M. Buchanan, *The Limits
   of Liberty: Between Anarchy and Leviathan* (Chicago; University of
   Chicago Press: 1975)
52 By a "distinctive" value, I mean one that members apply only to
   other members and not to persons more generally.

values of the group. Rather, it would most plausibly be interpreted as an exhortation to others to strike, and (*a la* Gilbert) as a conditional pledge to join them if they do.

The illocutionary force of this utterance, in this context, is best illuminated if we think of it as serving to overcome a free rider problem arising from the following array of preferences: each striker would most prefer to secure the benefits of a strike without the risks of joining a strike; but each would prefer to join a strike, with all the risks that this entails, if the only alternative were no strike at all. If the union members are to overcome this free rider problem, each member must have some assurance that others will make good on their conditional pledges to strike. This assurance against defection must be provided in the face of the knowledge that others lack any prior internalist commitment to strike. What is needed by the members of our hypothetical aggregative union is an all-purpose means of taking on commitments to do that which no one has prior internalist commitment to doing. This can be accomplished by an exchange of conditional promises—provided at least that members take their promises seriously and believe that other members do as well. Since this is the background need, it seems reasonable to interpret public announcements of intentions to strike as implicit promises to strike provided that others do. Here promises (or implicit promises) can play a role which simply could not be played by the sincere descriptive-commissive use of the verbs in Groups Four and Five. This is because group members do not have a standing intention to strike that they are in a position to reveal; they merely have a conditional willingness to strike if others do so as well.

In free rider problems like this—as more generally when one knows that others have a keen legitimate interest in one's intentions—one does wrong if one knowingly leads others to hold false beliefs about one's intentions. Thomas Scanlon has argued convincingly that misleading others in this way is wrong, and wrong for the same fundamental reason, whether one does it by promising insincerely or by some other means.53 In Scanlon's view, all

---

53 According to Scanlon, the locution "I promise" does have a distinctive function: it serves to indicate that one fully understands and appreciates that absent some powerful excuse, it would be wrong to fail to do that which one says one will do. However, Scanlon maintains that other locutions (e.g. "Trust me") can serve this same function. See Thomas M. Scanlon, "Promises and Practices," *Op. Cit.*, especially p. 211.

such wrongdoings are cases of unjustifiable manipulation.54 This seems to me to be true in the context of the social groups which I have called aggregations, or in the context of negotiations aimed at the creation of an aggregation. In such contexts, I believe, the commissive verbs in all five of the groups I have been considering can be used to manipulate others, and their commissive force is quite plausibly traced to the general moral prohibition against such manipulation. To return to our hypothetical aggregative union, it seems to me that one could commit oneself to join a strike simply by saying that one intends to strike, or that one favors striking. If one said such things without any intention of joining the strike oneself, this would ordinarily count as an unjustifiable manipulation of others. There is perhaps nothing more to be said about its wrongness. In the context of an aggregation, all of the commissives would seem to function like promises.

VB. ASSOCIATIONS

The same commissives function in entirely different ways in the conversational contexts provided by the other kind of social group in which I am interested: the association. Associations differ from aggregations in the following very general way: the activities of associations are viewed by members as valuable quite apart from their instrumental usefulness in securing ends which members hold *qua* individuals—that is, ends held *prior to* their membership in the group, or ends they would hold *apart from* their membership. Given only this very general characterization, it may be unclear what associations are. I will attempt to clarify the notion by discussing some of the different kinds of associations.

First, I will consider the category of association which is most like an aggregation, since this will help me to specify the difference between associations and aggregations more precisely. These are

54 *Ibid.*, p. 202. Of course, there might be cases in which this sort of manipulation is justified. Scanlon's principle, which he calls Principle M, is this: "In the absence of special justification, it is not permissible for one person, A, in order to get another person, B, to do some act, *x* (which A wants B to do and which B is morally free to do or not to do but would otherwise not do) to lead B to expect that if he or she does *x* then A will do *y* (which B wants but believes that A will otherwise not do) when in fact A has no intention of doing y if B does *x*, and A can reasonably foresee that B will suffer significant loss if he or she does *x* and A does not do *y*." (pp. 202–3)

goal-directed associations, in which members work together to bring about a worldly goal whose value has been made evident to them in and through their participation in the group (e.g. a socialist worker's party). Next, I will consider associations which are more sharply distinguished from aggregations, since they are not goal-directed at all. Members of these sorts of associations are united by their recognition of the intrinsic value of some shared activity. I will consider two varieties of non-goal-directed associations: *comprehensive associations*, the members of which are united by a "comprehensive conception"[55] of the good life (e.g. Catholicism); and *non-comprehensive associations*, the members of which are united by a conception of the good that they view as authoritative only for some delimited sphere of activities.

As I discuss these categories of associations, I will try to bring out the different features of associations that give to the commissive language under consideration the curious function that we have been considering. In particular, I will seek to answer to the two following questions: (1) How do the members of associations come to have particular reasons for caring about the descriptive accuracy of each other's commissive utterances?; and (2) How do the members of associations come to have a distinctive kind of authority to hold fellow members to their internalist commitments?

The first kind of association I will discuss is the *goal-directed association*. Like aggregations, so these associations have instrumental value to their members. What this means is that there is some worldly end which, if achieved in full, would leave associates with no further reason for association. What distinguishes these groups from aggregations is that the value of the goal at which the association aims can only be grasped in its entirety through an attachment to, or engagement with, the group. This is because one cannot grasp the value of the group's goal without first grasping the intrinsic value of the activities or states of affairs that the group seeks to promote (think here of leftist worker's movements and of the value that they place on unalienated labor). These associations do not appeal to new members based merely upon their pre-exist-

---

55 This term comes from John Rawls. For his use of the term, see Rawls, *Political Liberalism* (New York; Columbia University Press: 1993), pp. 13 and 175.

ing understanding of what is valuable; they also aim to enlighten new members about what is truly valuable. They have what might be called an *educative* function.[56] One finds this educative function not only in revolutionary groups with far-reaching doctrines of false consciousness, but also in a wide variety of reformist groups whose worldly aims cannot be appreciated, or cannot be attained, unless people reconsider what it is that they value. This is a wide umbrella, covering many civil rights, human rights, feminist, pacifist, nationalist and environmentalist organizations. Perhaps many apparent aggregations—including e.g. most unions—would prove on examination to be associations of this type.

These groups have a distinctive set of values, the affirmation of which is a necessary condition of membership. Of course, the distinctive values of these groups are not self-interpreting, and no single member enjoys unilateral power to dictate their content.[57] Such groups typically require shared deliberation about what is worth doing together, and this deliberation is not limited to instrumental consideration of how best to bring about agreed-upon ends. There is also need for deliberation about how precisely to specify the group's ends. The debate about these matters is guided by efforts to grasp aright the precise nature and concrete implications of the group's distinctive values. This might take place in a central forum, or in the course of more informal, person-to-person coordination of activities. In either case, when members deliberate about what they favor, or value, or intend (i.e. when they use Group Four and Five commissives), they are guided by the defining values of the group. However, since they endorse these values, this means nothing more than that they are guided by what they take to be valuable. Their utterances are presented as *representative*: they purport to represent the appraisal of what is truly

---

56 One problem with Gilbert's view is that it cannot account for the possibility of educative groups. In such groups, one cannot commit oneself all at once and from the beginning, since on first contact with other group members one lacks a fully adequate grasp of the values for which the group stands. In such groups, one's commitment grows as one is reshaped by one's contact with the group, and as one takes on the values of the group. It cannot be dated to anything like a single act of voluntary consent.

57 If one person is viewed as authoritative, this is only because his pronouncements are affirmed by others. This means that his authority is not really unilateral.

valuable, or what ought to be done, that would be reached by the sincere and conscientious deliberation of anyone who affirms the distinctive values of the group.

In the course of this sort of group deliberation, *sincerity* takes on a peculiar importance. Of course, sincerity is already critically important in the context of aggregations, at least when members commit themselves to each other. In aggregations, members must take on commitments sincerely—that is, with the intention of fulfilling them—and must believe that other members also commit themselves sincerely; otherwise their commissive utterances will not help them to overcome free rider problems. Members of aggregations have an egoistic interest in each other's sincerity, akin to the interest of promisees in the sincerity of promisers. Each member of an aggregation can achieve his/her own ends only if others carry through on their promise-like commitments, and others can be trusted to carry through on their commitments only if they undertake them sincerely. To put matters in terms of the two dimensions of integrity mentioned in the introduction to this chapter, members have an interest in the diachronic integrity of other members—that is, in the consistency of their words and actions over time. However, they have at most a derivative interest in their synchronic integrity—that is, their wholeheartedness at any particular time. This latter sort of integrity is important in the context of aggregations only to the extent that it makes diachronic integrity more likely.

Sincerity does have this sort of importance in goal-directed associations. The central aim of these groups is to bring about an end that all members affirm as valuable, and their coordinated efforts to bring about this end are likely to be far more effective if members can count on each other to act over time in conformity with their commitments. Furthermore, it is true in associations, just as in aggregations, that if member P speaks insincerely of his intentions or evaluations in order to prompt member Q to make costly sacrifices that serve P's interests, then P wrongs Q. This is the same wrong mentioned earlier—the wrong of unjustified manipulation.[58]

This, however, does not exhaust the importance of sincerity for goal-directed associations. These associations deliberate in

---

58 See Scanlon, *Op. Cit.*, pp. 202–3.

order to specify the ends at which they aim; that is, they seek to specify the concrete implications of the values they jointly affirm. With the possible exception of founding members, each member takes himself or herself to have grasped these distinctive values through conversation with other members of the group. This means that each member has a *cognitive stake* in the sincerity of other members. Since the group has an educative function, members believe that they owe their grasp of what is valuable partly to the evaluative insights of other group members. If they were to discover that these other group members had spoken insincerely about what they took to be valuable, this would throw into question their own warrant for the values they themselves affirm.

Why should this be so? It may be true that we feel greater confidence in our evaluations if others affirm them, but isn't this just an unfortunate psychological fact about us—the fact of our conformity? I don't believe so. To see why, one need only attend to the way in which we come to affirm claims about what is valuable or what would be best to do. We do not do so all by ourselves, in Zarathustrian isolation; we do so in serious conversation with others. In the course of such conversations, we extend a provisional trust to other evaluators. We give provisional credence to their evaluations, meaning that we assume they are offered sincerely, as considered assessments of what is valuable, and we dwell on them and see if we find them enlightening. (This, I take it, helps to explain how contact with an association can be educative.) It sometimes makes sense to extend this trust because our own experience is limited, and we often face predicaments which are new to us but familiar to others. However, it does not make sense to extend such trust indiscriminately. We extend it when we have an as-yet-inarticulate feeling that our interlocutor is right, or when we have independent reasons for thinking our interlocutor to be a good evaluator—perhaps because her past judgments have gained our affirmation in hindsight, or because she has experience relevant to our current predicament, or because she consistently acts in ways we find admirable. One way to think of associations is this: they are groups whose members regard each other as good evaluators, at least over some specific range of practical questions, and hence have reason to trust each other's evaluations by giving them a provisional credence.

The notion of trust at work here is not easy to make precise.

Negatively, it rules out taking the claims of others merely as elements of an opposing bargaining position that must be reckoned with in order to get the most we can of what we have antecedently determined to be valuable. More positively, it might require that we dwell on the evaluative claims of others and assess them in good faith, with a provisional readiness to accept them as correct. It is a form of trust because it requires us to believe that others are forwarding sincere and considered appraisals, and that they are not just manipulating us, or misleading us, or mocking us. It is also a form of trust because it requires us to place provisional credence in the *quality* of others' deliberations about the good.

In this and perhaps in other ways, we might independently affirm the judgments of others. When we do so, it is reasonable to derive added confidence from the agreement of other people whose deliberative capacities we trust. However, it ought not to increase our confidence if others voice their agreement with us rashly or insincerely. This means that we have a cognitive stake in the reflective sobriety and the sincerity of those with whom we engage in serious deliberation. Since associations require this sort of serious deliberation, the fellow members of associations have a cognitive stake in each other's reflectiveness and sincerity. When in the course of serious deliberation the members of associations say what they intend or what they value, it is important that their words accurately reflect their considered judgments. If they do, then there is a clear sense in which they will be *true* taken as assertions—though it is perhaps worth reiterating, *pace* Moran, that this does *not* imply that the speaker *offers* them as self-descriptions.

Still, there is another sense in which these same utterances might be descriptively false. It is possible for there to be a mismatch between the evaluations or intentions that we sincerely affirm after careful reflection, and those which must be attributed to us in order to provide the most cogent account of our behavior. If a person displays such a mismatch, then his own avowed intentions and evaluations are not fully his own—they are belied by his own impulsive thoughts and actions. A charitable interpreter of such a person would be forced to one of three conclusions: (1) he is insincere (I have stipulated that this is not the case); (2) he is self-deceived about his own real values or intentions; or (3) he is chronically akratic. If any of these interpretations is appropriate, this means that his self-reported intentions and evaluations do not amount to what I referred to above as internalist commitments. His acceptance of them is not complete and wholehearted, since they are not manifest in his characteristic thoughts and actions.

Now, the members of instrumentalist associations have good reason to want each other's commissive utterances to be descriptively accurate in this further sense as well. In this particular, however, this kind of association is not different from an aggregation. The insincere, the self-deceived and the chronically akratic are bad associates because they frustrate the efforts of the association to realize its ends. These associations rely for their effectiveness upon coordinated action in line with goals and values affirmed publicly by members. The anomaly that forces us to interpret others as insincere, self-deceived or chronically akratic is precisely that they do not characteristically act on the evaluations and intentions which they publicly affirm.

If we turn now to the case of *comprehensive associations*, we will see that their members often have yet a further reason to be concerned about the descriptive accuracy of the class of commissive utterances with which this essay is centrally concerned. They often have what I am calling a cognitive interest that these utterances accurately identify the evaluations or intentions which must be attributed to the speaker in order to make sense of the speaker's characteristic thoughts, reactive attitudes and impulsive actions.

Comprehensive associations are groups formed by individuals who share a creed which includes, among other things, a conception of the good life, and who join together to explore, perpetuate, or practice the dictates of this creed. When I say that these sorts of associations are comprehensive, what I mean is that their distinctive values have comprehensive implications for the conduct of life. What this means, in effect, is that there is a much wider range of topics in which members must attempt to specify what they take to be truly valuable.

It is possible for a comprehensive association to be formed voluntarily by people who share, or come to share, a common comprehensive conception of the good. However, I am most interested in those more typical comprehensive associations which span the generations, perpetuating themselves by schooling the children of their members in the distinctive values of the group. The paradigm example of the comprehensive association, the religious sect, is typically like this. Members of this sort of group take on the group's values in the course of socialization. They come to share a distinctive set of more or less inarticulate tendencies to approve or disapprove of actions and states of affairs, to notice certain things as reasons for action, to feel certain desires, to feel pride of shame in certain actions, and so on.

In these sorts of groups, the internalist commitments which members share are rarely articulated in their entirety. It is relatively easy to see why it might be important to the workings of these sorts of groups to try to articulate (in Taylor's sense) the evaluative reactions encoded in one's immediate, unreflective reactions of revulsion, admiration, shame, and the like. In certain cases it might be that one can only give precise content to the evaluative reactions that are one's own, and that are characteristic of the tradition with which one identifies, by attempting to bring them into words—by saying what if anything gives rise to them. Here is a place for commissive language uttered with one eye directed inwards towards one's own inarticulate reactions.[59] It is also relatively straightforward to see how the evaluations enunciated through this sort of self-interpretive effort would stand as representative with respect to the broader community of belief. They are representative because members share their socialization, or at least some significant part of it, in common.

As indicated above, the public articulation of the evaluations encoded in one's unreflective reactions is not driven by a purely theoretical interest in oneself. In interpreting these reactions, one is attempting to make clear what it is that one values.[60] If one cannot reflectively affirm the values that one attributes to oneself, then this sort of utterance must be hedged. It cannot be voiced in a full-

---

59 As noted above, it is only if such self-descriptive speech is disavowed explicitly that it is not commissive. Then it might be fodder for the best sort of criticism.

60 The combination of self-interpretation and commissive self-affirmation that I have in mind is captured quite eloquently by Josiah Royce in the following passage:

> Now, if this view of the application of our precept is right, you see how our principle is just to that mysterious and personal aspect of conscience upon which common sense insists. Such a loyal choice as I have described demands, of course, one's will,—one's conscious decisiveness. It also calls out all of one's personal and more or less unconsciously present instincts, interests, affections, one's socially formed habits, and whatever else is woven into the unity of each

throated and unreserved way, for this would carry the implication of reflective affirmation.[61]

When members of trans-generational comprehensive associations engage in this representative form of self-articulation, fidelity of self-description has cognitive importance not only to the speaker, but also to other associates. Since these associations are bound together by shared convictions about the good, members have reason to take each other to be good evaluators, and to trust each other as such. However, the evaluative capacities in virtue of which they trust each other are partly encoded in as-yet-inarticulate evaluative reactivities and sensibilities—both their own and those of other members. We are never entirely masters of the values we inherit and share with others. We consult our reactions and attempt to clarify where it is that we take our stand. There is no bright line between the description and the creation of commitments here: we give precise content to our commitments by interpreting ourselves faithfully. And as noted above, this faithfulness has cognitive importance. To see this, consider that members take their tradition to have been a source of enlightenment for themselves, not only because of its explicit teachings but also because they have been able to affirm the evaluations which they have found to be encoded in their own reactive attitudes. Given this, it is reasonable for them to extend a provisional credence to their own intuitive reactions, dwelling on them and attempting to discern and assess the evaluations implicit in them. But it is also rea-

---

> individual self. Loyalty, as we have all along seen, is a willing devotion. Since it is willing, it involves conscious choice. Since it is devotion, it involves all the mystery of finding out that some cause awakens us, fascinates us, reverberates through our whole being, possesses us. It is a fact that critical decisions as the direction of loyalty can be determined by our own choice. It is also a fact that loyalty involves more than mere conscious choice. It involves that response of our entire nature, conscious and unconscious, which makes loyalty so precious.

Josiah Royce, *The Philosophy of Loyalty* (Nashville; Vanderbilt University Press: 1995); (@1908 by The MacMillan Company), p. 91.

61 This might provide a conceptual space for an as-yet-unrecognized sort of charitable interpretation: self-interpretation that renders one's own characteristic reactions maximally affirmable. There are dangers lurking in this sort of charity—dangers of self-deception involving the misrepresentation of errant feelings. For instance, I might make sense of an anger that I ought not to affirm by inventing an appropriate occasion for it and/or by deceiving myself about its actual object.

sonable for them to extend provisional credence to the intuitive reactions of others, since these too have been informed by the tradition whose wisdom they have found worthy of affirmation in other instances.

This implies that when, in the course of serious deliberation, the members of comprehensive associations say what they intend or what they value, it is important that their words accurately reflect their considered judgments *and* that they accurately describe their characteristic thoughts, impulses and behavior. Other members have a cognitive stake in this descriptive accuracy. And when these utterances display *this* sort of descriptive accuracy, there is no remaining sense in which they could be thought descriptively false. If such an utterance were immediately reformulated by another in the third-person indicative, as an assertion about the original speaker, the reformulation would accurately describe the speaker's sincere avowals *and* would be part of the most coherent intentional explanation of the speaker's ongoing behavior.[62]

By focusing on the cognitive interest that associates have in each other's sincerity, I believe that I can make sense of an aspect of the phenomenology of mutual commitment and betrayal which otherwise might remain obscure. What I have in mind is the fact that one's convictions are often firmer and more confident if they are affirmed by others, and conversely the fact that one's convictions would be deeply shaken by the discovery that others who appeared to share them, and who helped one to articulate them, in fact did not share them. My account provides room for interpreting

---

62 Perhaps few of us moderns think of ourselves as being part of a traditional comprehensive conception of the sort that I have just described. To this extent it might seem that reflective self-scrutiny does not have the same role that it once might have had. This opens greater space for a more rationalistic mode of making one's identity precise, by determining for oneself what is valuable. But there are problems with this notion of autonomy. There is no ground, untainted by our characteristic reactions, from which to assess those reactions, so that we have no choice but to lend them a measured trust. And there is something very important at stake in our being able to presume that our reactions are somewhat similar to those of others, since we continually converse with others on the tacit presumption that we can work together on making our values explicit—that their suggestions about how best to put our reactions into words are potentially enlightening. We make our values articulate in conversation with others, but we take it that the values we are making explicit are *ours*.

this as something more than mere weakness or conformity (though I do not wish to deny that it *could* arise from mere weakness).

My examination of these groups also puts me in a position to illuminate what I take to be the deepest sense in which the fellow members of associations are dependent upon each other's sincere attachment to the values of the group. The joint activities that members engage in with each other, and that they take to be intrinsically valuable, often require for their successful enactment that each member engage in them out of a recognition of their intrinsic value, and not for some further reason. If members have engaged in them for the wrong reasons, this casts doubt on whether these shared activities really do answer to the description under which members took them to be valuable. This, I think, is the deepest sense in which sincerity matters amongst associates. The correct description of the group's activities, and the correct assessment of their value, are quite often contingent upon the reasons that prompt other members to engage in the activity. To illustrate, it is a different activity—and arguably a far more valuable one—to farm fields and raise children with fellow members of a commune who share ideals of simple living and self-sufficiency, than to do so with people who merely give every appearance of affirming those ideals. One can neither describe these shared activities nor evaluate them definitively without reference to the motives of one's collaborators. To do so would be nearly as misguided as it would be to characterize and evaluate one's friendships or love relationships without reference to the motivations of one's friends or lovers.

I turn now to *non-comprehensive associations*. These are associations of people who seek to sustain or promote an activity, or a mode of conducting some aspect of life, which members view as intrinsically valuable. What binds together the members of this sort of association is the common affirmation of a set of values or norms as authoritative guidelines for some particular, delimited sphere of activity.

One common kind of non-comprehensive association is formed by the devotees of what Alasdair MacIntyre calls a "practice"—roughly, a complex activity with its own internal standards of excellence which help to define and to guide engagement in the activity.[63] People dedicated to such activities as jazz, poetry, mountaineering or philosophy constitute associations of this sort. These groups do not necessarily have a formal, centralized organizational structure or deliberative procedure. This, however, is not a necessary features of all associations. Associations are constituted by conscious recognition of shared values. These far-flung collections of people count as associations because any two people who are able to recognize each other as fellow practitioners of the practice must affirm an overlapping set of evaluative standards as authoritative for the practice. If they did not, they would not be engaged in the same practice. This is because one cannot grasp what a practice is, much less engage in it, unless one grasps what it would be to excel or succeed in the practice.[64]

These groups are like comprehensive associations in that they serve as the custodians of a distinctive set of values, and perhaps also of a distinctive evaluative language. These values are affirmed, by and large, by those who engage in the practice. Consider jazz musicians. They might be drawn to the music in the first instance simply because they like it. However, by listening to jazz music and talking to others who like it, they give definite shape to their conception of excellence in jazz. They learn how to make fine-grained distinctions between inspired riffs and imitative sounds. While they demand that these evaluations command their own conviction, they give weight to the evaluations of those who are more experienced than they are. These evaluations serve as provisional guideposts for articulating what it is that they like about jazz, and for extending their capacity to appreciate qualities of jazz which they are not initially able to discern.

---

63 In MacIntyre's words, a 'practice' is "any coherent and complex form of socially established cooperative human activity through which goods internal to that form of activity are realised in the course of trying to achieve those standards of excellence which are appropriate to, and partially definitive of, that form of activity, with the result that human powers to achieve excellence, and human conceptions of the ends and goods involved, are systematically extended." Quoted from Alasdair MacIntyre, *After Virtue: A Study in Moral Theory* (Notre Dame, Indiana; University of Notre Dame Press: 1981), p. 175.

64 To illustrate, one cannot understand what philosophical argumentation is, and certainly cannot produce it, without understanding what it is to argue *well* or *successfully*. Similarly, one cannot fully grasp what a jazz composition is, and certainly cannot compose jazz, unless one has a grasp (perhaps not entirely articulable) of what it is for a jazz composition to be *successful* or *good*. This is why two people who had no overlap in their idea of the defining excellence of their practices would no longer be engaged in the same practice (though they might be engaged in a struggle to be the authentic continuant of the same practice).

In order to engage in a practice (rather than in some new, entirely self-defined activity), one must accept certain evaluative standards which are internal to and partly definitive of the practice. Those who would play jazz are not entirely unconstrained; not any noise they could make would count as jazz. The practice carries with it internal standards of excellence, and musicians who stray too far from these standards are no longer playing jazz. On the other hand, practitioners are not entirely constrained either. What counts as jazz changes over time, as practitioners extend and refine the forms of success that they recognize and aim to meet. The practitioners of a practice are collectively responsible for giving definite form to the semi-articulate and continually evolving standards of excellence which partly define the practice. If a practice is to remain vital, attracting and inspiring a new generation of practitioners, this will only be because the practitioners have managed to specify the evolving conception of excellence in a way that commands their enthusiasm and conviction.

It is not hard to see why one's commitment to the evaluative standards of a practice ought to be internal commitments. The evaluative commitments shared by practitioners are conditional, in the sense that they specify what one ought to do if one engages in the practice. Practitioners need not believe that anyone who fails to engage in the practice is making a mistake about what is valuable. However, they do share beliefs about what anyone who engages in the practice ought to do. If a practitioner were to find that these evaluative standards ceased to be compelling—that they ceased to define an intrinsically valuable activity—then that practitioner is left without the right sort of reasons for engaging in the practice. Such a person still might have *a* reason to engage in the practice—think here of a jaded saxophonist playing the same old tired "improvisation" for money—but she is no longer able to engage in the activity out of a recognition of its intrinsic value.

A practice, then, is only valuable to practitioners if their engagement in it springs from and is guided by an internalist commitment to the standards of excellence which partly define the practice. Thus, practices provide an important sort of forum for the hybrid descriptive-commissive speech that I am investigating. It is the speech by which practitioners can specify the values that they affirm as authoritative for their shared practice, while simultaneously committing themselves to exemplifying those standards of excellence.

Sincerity takes on the same sort of cognitive importance in the context of practices that it has in associations. To bring the point home, imagine what it would be like to find out that no one else really finds philosophy valuable—that everyone else sees it as a set of amusing puzzles, or as a tolerably comfortable career. It might seem that this ought to change nothing. After all, whatever reasons one has for valuing philosophy can still be rehearsed, and these reasons ought to be just as convincing (or unconvincing) as before. But I suspect that few of us would be fully immune from a loss of confidence upon this discovery. On my account, we can render this loss of confidence rational. What this fact about us reveals, on my account, is that at each step, as we commit ourselves to philosophical thought, we are in effect trusting others who have seen farther into the subject matter, or who have approached it from different vantage points, and whose like commitment provides us with an indication that we are not wasting our energies.[65]

Often, we will be engaged with other practitioners in ways that give us a further stake in the wholeheartedness of their engagement in the practice. Here again, one can neither describe nor evaluate one joint engagement with others in a practice without reference to the motivations of collaborators. It is a different and arguably more valuable activity to play in a jazz band or to participate in a poetry discussion group with others who find their participation intrinsically valuable than with others who are merely blowing hot air.[66]

---

65 Of course, not every report of every accomplished philosopher is terribly encouraging (think of Wittgenstein's warnings to young philosophers). But these discouraging reports haunt the field, and I think it makes sense that they do.

66 I do not think that my discussion has exhaustively characterized the value of membership in associations. I have omitted at least one thing of considerable importance. When one engages in coordinated actions guided by shared convictions, one acts in concert with people who share precisely those convictions that prompt one to act. What this means is that one's actions are coordinated with others who are able to endorse one's actions all the way down, right to their deepest motivations. This permits a less alienating, more fully unified sort of membership than is possible in an aggregation. Perhaps it is only this sort of group that deserves the name of "plural subject"—a name that I think Gilbert applies too indiscriminately. Such groups count as plural subjects because they are composed of individuals who are of one mind not only about what ought to be done, but also about why it ought to be done.

Vc. Personal Relationships

While friendships and love relationships cannot be assimilated entirely into the class of associations, they do provide an important scene for the hybrid descriptive-commissive speech under investigation in this chapter. This can happen in two ways. First, one cannot describe one's feelings of affection and concern for another without taking on certain commitments to the other. Second, one's friends play an important role in helping one to articulate the values by which one lives, and come to have the standing to serve as allies of those values in times when one is tempted to stray from one's own reigning commitments. Here, I think, we can see an important difference between friends and associates: we grant to friends a delimited authority to speak in the name of values which are ours, but which they themselves do not share, because we grant them the status of allies of our best or truest convictions.

Some friendships and love relationships are clearly unlike associations. It is possible for a personal relationship to arise from mutual attraction, or a twist of fate, or a recognition of mutual usefulness, and to endure simply because it serves the pre-existing aims of the parties to it.[67] However, many personal relationships have much in common with associations, since the parties to them endeavor to articulate ideals or values which command their conviction and which they are ready to stand by as guidelines for their shared activities. The difference is that friends are not brought together entirely by an acknowledgment of shared values. In order to be friends, they must enjoy spending time together, and this enjoyment is not entirely a matter of sharing values. While a fundamental disagreement in evaluations might call a friendship into question, still (Aristotle notwithstanding) true friends need not share all values in common, and indeed a friendship might be enhanced by differences.

Like the "educative" associations described above, so these more intimate associations are such that one cannot commit oneself to them all at once and from the beginning. The abstract commitment to a person *tout court*—without particular, substantive values to guide and structure the commitment—would not count

---

67 This observation that personal relationships can be purely instrumental is an ancient one, dating back at least to Aristotle (see *Nichomachean Ethics*, Book viii, Chapter 3, 1156a-b).

as a friendship or love relationship. It would be nothing more than a particularly concentrated variant of Kantian benevolence: a focused readiness to further the ends of a particular person, regardless what those ends might be. This would fall short of friendship because it would imply no particular approval of any of the other's ends, nor of the evaluative judgments which determine these ends.

One commits oneself to a friend or an intimate under a particular, somewhat restrictive description of the other's core convictions, hence of what would count as good for the other. Friends and intimates serve each other as sounding boards, helping to bring each other's idiosyncratic values into full articulation. The full-throated and responsible use of Group Four and Group Five commissives plays a critical role in this process. When in the context of an intimate relationship we try to say what it is that we care about, what we are trying to make of ourselves, or what we hope to do, our language is both descriptive and commissive. These utterances help to make of the friend a faithful externalization of one's own conscience. When friends call each other to account, and insist upon something to which the other is supposedly committed, their authority—supposing that it goes beyond the threat of withdrawal of love and affection—stems from their insight into the friend's true values, which after all one can forget, or misconstrue, or shrink from or betray. Consider the difference it makes whether a stranger or a friend says, "I did not think that you were that kind of a person." It is rather hard for a friend to say these words without registering an admonition, and it seems to me that one of the things that distinguishes our friends is precisely that we are disposed to hear such utterances, when they speak them, as *prima-facie* reasons to rethink what we are doing.[68]

There are a more restricted set of commitments that interest the friend more directly and obviously. These are the commitments

---

68 I do not take this brief discussion to provide an exhaustive characterization of the ways in which intimate relationships matter to us. One thing I have omitted is that intimate relationships provide a particularly important forum for confessional speech—a forum which is far riskier than therapy but which permits the loving acceptance of deep-rooted character flaws. In the professional relationship of therapy, acceptance of flaws is nearly a foregone conclusion and certainly not a sign of mature un-blinkered love, as it can be in an intimate relationship.

that one commonly has in mind when one thinks of the bonds of friendship. These are commitments to remain together and to help each other in hard times. These commitments, too, are entered via the full-throated use of the descriptive-commissives under investigation. The commissiveness of the utterance "I love you" works like this. In ordinary circumstances it is inappropriate to say this unless it is descriptively accurate, and these words convey important information, yet these words are also clearly commissive. Indeed, it may be hard to distinguish clearly between the two uses, because part of the vitally important information that these words convey is precisely that one now stands in a particular sort of normative relation with another.

When one undertakes the central commitments of friendship—for instance, the commitment to help one another in hard times—one's sincerity has a peculiar importance. If one insincerely utters the sorts of words that are used to enter into these commitments, then it is not at all clear that one actually undertakes the commitments in question.

When it comes to the more central set of commitments, those owed directly to each other, sincerity is even more important. For what is at stake here is a recognition of particular value. One is affirming the other, though under a somewhat demanding description. To use Austin's terms, it seems that insincere self-revelations in such contexts are not merely "unhappy" (i.e. inappropriate), they actually "misfire" (i.e. they do not actually have commissive force). While perhaps such words give to another a formal right to expect and even to insist on certain future performances, their utterance does not in fact signal the conditions under which these future performances would be acts of friendship.

For purposes of illustration, let us consider the case of Arthur, who systematically deceives Bernard into thinking that he is his friend. Arthur says that he places great value on Bernard's well-being, and on time spent together with Bernard, and on certain ideals which Bernard himself affirms. As a result of Arthur's deceptive characterization of his own values (i.e. his deceptive use of Group Five commissives), Bernard comes to think that Arthur is his friend. Now something happens to Bernard which triggers the commitments ordinarily associated with friendship. Let us say that Bernard's brother dies, and he is in need of emotional support from his friends. At the same time, Bernard discovers that Arthur has been systematically deceiving him. The question is, will Bernard now think that Arthur is committed to helping him through his dark time? It seems most natural to say that when Bernard discovers Arthur's deception, what he discovers is that Arthur is not the sort of person he had led Bernard to believe, and in particular not the sort of person who could make the commitment he pretended to make. It would seem odd for Arthur to locate the wrongness of Bernard's behavior in the fact that he implicitly undertook a commitment which he *now* refuses to fulfill. What Bernard has discovered is precisely that *nothing* Arthur could possibly *do* would count as a fulfillment of the commitment in question, and this is because he never had the internalist commitments whose existence he had asserted in the same utterances which—had they not misfired—would have initiated a commitment to help Bernard through hard times.

My position, then, is that Arthur has not in fact entered into an associational commitment with Bernard, and hence is not bound now by the obligations which structure friendships. However, this does not mean that Arthur has done Bernard no wrong. It simply means that the wrong is retrospective: it throws into question the nature and value of the activities the two have engaged in together in the past. What is revealed is that these activities did not answer to the description which Bernard thought them to meet, and hence that they did not have the value Bernard had assigned to them. By misrepresenting his true commitments, Arthur manipulated Bernard into engaging in shared activities which lacked the value that Bernard believed them to have. This, however, does not imply that breaking associational commitments is wrong because it is a form of unjustified manipulation. If Arthur had entered into association with Bernard, his commitment would be grounded directly in the evaluative commitments which they had come to share and which invested their shared activities with value.

PART VI: INTERNALIST COMMITMENT, INTEGRITY AND AUTHORITY

The commitments which bind associations together are precisely the paradoxical sort discussed above: the sort which are appropriately undertaken only by being revealed. Associations are kept vital by the ongoing efforts of members to give voice to com-

mitments that are already theirs in a semi-articulate form, and this
is done with commissive verbs like the ones in Groups Four and
Five. A number of verbs that Austin did not list among his commissives can be added to these groups, since they also have commissive uses in associations:

Group Four additions:	stand by, aim to, aspire to, adhere to
Group Five additions:	value, esteem, care about, attach importance to, set store by, honor, have the conviction that, deplore, protest, challenge, commend, applaud, approve[69]

These verbs are the linguistic tools by which individuals might
articulate the goals, ideals, principles and values in terms of which
they all stand ready to govern their shared projects and activities.
As I have argued, such speech cannot exhaustively be analyzed, *a
la* Gilbert, as the conditional expression of willingness to act in certain ways provided that others do likewise. This seems to be the
source of the normative bonds that structure the groups I have
called aggregations, but it is not what ties together associations.
What Gilbert's analysis leaves out is that when we speak commissively, we are often seeking to articulate the practical dictates of
the values that we actually affirm. The commissiveness of this
speech owes to the speaker's acknowledgment of the values for
which she speaks. Agreements that come about in this way matter
to us because they reflect who we are.

VIA. Synchronic and Diachronic Integrity Revisited

I noted in the introduction that this essay aims to draw attention to an under-appreciated sense of 'integrity' that corresponds

---

69 The last six verbs are taken from a list provided by Austin of what he
calls "behabatives"—verbs that register our reactions to the behavior
or plight of others. Austin himself notes that these verbs can function
as commissives. See Austin, *How to Do Things with Words* (*Op.
Cit.*), pp. 160–61.
  Another verb on Austin's list which might also merit inclusion
is 'apologize.' It seems that when one says one is sorry, one commits
oneself to act like it, where this means at least not repeating the performance for which one has apologized. The related verb 'am sorry' is
like other Group Five commissives in that it has a descriptive meaning, and in that it is often inappropriate to say "I am sorry" when it
is not descriptively true—that is, when one does not *feel* sorry. (I owe
this point to Richard Moran, who raised it in a recent seminar)

to the under-appreciated sense of 'commitment' on which I have been dwelling. If integrity is the virtue of those who keep their commitments, and if promises are taken to be paradigm commitments, then integrity appears to be a formal diachronic relationship of consistency between current actions and past commissive actions or utterances. I do not think that this is an exhaustive analysis of integrity. As I see it, the distinctive sorts of commitments that are the central topic of this paper can be linked to a different, yet still immediately recognizable kind of integrity. We exhibit this alternative sort of integrity when we reflect carefully on what is in fact valuable, speak sincerely in line with the outcome of this reflection, and think and act characteristically in ways that manifest our considered and un-blinkered assessment of what is valuable. When one speaks and acts in this way, one undertakes commitments by revealing them, and one fulfills commitments by remaining true to one's own considered judgments about what one has most reason to do. One's commitments do not enter into this deliberation *as commitments*—that is, one does not deliberate by reflecting on what it is that one is committed to do. Rather, one honors one's commitments by deliberating about what one's firmest and most deeply entrenched values give one most reason to do, and by acting in line with this deliberation. This, I think, is the fundamental sort of integrity Gabriele Taylor commends to our attention when she characterizes the integral person as the one "who 'keeps his inmost self intact', whose life is 'of a piece', whose self is whole and integrated."[70]

This sort of integrity has both a diachronic and a synchronic dimension. It has a diachronic dimension, because it is criterial of genuine internalist commitments that they endure over time, that they be held for good reasons, and that they not evaporate without sufficient reason. It has a synchronic dimension because one lacks the wholeheartedness necessary for genuine internalist commitment if there are serious discrepancies between one's desires,

---

70 Taylor writes: "But the notion of integrity may also be approached not by picking out such moral qualities as are normally associated with it, but by thinking of the person possessing integrity as being the person who 'keeps his inmost self intact', whose life is 'of a piece', whose self is whole and integrated." Taylor goes on to argue that this conception of integrity is the fundamental one, and that the sort of integrity we exhibit when we tell the truth, or keep our promises, is merely derivative. See Taylor, "Integrity" (*Op. Cit.*), p. 143.

one's considered judgments about what one has most reason to do, and one's deliberate actions.

If I am right that integrity has these two dimensions, and that both dimensions are relevant to the question whether one's actions are consistent with one's internalist commitments, this raises an analytical puzzle. The trouble is that the two dimensions of internalist commitments, and hence of this sort of integrity, can come into practical conflict with each other. That is, there are circumstances in which one action would be consistent with one's past word and another would be consistent with one's considered evaluative judgments about what it would now be best to do. One central burden of the next chapter will be to explore this difficulty, in the context of intractable marital conflicts. My conclusion will be that it is sometimes morally permissible, and perhaps even morally required, to act consistently with one's current evaluations even when this means that one will break with the terms set by past commissive utterances and actions. On the other hand, one cannot do this too often and still expect to be viewed as the sort of person who is capable of internalist commitment.

VIB. Authority and Interpretation by Outsiders

It may be that the distinctive values of many different associations cannot be grasped by those who are not actively engaged in the group. It would be incautious to insist upon this, however. An understanding of the distinctive values of an association may or may not presuppose a recognitional capacity which could not be mastered by an outsider—i.e. by someone who is not internally committed to living in accordance with the association's defining values.

However, there is another, quite different kind of limit on the authoritativeness with which outsiders can apply the distinctive values of an association. Once we see what role is played by the efforts of the members of a living and evolving group to articulate the implications of their own values, we can see that only the members of such a group can really speak authoritatively about the implications of these values. This stems from two facts. First, these people are the ones who stand ready to guide some range of shared activities in line with these values. Second, the content of these values is not fixed once and for all, but is subject to change depending upon the evaluations that members are willing to make and stand by. Together, these facts imply that even if an outsider (e.g. a field anthropologist) were to observe precisely how the members of a particular group use a certain evaluative term, and were to formulate a set of rules for applying the term, these rules would be merely descriptive and not *authoritative*. If the anthropologist has done his work well, and if group members go on using the term precisely as before, then the anthropologist's predictions might hold good. However, if those who actually assess their actions in terms of these evaluative terms (i.e. the practitioners) were to go on in a different way than predicted, the anthropologist would not be in a position to correct them, any more than a dictionary definition, originally culled from actual usage patterns, can provide good grounds for condemning changes in that practice (rather than good grounds for updating the dictionary).

Insofar as evaluative concepts are used commissively, as they are in vital associations, it seems to me that no naturalistic reduction of these concepts could ever be authoritative. No naturalistic reduction can be authoritative because each new generation must affirm those values, and reaffirm them again and again over time, if the tradition is to continue to be a living one. As is perhaps by now quite clear, I take it that this is achieved by the full-throated descriptive-commissive use of the locutions under investigation. Such uses do not merely describe a set of standing dispositions to act in particular ways, or to assess things in particular ways. They also imply that the speaker affirms herself under the proffered description. It is this implied self-affirmation that makes the use commissive.

This, as I have indicated, is the key difference between the anthropologist's projections of the evaluative terms of a group united by a particular practice, and the otherwise similar speech of group members. The group members affirm themselves under a particular description, and commit themselves to exemplify this description, while the anthropologist does not. To put the point in another way, the group members engage in the sort of speech that creates and sustains associations, while the anthropologist does not. This, at heart, is why any failure of prediction on the part of the anthropologist is a failure of the anthropologist and not of the group members.

To illustrate, suppose that an ethnomusicologist were to devel-

op an account of what distinguishes a successful jazz improvisation from an unsuccessful one. Supposing that the account is reasonably accurate, this researcher would be in a position to make
judgments of the form "That was a good improvisation" with
some confidence that her assessments will accord with those of
many jazz aficionados. However, if discrepancies arose between
her reductive account and the reigning judgments of jazz practitioners and aficionados, her account could not be presented as an
authoritative basis for correcting the judgments of others. She is
not committed to the values which define the practice, and authority rests with the judgments of those who are so committed, since
their commissive evaluations determine what counts as the continuant of the practice.

CHAPTER 4

Special Non-Promissory Obligations

INTRODUCTION

In the last chapter, I developed an "internalist" conception of commitment and I suggested that the normative bonds of certain social groups could be explained in terms of this conception of commitment. I will develop and defend this suggestion further in this chapter. I will try to show, among other things, that this conception of commitment can serve as the basis for a satisfying theory of obligations as diverse as the obligation to risk one's life for the (good) state and the obligation to remain faithful to the (good) spouse.

The obligations which I wish to investigate are all *special non-promissory obligations*. When I call these obligations *special*, I mean that they bind persons in virtue of contingent facts about who they are or what they have done.[1] When I call them *non-promissory*, I mean that the contingent fact in virtue of which they

---

1 I remain agnostic about the existence of general obligations—i.e. obligations which are necessarily binding on all persons. My doubts are primarily terminological. I believe it is true that all persons ought to refrain from murder, and perhaps that all ought to aid those in need when it is not terribly costly. However, since these obligations are not owed to particular (rigidly designatable) persons, it is perhaps more apt to call them duties.

are binding is *not* that one has publicly promised or contracted or consented to fulfill them. I remain agnostic as to whether the theory elaborated in this chapter can account for all special non-promissory obligations. It is not clear to me, for instance, that it can account for parental obligations. However, I believe that I can account for a large number of these obligations.

The class of special non-promissory obligations is theoretically puzzling—puzzling enough that in the course of philosophical speculation we might be tempted to deny that there are such obligations, though when speculation ceased I believe we would find this denial hard to sustain. There is no comparable mystery about the existence of special *promissory* obligations—we routinely undertake them when we promise, sign contracts and otherwise signal our agreement to terms binding on our future actions. However, the existence of special *non-promissory* obligations can only be demonstrated by showing that we have certain obligations whose normative force is fundamentally different from that of promises, contracts and the like. This, in turn, is best done by providing an alternative, non-promissory analysis of obligation, and showing that this account captures the normative force of certain of our obligations better than the promissory account. In my attempt to do so, I will draw heavily from the suggestive treatment of obligations offered by Michael Walzer in his early book on the subject.[2]

Let me provide some examples of special obligations that I take to be non-promissory. Given that I am a member of this family, this community, or this political society, I might find myself obligated to the other members of this family, community or political society. I am obligated to these people in virtue of particular facts about me, but I have not made a promise, nor have I said or done anything that could plausibly be construed as an implicit promise. These obligations, I will argue, are non-promissory.

This classification is perhaps most persuasive for the obligations that bind intimate friends and relatives. For example, we do not take the obligations of friendship to arise *simply* from the fact that we have made a series of voluntary choices to be someone's friend. Perhaps this fact alone is enough to establish *an* obligation,

2 Michael Walzer, *Obligations: Essays on Disobedience, War and Citizenship* (Cambridge; Harvard University Press: 1970).

but it is not all that is at work in establishing *the* obligations that many friends believe themselves to have to each other. We can catch a glimpse of the inadequacy of the promissory account of the obligations of friendship by reflecting on just how strange a notion of consent we must accept if we are to treat the motley words and actions by which we enter friendships as signs of voluntary consent to all of the many and varied obligations of friendship. We can attain a somewhat fuller view of the inadequacy of the promissory account by reflecting on our intuitive reactions to those whose sole motivation for fulfilling their obligations to their friends is that they voluntarily entered the friendship. There is a distinct temptation to say that such persons could not fulfill all of the obligations of friendship unless they had a different sort of relationship with their friends—a relationship which afforded them a more direct apprehension of the value of their friends' flourishing.

Let me turn to another set of examples. Given that I am a member of this or that association, I might find myself obligated in certain ways to my fellow members. I am obligated because I am a member, but I might never have taken an oath of membership or made anything like a promise to all other group members. These are also non-promissory obligations—or so I will seek to show. Here too we can adduce support for the classification from two sources. First, we enter into many associations without saying or doing anything that is plausibly be interpreted as a voluntary agreement to the terms of membership. Second, the members of many associations do not view their mutual obligations as arising *simply* from the fact that they have chosen to join the group or promised to heed its standards, and they would be dismayed to learn that their associates took this view of their obligations. In a vital association, members take their obligations to arise from and to be justified by the ideals and values which they affirm in common with other group members, and which prompted them to join the group in the first place.

These putative obligations present a theoretical puzzle precisely because it is so implausible to trace their genesis to anything like a promise, contract, or any other public sign of voluntary agreement. They present a puzzle, that is, because we are prone to think that nothing but our free agreement or consent could possibly give rise to a new commitment. This latter idea, which I call the *bare voluntarist thesis*, has an intuitive hold on many of us. However, if we take this as an axiom of a systematic theory of obligations, we are forced towards one of two equally unattractive options: we must either constrict the domain of obligations implausibly, ruling out of court many of the interpersonal bonds we ordinarily think of as obligations, or we must introduce a doctrine of "tacit" consent which stretches the notion of consent beyond the bounds within which it illuminates the normative authority of our obligations. These familiar alternatives might be called the Scylla and Charybdis of consent theories of obligation.

I think it best to avoid both of these alternatives by rejecting the bare voluntarist thesis that drives us towards them. There is, however, an element of truth in the thesis, and this must be preserved: we cannot be coerced into undertaking a new non-promissory obligation.[3] I call this the *refined voluntarist thesis*. I believe that we ought to accept this thesis, but not as a fundamental axiom; rather, we ought to accept it because it is a direct corollary of the most persuasive account of what non-promissory obligations *are*. This thesis is considerably weaker than the bare voluntarist thesis, since it allows for the existence of obligations which we have not chosen to undertake yet have not been coercively forced to undertake. Indeed, the obligations we have taken as our prime exemplars—those which bind us in virtue of our significant social attachments or in virtue of the convictions we find ourselves compelled to affirm—fit this mold strikingly well.

As noted above, my aim is to account for special non-promissory obligations by reducing them to *commitments*. Stated in such general terms, this strategy is uncontroversial enough. There is an extremely close relationship—perhaps in some contexts an identity—between obligations and commitments. Given this, one might wonder whether analyzing obligations in terms of commitments could possibly be revealing. One might also wonder how my view could represent an *alternative* to the promissory analysis of obligations. After all, those who analyze obligations as promises presumably do not wish to deny that our promises commit us and that the resulting obligations are commitments. Indeed, such theorists would presumably claim that nothing but a voluntary, promise-like agreement could possibly generate a new commitment of any moral significance.

---

3 I do not wish to tangle with the question whether promises made under coercive conditions are binding.

As I tried to show in the last chapter, this bare voluntarist regimentation of the concept of 'commitment' does a violence to the ordinary, admirably complex understanding of the concept. It highlights what might be called the "externalist" sense of 'commitment'—which involves remaining true to one's past word—while obscuring the "internalist" sense of 'commitment'—which involves remaining true to one's own core ideals and values. My position, in essence, is that the obligations under consideration are grounded in the internalist commitments of individuals, as worked out in their significant face-to-face interactions with others. As will become evident, this claim is neither empty nor uncontroversial.

PART I: WALZER ON OBLIGATIONS AND COMMITMENTS

In my attempts to develop a theory of special non-promissory obligations, I will take my bearings from Michael Walzer's *Obligations: Essays on Disobedience, War and Citizenship*.[4] There are several reasons why this might seem an odd starting point. First, Walzer limits his attention to political obligations, while my topic is considerably broader. Second and more seriously, Walzer writes explicitly that he does not intend to provide a novel theory of obligations, but simply to apply an old theory to the peculiar predicaments of his contemporaries.[5] Third and most seriously, the theory that Walzer himself claims to be applying is consent theory, and this is precisely the theory I hope to supplement or to supplant entirely.[6]

Self-characterizations to the contrary, I think that Walzer's text does contain the seeds of a novel theoretical account of obligations. Furthermore, I believe that the theory can be developed in a way that simultaneously substantiates the existence of special non-promissory obligations and illuminates their normative force.

According to classical consent theory, as found in Locke and in the philosophical tradition which descends from him, obligations must be grounded in acts of voluntary consent such as the

---

4 Walzer, *Obligations* (Op. Cit.).
5 *Ibid.*, pp. ix-x and xvi. The peculiar predicaments that interest Walzer most are those of the revolutionary, the civil disobedient, the Afro-American, and the alienated citizens of oversized and over-bureaucratized modern liberal states.
6 *Ibid.*, p. ix.

making of a promise or the signing of a contract.[7] Special obligations are explained as particular instantiations of a universal moral
principle—call it *the principle of consensual obligation*—to the
effect that one must do what one has freely consented to do.

As I read him, Walzer has a different account of how we come
to be bound by obligations. We catch glimpse of Walzer's alternative account in his general formulation of consent theory: "The
paradigm form of consent theory is simply, *I have committed
myself (consented): I am committed (obligated)."*[8] What is distinctive about this formulation is that consent and obligation are
both defined in terms of a single more basic phenomenon: commitment. On Walzer's account, to say that someone has consented
to certain terms governing future actions is to say that she is committed to these terms, and this in turn is to say that she is obligated to observe them. The principle of consensual obligation has no
role to play in this version of consent theory. Once we have properly understood what consent is, and what obligations are, we can
see that one cannot truly consent to terms governing one's future
action without coming to be obligated. The connection between
consent and obligation is seamless.

In order to grasp the distinctiveness of Walzer's theory, it is
essential to understand his notion of commitment. For Walzer,
entering into a commitment is best understood as a sort of inner
conversion—a transformation (or renewed affirmation) of what
one cares about or values. In this sense, one does not necessarily
commit oneself simply by performing acts or uttering phrases that
signal one's commitment, nor can one commit oneself to just anything. If one's acts or utterances are to signal commitments, they

---

7 As Professor Thomas Scanlon has pointed out to me, consent-giving
   normally has a "licensing" function as opposed to the "binding" function that promises have. For instance, I might give someone consent to
   pick apples from my tree, without making anything that would ordinarily be called a promise. However, in the philosophical literature on
   political obligation, consent is often conceived on the analogy of a
   promise. This analogy seems to me to be in good order for three reasons: (1) giving one's consent and promising are both ways of offering
   others valuable assurances about one's future actions to others, and
   both give to these others rights that they did not previously have to
   demand certain future performances or restraints; (2) the normative
   force of both instruments stems from the fact that one has made
   explicit *that* one is agreeing to certain conditions on one's future
   actions, and made explicit just *what* these conditions are.
8 Walzer, *Obligations*, p. x (Introduction).

must accurately reflect one's own settled convictions about what one has most reason to do. This is true because internalist commitments just *are* settled convictions about the good or the right, or the practical dictates of these convictions, and as such they determine what one has most reason to do in a certain range of circumstances.

I noted above that this approach promises to spare us the dilemmatic choice between a parsimonious constriction of the domain of obligation and the introduction of an implausibly broad doctrine of tacit consent. It is worth mentioning two other potential attractions of the approach. The first is that it obviates the need for a special account of the most essential and perhaps most puzzling feature of obligations—their bindingness. On the account under consideration, if person P is obligated to ø, this can only be because P is committed to some value that gives her reason to ø. P is bound in the rather compelling sense that in fulfilling the obligation, she is doing what she is committed in the internalist sense to do. P has what Bernard Williams could call an internal reason to fulfill her obligation.[9] The position, then, seems to be immune from the neo-Humean skepticism pressed by Williams and others about the reason-giving force of the putative obligations described by some contemporary moral theories.[10]

A second potential attraction of this approach is that it connects obligations to substantive, value-conferring bonds of membership and to substantive convictions about the good. As I indicated in the introduction, I think that this permits a phenomenologically accurate account of the way we think about many obligations, including those owed to intimates and to fellow members of associations united by common ideals and values.

Given these attractions, it is worth considering whether Walzer's explication of consent and obligation in terms of commitment is defensible.

---

9 Williams maintains that a person P has an internal reason to ø only if there is a sound deliberative route to the conclusion that P ought to ø which takes P's actual aims, desires, loyalties, dispositions of evaluation and projects (Williams calls these "commitments") as its sole premises. See Bernard Williams, "Internal and External Reasons," in *Moral Luck* (Cambridge; Cambridge University Press: 1981), pp. 101–113.

10 Williams, *Ethics and the Limits of Philosophy* (Cambridge; Harvard University Press: 1985), Chapter 10, especially pp. 178, 180–85 and 191–4.

PART II: INTERNALIST AND EXTERNALIST COMMITMENTS

Recall that Walzer equates consenting with committing oneself, and having an obligation with being committed. These equations both sound plausible, and they suggest that there is a seamless relationship between consenting and coming to have an obligation. One might suspect, however, that Walzer's case gains spurious plausibility by trading on the above-noted ambiguity of 'commitment.'

This suspicion is fed by the fact that in ordinary speech there seems to be room for committing oneself without becoming truly committed. To use the example I mentioned in the last chapter, a defendant on trial might promise to testify truly, thus *committing herself* (in the externalist sense) to telling nothing but the truth, yet remain secretly *committed* (in the internalist sense) to concealing the identity of her co-conspirators. These two senses of 'commitment' tend to come apart in precisely those instances in which disputes over obligations are most likely to arise. Unless one specifies which sense one has in mind, one cannot shed light on obligations by reducing them to commitments. And unless one opts for the second sense of 'commitment', the equation of commitment and obligation is not terribly revealing, nor does it rule out a Williams-style skepticism about the reason-giving force of putative obligations.

On the other hand, if one reduces obligations to internalist commitments—as I propose to do—one runs the risk of losing the moral dimension of obligations. If obligations require fidelity to one's own most firmly held values and not to one's past word, they might seem to be nothing more than dictates of prudence. As such, they might seem to lack categorical force, since their terms could presumably be met either by fulfilling their terms or by a change of convictions. Further, it might seem that these putative "obligations" are not owed to other persons in the way anything deserving to be called an obligation would have to be. After all, it is not clear how third parties could come to have legitimate grounds for demanding that one act on one's own convictions. I hope to meet these *prima-facie* doubts in the course of this essay.

IIA: What Are Internalist Commitments?

Walzer does not provide a systematic development of the idea of commitment at work in his writings. I order to proceed, I will have to supply an account which fits with Walzer's general claims, and which includes some nuances which I did not bring out in the last chapter. It is tempting to think that the internalist sense of 'commitment' is descriptive and the externalist sense normative. On this account, to say that P is committed in the internalist sense to ø would be to claim that all else equal P will ø, while to say that P is committed in the externalist sense to ø would be to claim that P ought to ø. I believe that this interpretation of the ambiguity is mistaken, and that both senses of 'commitment' are normative. This is a good thing, since it would be a clear mistake to reduce obligations to something non-normative.

One way to bring out this point is to think again about our imagined witness. It seems to me that it misdescribes the case to think of her inner resolution not to tell the truth as a belief or silent prediction that she will lie. Her inner resolution is a kind of summary of the reasons for action which she herself recognizes and stands ready to act on. If it is true that she remains committed to lying, this implies that she takes herself to have good reason to lie, and of course that she does not recognize her oath as a sufficient reason to tell the truth. If, when the time comes, she can tell the lie but chooses to tell the truth, she has not merely made a false prediction; she has either let herself down or had a change of heart (that is, a change in her internalist commitments).

It is closer to the truth to equate internalist commitments with firm intentions to do some particular thing or to act in accordance with particular goals or values. However, this proposal too is flawed. As I pointed out in the last chapter, some firm intentions are not commitments. One must generally be able to act as one firmly intends in order for one's firm intentions to count as internalist commitments. This may require, among other things, that one's affects and patterns of salience ensure that one will notice and respond appropriately to the features of the world which are counted as reasons for action by the commitment.

We are now in a position to see why the internalist sense of 'commitment' might have seemed, at first blush, to concern predictions about future actions, and hence to be descriptive rather than normative. When I have an internalist commitment, there are good grounds for predicting that in the absence of external impediments, I will act in accordance with my commitment. This is because a commitment penetrates more deeply into one's actual perceptions, motivations and behavior than a mere intention, and it provides greater protection against *akrasia*. I argued in Chapter Two that we would not assign a maxim to someone who sincerely avowed the maxim but who lacked the background desires and sensitivities needed to respond to changing situations in the way in which the maxim specifies. The same point holds here: we would not assign an internalist commitment to someone who lacked the desires and sensitivities needed to act in line with the commitment most of the time.

When we speak in the internalist sense of a person P's commitments, we often mean to refer to P's convictions—that is, to the ideals, values, goals or principles that P reflectively judges to be worthy of allegiance, and hence stands prepared to act on. This is what we mean, for instance, when we say that Martin Luther King was committed to racial justice. However, 'conviction' is not an exact synonym for (internalist) 'commitment.' We sometimes speak of what we have a(n internalist) commitment to do, as when we say that King had a commitment to march on Birmingham, yet we would not say that King had a conviction to march on Birmingham. Still, when we speak of what we have a(n internalist) commitment to *do*, we mean to refer to the practical dictates of our convictions—that is, to what our ideals, values, goals or principles give us reason to do under prevailing circumstances. This means that if we are to speak authoritatively of the internalist commitments of another in either of these two senses, we must be in an authoritative position to identify the other's convictions.

Once we grasp this link between internalist commitments and convictions, it is clear that internalist commitments are normative—they are either the sources of what we regard as weighty reasons, or the things we take ourselves to have weighty reasons to do. What might be less clear is why internalist commitments are particularly proof against *akrasia*, as I claimed they were above. The quick answer is that they are determined by or identical with our considered and firmly held judgments—i.e. our convictions. But to see why this is any answer at all, we need to bring out what convictions are and how we go about identifying them.

IIB: The Authority of First-Person Avowals of Conviction

When we seek to identify the guiding convictions of other agents, we have two different avenues of approach: we can *converse* with them and take their avowed judgments as authoritative, or we can *observe* them and attribute to them the ideals, values, goals or principles that figure into the best intentional explanation of their behavior.[11] What is easily overlooked here is that the conversational approach cannot be subsumed without loss under the observational approach. First-person avowals have a certain delimited authority in the identification of another's convictions. Thus, it is ordinarily inappropriate to regard the avowed convictions of another agent as additional bits of data that must be rendered intelligible by any adequate intentional explanation of the agent's behavior. Of course, one *can* regard the avowals of another in this way, merely as signs of behavioral dispositions, but to do so constitutes a decisive breach in the quality (I am tempted to say the *moral* quality) of one's relation to that other.

What precisely is this authority that we normally extend to first-person avowals of goals, values, ideals, principles and the like? We can sharpen the question as follows: What authority do we normally grant to the commissive utterances to which I attended in the last chapter — utterances formed by the first-person present indicative conjugations of verbs such as 'value,' 'esteem,' 'care about,' 'approve of,' 'deplore,' 'aim to,' 'aspire to,' and 'adhere to'? The utterances in question have the surface grammar of assertions: they seem to be descriptions of the mental states of the speaker. Thus, it is tempting to think that the authority we grant to them is like the authority we grant to descriptions of worldly events offered by well-positioned and trustworthy eye-witnesses.

I believe that this is wrong, and that these utterances are governed by an entirely different set of proprieties than descriptions

---

11 Stated this way, the dichotomy is overly neat. This is because many wordless actions play the role of signifying our convictions, and are known by agents to play this role. I will acknowledge and discuss this complexity below. I do not believe that my current argument is undermined by my use of the simplified dichotomy. I depend here only on the claim that there is a distinction between taking the words/acts of another as expressions of their convictions and taking them as evidence of their convictions. I believe that this distinction is genuine, even if the same words/act could be taken up in either way by third parties.

(including those closely related descriptions formed by the same verbs in their past-tense or third-person conjugations).[12] In the last chapter, I drew attention to the fact that when we prepare to say what we intend, value, etc., we do not ordinarily direct our attention to *ourselves*, taking care to attribute to ourselves the intentions and evaluations that make most sense of the data at hand— i.e. our behavior, thoughts, characteristic fantasies and the like. Rather we think about what it would be best to do, or what is really valuable, and our words reflect our considered judgments of these matters. Thus, while the utterances under investigation appear to be self-descriptions, they cannot be voiced in a fully responsible way if the speaker offers them merely as self-descriptions. Whenever one says what one intends or values, one implicitly claims that one has good reason for holding those intentions or affirming those values, and this implicit claim cannot plausibly be understood as a further description of one's dispositions to act or judge in particular ways. Third-person attributions of intentions and evaluations do not carry this same implication. They are formulated by attending to the characteristic words and actions of another agent, and not by deliberating directly about what is worth doing or what is valuable.[13]

IIC: The Presuppositions of Internalist Commitment

These considerations help to illuminate the peculiar authority that we grant to first-person avowals of intentions, evaluations and the like. As suggested above, we do not grant this authority because we take the agent's avowals to be the best *evidence* of her real reasons for action, though no doubt it often *is* the best evidence. We grant it, instead, because we must do so in order to acknowledge other persons as sincere interlocutors and as practi-

---

12 My view of commitment has been deeply influenced by Richard Moran—not just by the writings I have cited, but also by a seminar on belief and testimony that he gave at Harvard in the spring of 1996.

13 I owe this point to Moran, though I am not entirely certain that he would approve of the way I put things. Moran makes this point about avowals of belief. He points out that first-person avowals of belief imply that the speaker endorses the belief as true, while third-person attributions of belief do not carry the implication that the speaker endorses the belief as true. See Moran, *Op. Cit.*, pp. 28 and 30.

cal agents who act on what they judge to be good reasons.

These cursory remarks require some elaboration. Ordinarily, our interpretations of other agents are governed by the following key presuppositions (among others):

(1)Their avowed judgments are *sincere*, faithfully expressing their actual judgments.

(2)Their actual judgments are thoroughly *considered*, hence supported by good and sufficient reasons.

(3)Their actions are *continent*, and hence reflect their actual judgments of what they have reason to do.

All three of these presuppositions must be in place if we are to view others as full participants in the wide range of conversations within which we give an account of ourselves—either by making known to others what it is that we stand for (while simultaneously committing ourselves to stand by it), or by engaging with others in clarificatory discussions of values that we have not yet made fully articulate (simultaneously expressing our values and committing ourselves to their implications). These presuppositions, then, partly characterize the authority or standing that we grant to other agents to engage as full participants in the conversations by means of which we seek to coordinate our activities in line with shared convictions.

When these presuppositions are all in place, third persons can attribute convictions, and hence internalist commitments, from one's speech and from one's actions. Ordinarily one's actions are less determinate than one's speech, in that they leave the third-person interpreter with greater flexibility in attributing internalist commitments. However, this flexibility has its limits. The interpreter might be pushed to renounce one of these three presuppositions if word and action became too hard to reconcile. This helps to specify the limits of the authority that we grant to first-person avowals. Although such avowals are neither offered nor received merely as self-descriptions, they must meet a minimal test of plausibility as an account of how things are. At minimum, it must be possible to incorporate them at face value into *a* coherent account of the speaker's manifest behavior, though in most circumstances they need not figure into the *most* coherent account of that behavior. The authority that we grant to first-person avowals is this: we accept them at face value even at the cost of affirming a somewhat strained or implausible intentional explanation of another's actions. The measure of this authority is the degree of implausibility we are willing to countenance.[14]

We can withdraw from person Q the authority to speak definitively of her own convictions by cancelling any one of the three presuppositions listed above, interpreting her either as *insincere*, *capricious* or *akratic*. If the breach takes either of the last two forms, then one regards Q as someone incapable of convictions and hence incapable of internalist commitments. This is because convictions are firm and motivational efficacious judgments.[15] If the breach takes the first form, we still view Q as capable of convictions, but we are unlikely to see ourselves as having any reason to hold Q to the particular internalist commitments stemming from her convictions.

We interpret Q's avowals as *insincere* by attributing to Q an alternative set of intentions and evaluations that explain why Q would deliberately misrepresent her own convictions. In this sort of case, we see Q as someone who has internalist commitments but who cannot be counted on to make them known to others. This, however, does not mean that we have usurped from Q the authority that we ordinarily grant to other persons to say what their internalist commitments are. It is true that we have *withdrawn* this authority from Q, but we have not *usurped* the authority because we have not assumed it for ourselves. That is, we do not think that *our* characterization of Q sets down morally binding terms on Q's future actions.[16] Rather, we come to regard Q as an unwilling or

---

14 There is no perfectly general way of specifying how great an implausibility we ought to be willing to accept. There is no precise level of interpersonal trust that is appropriate to, or demanded by, all social relationships.

15 It is true that one still regards the other as a rational system, since one still seeks to explain the other's behavior by attributing to her the beliefs and desires that render her behavior maximally intelligible. However, one effectively withdraws from her the authority we normally grant to other persons to give a definitive account of their own practical reasons.

16 On the contrary, we might well think that Q is bound morally to keep the commitments she has avowed and not the commitments we attribute to her. We might think this if we are in the sort of relationship with Q that gives us reason to insist that she act as she has indicated that she will. If so, then we take Q to have an externalist commitment to us, on the model of a promise.

unfit participant in those important human relationships—including friendships, family relationships and civic and religious associations—which require serious conversation about what values are worth affirming and acting on. I will go on to argue that these forms of relationship, within which participants attempt to work out terms that each affirms as authoritative for the regulation of their shared activities, are precisely the settings in which internalist commitments matter most, and in which we can come to have grounds to hold each other to internalist commitments. The three presuppositions under discussion can be conceived of as specifying a social background of interpersonal trust that makes these important relationships possible.

If Q's avowals of convictions seem to change frequently and arbitrarily, we might come to interpret these avowals as *capricious*. That is, we might think of Q as disposed to avow intentions and evaluations without careful deliberation, and prone to change avowals without good reason. If we take this view of Q, we do not interpret Q as having an ever-changing series of internalist commitments. Rather, we think of Q as someone who is incapable of internalist commitment. This is because internalist commitments just are the sort of things that do not change except for good and weighty reasons. This is what distinguishes them from mere whims.

Finally, we might interpret Q as someone who is careful in deliberating and sincere in avowing her judgments about what she has most reason to do or to value, but who fails to act on these judgments. That is, we might view Q as *akratic*. If we were to attribute to Q a *chronic akrasia*, we would cease to view Q as having convictions, since evaluative judgments do not count as convictions unless they are characteristically manifest in action.

This might seem a perverse view of *akrasia*. Wouldn't it be more reasonable to maintain that Q's judgments have the same standing as anyone else's—i.e. that they count as convictions if anything does—but that Q is plagued by extraordinarily strong and perverse desires or emotions that lead her to act against her own best judgments? I believe that this alternative rests upon an implausible interpretation of desires and emotions. In Chapters One and Two, I sought to show that desires and emotions cannot plausibly be thought of as natural forces external to the workings of practical reason. Rather, our desires and emotions have a cognitive aspect. If we desire something, we take it as a *prima-facie* good; likewise, if we fear something, we take it as a *prima-facie* threat. These "takings as" are part of the way in which we order our perception of the world in which we must act, and they provide the initial, judgment-laden framework within which practical deliberation begins. To say that this framework is judgment-laden is to say that reasons for action are already provisionally mapped (so to speak) into it. If this is right, then the conflict that plagues the *akratic* is in an important sense a *cognitive* conflict. The conflict makes manifest that one's judgments have not yet done the work of reorienting one's characteristic way of ordering the world for practical deliberation. As I argued in Chapter Two, chronic conflicts of this sort manifest that one's judgments lack the status of convictions.

We are now in a position to see why internalist commitments are proof against *akrasia* in a way that mere intentions are not. One can routinely fail to do that which one says one will do, even that which one intends to do. However, one cannot routinely fail to act on one's convictions that is, to fulfill one's internalist commitments. If one routinely failed to act on them, they could not be counted as convictions.

PART III: WALZER AND INTERNALIST COMMIT-MENTS

I have thus far provided scant textual evidence for my claim that Walzer has *internalist* commitments in mind when he equates obligations with commitments. The clearest evidence, I think, is found in his argument that the obligation to risk one's life for the good of the state cannot have its origins in Lockean consent.[17] Walzer describes the Lockean social contract as an agreement among freely willing individuals to cooperate in an effort to secure certain results which are in the interest of each of these individuals. Because its terms must be in each individual's interest, Walzer concludes that the Lockean contract "would seem by its very nature incapable of describing ultimate obligation [i.e. the obligation to risk one's life for the state]."[18]

---

17 Walzer, *Obligations*, p. 89.
18 *Ibid.*

Walzer's argument, in this abbreviated form, is not by itself conclusive. If we accept the Lockean principle that we are obligated to do what we have consented to do, then we can describe "ultimate obligations" as easily as any other obligations. We are bound to risk our lives for the state provided that we have agreed to do so. If there were an actual contract that contained this provision, we would be obligated to keep it. So there is a sense in which Locke's theory could describe "ultimate obligation."

There is another way of reconstructing Walzer's argument against Locke that works a bit better. On this reading, Walzer's claim is that Locke cannot account for ultimate obligation because Lockean obligations must serve the prudential interests of the citizens they bind, and it would not be prudent to undertake ultimate obligations—at least not in exchange for the benefits offered by a state. Walzer suggests this reading when he claims that Locke's "general pattern" is to "treat politics and the state as instrumental to the achievement of individual purposes..."[19] Since the agreements of most actual citizens are not set out in explicit contracts, their obligations must be inferred hypothetically by considering what it would have been rational for them to accept if the state had been formed with their voluntary consent. If Walzer is right that citizens could have no prudential reason for accepting ultimate obligations, this implies that most actual citizens are not bound to risk their lives in the defense of the state.

This argument might work as a refutation of Lockean justifications of ultimate obligation, though it hinges on a controversial claim about the limits of prudential reasoning. If this were Walzer's argument, however, Walzer would present us with no reason to question the basic tenets of Lockean consent theory. His objection to Locke would leave untouched the central Lockean claim that voluntary consent is the best and perhaps the only possible grounding for political obligations.

IIIA: Walzer's Real Objection to Lockean Consent Theory

As I read Walzer, he offers a more fundamental and potentially more devastating objection to the Lockean consent tradition.

19 *Ibid.* A. John Simmons takes this to be a fundamental element of the traditional consent theory of obligation. See A. John Simmons, *Moral Principles and Political Obligations* (Princeton; Princeton University Press: 1979), pp. 68–9.

Walzer's real objection, I think, is that mere consent—construed on the model of a past promise—is too insubstantial a grounding for the weightiest political obligations such as the obligation to risk one's life and perhaps to kill other humans (i.e. enemies) in furtherance of the state's military aims.[20] The strongest ground for ultimate obligation would be that one has affirmed and continues to affirm goods which are actually realized by the state and which are worth risking one's life to preserve.[21]

It is true that Walzer consistently states his case in the language of consent theory, but this language provides an increasingly procrustean setting for the intuitions that are driving him. According to Walzer, the only sort of "contract" that really could provide a proper underpinning for ultimate obligations "must involve some acknowledgment of the reality of the common life and of the moral transformation which it makes possible."[22] This proviso would be implausible if read as a specification of the language a contract would have to include in order to ground ultimate obligations. Like promises, so contracts are all-purpose tools for undertaking contracts. They bind us by making known that we voluntarily agree to certain terms and conditions on our future actions, and by making explicit what those terms and conditions are. When we promise or agree contractually to ø, we do not imply that we have any (prior) reason to ø. Our obligation does not hinge on our acknowledgment that øing would be good, and it would not be canceled if we were to make known that we believe øing to be bad.

---

20 I owe to Thomas Scanlon the idea that this is the best reading of Walzer and the idea that this interpretive option contains the seeds of an extremely interesting theory of a class of obligations.

21 I believe this to be a striking and original criticism of Locke. Locke's theory is widely criticized on the grounds that it maps poorly onto the world, failing to account for the obligations of that great legion of citizens who have neither explicitly consented to be governed by the state, nor said or done anything that could plausibly be interpreted as a sign of tacit or implicit consent to be governed by the state. However, Locke's critics typically leave uncontested the claim that if it were given, voluntary consent *would* provide a more-than-adequate grounding for political obligations. For instance, in the course of a devastating dissection of Lockean consent theory, A. John Simmons traces the attraction of consent theory to the fact that it models political obligations on promises. This is attractive, he claims, because promising "is surely as close to being an indisputable ground of moral requirement as anything is." Simmons, *Op. Cit.*, p. 70.

22 Walzer, *Obligations*, p. 97.

It is more plausible to read Walzer as asserting that those citizens who acknowledge the goodness of existing political arrangements thereby incur certain obligations, perhaps including the obligation to risk their lives in defense of the state. But if this reading is correct, then continued talk of contracts seems otiose. Those who acknowledge the moral transformation made possible by their civic engagement presumably have an internalist commitment to do whatever it is that those who have undergone this transformation have most reason to do. If this means that they are bound to risk their lives in defense of the state, they are not bound contractually but by their own considered judgment of what is good.

This implication quickly surfaces when Walzer notes that his position "comes dangerously near to suggesting that a man is obligated to die only if he feels or thinks himself obligated."[23] This is indeed a danger for any theorist who treats obligations as internalist commitments, though I will try to show below that it is not fatal. However, it does not seem to be an objection to a consensualist theory of obligations—at least not one that models the normative force of consent on promising or contracting. It is essential to the normative force of promises and contracts that their terms are clear and interpersonally specifiable; they are particularly appropriate implements for establishing obligations in conditions where the primary need of those involved is to count confidently on others to act in particular ways in the future.

One way to bring out the intuition that I believe to be at work in Walzer's text is to think about what the fellow citizens of a front-line soldier might tell her if they were asked to explain why she ought to risk her life in defense of the country. It would ring hollow to say that she is obligated to risk her life merely because she promised. Any adequate answer, it seems, would make essential reference to the goods and ideals that the state actually embodies and that the soldier has good reason to endorse.[24] Without

---

23 *Ibid.*, p. 98.
24 In our response to the soldier, we might make reference to what the soldier herself would judge that she ought to do if she were to think about the matter calmly and deliberately, without the distorting effect of her current fears. However, this thought experiment would not be a way of bringing out what the soldier has actually or tacitly consented to do; rather, it would be a way of clarifying the implications of the soldier's own deepest convictions.

such a backdrop of shared goods and ideals, a promise seems too thin a reason to fulfill so costly an obligation.[25]

IIIB: Internalist Commitments and "Significant Actions"

There might still seem to be an important remnant of consent theory in Walzer's position. The reason is that he insists that one can only come to have political obligations through one's own "significant actions"—actions repeated over time which signal one's self-conscious and voluntary participation in a morally transformative common life.[26] This raises two questions for my interpretation of Walzer. First, if obligations are understood in terms of internalist commitments, it might seem that one could have them even if one had not signaled this fact to anyone else through one's significant actions. Second, it might seem that "significant actions" could only play an important role in determining one's obligations if they were regarded—on the paradigm of consent theory—as implicit signs of voluntary consent to the obligations of citizenship. I will discuss these difficulties in order.

Recall that one's internalist commitments are one's convictions and their practical dictates, where convictions are understood as stable, well-reasoned and motivationally efficacious evaluative judgments. Now, it is perfectly possible to have convictions, and hence internalist commitments, that one has not (or not yet) expressed in one's actions. One has such a conviction if one holds a particular evaluative judgment and is prepared to act in conformity with it. However, until a conviction has been expressed in action, others are not yet in a position to assert authoritatively that one has the conviction in question. This means that others are not

---

25 This is not merely because military service poses a grave mortal risk—though this figures importantly into my argument. It is also because military service differs from other, more ordinary political obligations—such as the obligation to obey the law—in that it requires us to carry out state policies actively rather than merely to submit to them, and even to attempt to kill opposing soldiers in the process. When citizens are required to fight in a war they take to be misguided, they are required to kill other humans for reasons they take to be insufficiently weighty. In other words, they are required to perform an act that they can only regard as murder. This clearly imposes a far more serious affront to their conscience than does the ordinary duty to be lawful. (I owe this observation about the distinction between military service and peacetime political obligations to Walzer. See Walzer, *Obligations*, pp. 135–6 and 140.)

26 *Ibid.*, p. 98.

yet in a position to hold one to one's internalist commitments. These internalist commitments lack what seems to me to be an essential feature of obligations, since there is no one to whom they can plausibly be thought to be owed and no one who can insist authoritatively on their fulfillment. Rather than calling them obligations to oneself, it seems to me best to say that not all internalist commitments are obligations.

I think that the best way to understand Walzer's talk of "significant actions" is to think of them as actions which give others good grounds for attributing convictions, and hence for identifying internalist commitments. If this is right, then the class of significant actions has fuzzy borders. I simplified matters earlier when I distinguished two approaches to the identification of others' convictions: the conversational approach, in which one elicits avowals, and the observational approach, in which one observes actions. As Walzer's apt phrase 'significant action' suggests, there are a wide range of actions that signal one's convictions, and many of them are performed without saying a word. One can signal one's convictions by raising a hand to vote, marching in a protest, joining a picket line or enlisting in the army. In general, it seems to me that there is no clear line between the sorts of actions which express one's convictions, on par with verbal avowals, and the sort which merely evidence one's convictions. Even relatively "insignificant" actions might be construed as expressions of self-consciously held convictions if they are repeated deliberately over time.[27] However, when we take this view of a series of actions, the resulting attribution of conviction ought to be cautious and tentative, subject to revision on the basis of clearer and less equivocal signals. This is part of what it means to recognize the authority of first-person avowals of convictions.

These considerations provide a way of understanding Walzer's insistence that "we commit ourselves very often by degrees" and that "the expectations that others form as to our conduct are or ought to be similarly graded."[28] This claim is very hard to assim-

---

27 Cf. Walzer, *Obligations*, p. xiii: "Consent itself is sometimes signified not by a single act but by a series of acts, and the determining sign is always preceded, I think, by something less than determining: a succession of words, motions, involvements that might well be analyzed as tentatives of or experiments in consent."

28 Walzer, *Obligations*, p. xiii.

ilate to the promissory model, since we have no clear notion of what it means to give a partial promise. When we make promises or enter contracts, we aim to give valued assurances to others regarding our future actions; these assurances are most valuable if their terms are clear and uncontroversial. However, if I am right that Walzer thinks of consent as internalist commitment, his observation seems correct for two reasons. First, the results of deliberation can always be more thoroughly considered—not just because one could always spend more time deliberating, but also because one is limited by the breadth of one's experience, which partly determines the scope of considerations one can take into account. Second, the grounds that others have for identifying one's internalist commitments can be weaker or stronger, and are perhaps never absolutely conclusive.

IIIC: Significant Actions and Freedom

Once we see what significant actions are, it ought to be clear that they do not function as implicit voluntary agreements on the paradigm of promises and contracts. They function instead as signs of one's convictions. Interestingly, however, the conditions under which an action can plausibly be regarded as a sign of one's convictions are strikingly similar to the conditions that are sometimes thought to be required in order for promises or contractual agreements to be binding. Indeed, the non-promissory approach that I favor has an advantage here, since it makes clearer *why* these conditions obtain. There are great theoretical obscurities concerning contracts and promises made under duress. Choices made under duress do appear voluntary, at least in the familiar sense that we could have made some other choice. If we think of promises and contracts as binding because we voluntarily choose to make or enter them (that is, if we adopt what I have called the principle of consensual obligation), it would seem that promises and contracts made under duress would be just as binding as any others. However, we might balk at the notion that we could be bound irrevocably by a state-founding contract if we agreed to it under duress (i.e. to stave off life-threatening hunger) or coercion (i.e. at the point of a conqueror's sword). If by contrast we are bound by the internalist commitments signified by our words and actions, then it is clear why we cannot commit ourselves under duress or mortal threat. What we say or do in such conditions does not provide a straightforward expression of our internalist commitments. For instance, joining a picket line under duress does not indicate that we affirm the guiding convictions of the picketers, and thus does not commit us to sticking by other picketers come what may.

PART IV: THE CONDITIONS OF ULTIMATE OBLIGATION

On my reading of Walzer, those who perform significant actions that commit them to risk their lives for the state are not really bound *contractually* to defend the state. That is, they are not bound because their civic participation signals a tacit agreement to risk their lives for the state. Rather, they are obligated because they have been transformed morally by their public political participation, and their own deepest convictions give them good reason to risk their lives for the defense of the state.

IVA. Ultimate Obligation and Motivation

According to Walzer, the moral transformation in virtue of which one becomes obligated to defend the state is (at least in part) that one comes to be *motivated* to risk one's life for the state, at least under certain conditions. This motivation presumably arises from an identification of one's own fate with the historic fate of the political community. It is not easy to say just what this identification amounts to, but it must imply at least that one has come to prefer the survival of the political community even at the cost of one's own life.[29] If one held such preferences, then one might be motivated to put one's life at grave risk if doing so would materially improve the chances for the political community's survival. That is, one might view the political community's demise as "a fate worse than death."[30]

---

29 Of course, the identification could be more complete. For instance, one might see little or no value in the continuation of one's own life outside of the political community—perhaps because one holds membership in the community to be a "constitutive good," without which one could not recognize oneself as the same person. This would considerably widen the range of circumstances in which one might be motivated to die or risk death for the state.

30 Walzer, *Obligations*, p. 93.

Walzer attributes this republican account of "ultimate obligation" to Rousseau. However, he balks at the Rousseauvian claim that the citizens of the true republic can be forced, for their own sake, to risk their lives and even to die for the state. In Walzer's words, "There is a crucially important sense in which the obligation to die can only be stated in the first person singular." More specifically, "no man can be obligated to die unless he admits or has at some time in the past admitted" the existence of "moral goods for which political dying is conceivable."[31]

As Walzer himself notes, his position "comes dangerously near to suggesting that a man is obligated to die only if he feels or thinks himself obligated."[32] This is a danger because it seems that anything that deserves to be called an obligation might in some circumstances pose demands that one feels no motivation to meet. I do not think that this danger is fatal to the internalist project. As I understand them, internalist commitments are determined by the goods we affirm on considered reflection, and our momentary inclination need not reflect these goods. After all, one might be overcome by a momentary fear that eliminates any motivation to act on one's deepest convictions. In such cases, one is obligated to resist the fear.

On the other hand, inclinations to deviate from what one has previously taken to be one's commitments need not always be understood as temptations to act immorally. Such sentiments might be signs that one has mistakenly identified one's own deepest convictions, or they might be harbingers of a change in these convictions. The soldier's fear might be the first inkling of pacifism, announcing the inadequacy of an ill-considered militarism to the previously unimagined, hellish reality of war. The important truth in Walzer's claim is that the impersonal bureaucrats of the state are in a particularly bad position to second-guess the commitments of citizens who feel no motivation to risk their lives for

---

31 Walzer, *Obligations*, p. 97.
32 *Ibid.*, p. 98.
33 Walzer maintains that state officials ought to grant conscientious objector status to anyone whose refusals "follow from some more or less consistent pattern of interpersonal commitment and group action." He adds, "Since the persons involved are likely to be young, however, this criterion cannot be strictly applied, and any coherent statement of personal convictions likely to lead to group action must be taken as a sufficient sign of conscientiousness." See Walzer, *Obligations*, p. 141.

the state.[33] Any sustainable objection to these citizens would have to rest on a plausible interpretation and application of the ideals and values which they have manifested over time in their words and actions. Such objections are most plausible if raised amongst those who have participated together in a long-standing effort to give shape and clarity to some array of common values.

IVB. Ultimate Obligation and False Consciousness

While a conscious attachment to what one takes to be values that give one reason to die for the state is a *necessary* condition for the existence of an obligation to risk one's life for the state, it is not a *sufficient* one. It is not a sufficient condition because one might be convinced that one is obligated to die for the state because one has been duped into believing that there is a common life worth defending. As Walzer puts it, "I do not mean to defend all those nationalistic or ideological mystifications that lead men to believe they are living in a community when in fact they are not."[34]

This passage is difficult to interpret. On my reading, when Walzer speaks of "living in a community," he means living among others who actually do share a commitment to some range of common values, and who do not merely *profess* such a commitment—perhaps for self-serving reasons, or perhaps because they have failed to understand each other. In the context of the present example, the soldier cannot be called upon to risk life and limb to secure some valuable thing for which others—particularly those in power—would not similarly risk their lives.

This proviso might seem unmotivated, at least on the internalist reading of Walzer that I have been pressing. After all, such a soldier might still have an internalist commitment to risk her life in defense of the state. Yet Walzer's point is surely a forceful one, since it would be an alarming consequence of any theory of obligation that citizens could be given new political obligations by effective propaganda.

As suggested above, I believe that internalist commitments play the role I have assigned to them—that of determining mutual obligations—only in certain kinds of human relationships. I think that Walzer's passage is best understood as an effort to delimit the forms of political association within which the obligations of citi-

---

34 Walzer, *Obligations*, p. 98.

zens can properly be equated with their internalist commitments.

If this is right, then Walzer's critique of Locke might be put as follows. Lockean consent theory is an appropriate model for understanding the mutual obligations of a class of social groups that I have labeled *aggregations*. One key aim of Walzer's book is to argue that any political society with the underlying normative structure of an aggregation would have certain deficiencies. The deficiency on which I have been dwelling is that such a society lacks any legitimate grounding for military obligations, and can defend itself successfully only by duping its "citizens" into thinking that they have an obligation to risk their lives for the state, or by forcing "citizens" to so risk their lives. Another key deficiency is that when the citizens of an aggregative state participate in political deliberation, they are guided by their unregenerate self-interests, subject only to the limits on self-interested action that they have promised to observe.[35] One way to make this second deficiency more palpable is to note that the laws specifying the rights and obligations of citizens are not fixed once and for all by an original promise (as the originary tale of consent theory encourages us to imagine), but must be negotiated and/or renegotiated at every turn. In effect, the justice of the political order rest upon an unending series of agreements, each of which further specifies the terms of political association. It is plausible to suppose that if these (re)negotiations were bounded only by rules limiting self-interested actions, and not guided by a substantive internalist commitment of participants to the good of the whole, the justice of the political order could not be sustained. One might promise always to seek fairness in important political decisions. But there is a difficulty in importing the language of promises at this juncture. As noted above, it is perfectly proper to promise to do that which one has no prior internalist commitment to do, yet it is not at all clear that one can make one's political deliberations just by a voluntarily act of will, even in the absence of a more visceral attachment to justice.[36] As I argued in Chapter Two, one cannot ensure that one will be appropriately responsive to the needs and interests of fellow humans simply by affirming an abstract principle which requires

---

35 Walzer, *Obligations*, p. 215.
36 I set aside the further difficulty that it would be extraordinarily difficult to verify the fulfillment of such a promise, since selfish pursuits are notoriously easy to hide under the rhetoric of common interest.

such responsiveness. I believe that the same can be said for fellow citizens. In order to act consistently on a principle which grants due importance to the needs and interests of one's fellow citizens, one must actually have an affective concern for the fulfillment of these needs and interests.

We might approach the difficulty more directly by reflecting that the promissory account subtly misdescribes the sort of commitment that many of us take ourselves to have, and hope that our fellow citizens have, to social justice. Many of us believe, and hope that others believe, that we are bound by the dictates of justice not because we have promised to abide by these limitations, but because these dictates stem from a social ideal that we affirm, or because they properly reflect the value of our fellow citizens. If the citizens of a particular state did think of their mutual commitments on the promissory model, this might indicate that there is something amiss with the conception of justice expressed in the state's laws, or with the nature of the state's public political deliberations, or with the character of the citizens.

The loosely Rousseauvian account of political obligation which Walzer favors is appropriate for the other class of social groups which I isolated in the last chapter: *associations* (sometimes I will call them *communities of conscience*). In a political society with the underlying normative structure of an association, citizens deliberate by seeking to articulate their political convictions concerning the good of the whole. According to Walzer, one advantage of this sort of political society is that it can arrange for its own defense without resorting to coercion or to "nationalistic or ideological mystifications."[37] Walzer's book suggests that such a political society has two other important advantages. First, it provides for thicker and more significant bonds of citizenship than the

---

37 Walzer, *Obligations*, p. 98.

38 According to Walzer, this livelier sense of mutual responsibility might help to stave off certain forms of alienation and despair. Walzer maintains that it is a characteristic mark of the modern state that the suicide of citizens is permissible as far as the state is concerned. He maintains that in more intimate communities, members take on an obligation to live for each other, and that the absence of the sort of communal attachment amongst citizens reflects (or creates?) a vacuum of meaning—a lack of mutual responsibility, and a corresponding sense of alienation and uselessness—that might well have exacerbated suicide rates by producing "a new and profound readiness to die." (See Walzer, *Obligations*, pp. 186-7.)

aggregative state.[38] What Walzer might mean is that fellow citizens value each other not just as instrumental aids to the pursuit of their own ends, nor just as fellow cooperators who must not be expected to make unreciprocated sacrifices, but as partners in the project of articulating a worthy conception of the good life and enacting that conception in practice. Second, the associative state is better equipped then the aggregative state to realize the ideal of participatory self-rule, and the associated republican ideal of freedom. If the obligation to obey the law is tied to the capacity of the citizen to see himself or herself as the author of the law in some significant sense, then this would imply that not merely ultimate obligations, but also more ordinary political obligations, can have a firmer and more compelling footing in the associative state than in the aggregative state.

This does not necessarily mean that the associative state has a convincing claim to the obedience of all citizens. While participatory engagement in political decision makes it possible to sustain a lively commitment to the law, such engagement is mediated by convictions about the good, and the convictions of some citizens will almost inevitably be contradicted by some laws. Thus, as Walzer insists, the ideal of the associative state contains the seeds of a justification of principled opposition to the state's dictates.[39]

IVC. Ultimate Obligation and the Refined Voluntarist Thesis

On Walzer's view, obligations arise from significant words and actions within the context of such groups, they are owed to the fellow members of such groups, and they are constituted by a commitment to shared goals or values of the group.[40] Walzer claims, however, that the mere fact of group affiliation is never enough to give rise to obligations; though one may be affiliated with some group from birth, this adherence must become "willful membership" through a free act of consent before it can support obligations. Furthermore, it is not enough for coercion to be absent at the moment in which one becomes a willful member;

---

39 Walzer argues that the state must recognize the possibility of obligations to disobey the law in order to acknowledge the moral seriousness of the particular commitments of its citizens. See Walzer, "The Obligation to Disobey," in *Obligations*, pp. 3–23.
40 See Walzer, *Obligations*, pp. 4–5, 20, and 23.

obligations to the shared goals of some group can only arise if one has the freedom to pursue a wide range of alternative goals throughout one's life.

It is here, in the nature and conceptual foundations of the freedom condition, that Walzer's treatment of political obligation breaks most decisively with more familiar attempts to ground political obligation in consent. In Locke's view, for instance, political obligations must arise through freely expressed consent because there is no other way for them to arise consistent with the natural freedom of man. One might suspect that Walzer is invoking a similar principle when he insists that obligations must be undertaken freely. If so, this might seem adventitious to the internalist account of obligations, since it is not clear that freedom is a necessary condition for the formation of internalist commitments.[41] Yet if the 'full freedom' condition or something like it cannot be sustained, then the internalist view seems to conflate obligations with *de facto* commitments, and this conflation leads to troubling results. For instance, it leads to the conclusion that those who live under a totalitarian political system—one which indoctrinates them in a particular way of life and leaves them completely unaware of alternatives—are nevertheless obligated to uphold prevailing norms.

I believe that the internalist has a persuasive answer to this difficulty, and I will try to formulate it. First, however, I will discuss Walzer's interesting though not entirely convincing answer.

Walzer's argument is that the state—or at least the geographically expansive, bureaucratic and faceless modern state—cannot curtail freedom of expression and association, nor ban secondary groups, without eroding the capacity of its citizens to enter into obligations of any sort, including political obligations.[42] The argument turns on the claim that face-to-face relationships in a variety of social groups—from families and neighborhoods to church congregations, unions, and political parties—play an indispensable

---

41 It would also be deeply at odds with Walzer's political philosophy as developed in subsequent works, and in particular with his "moral minimalist" rejection of universal moral principles. See Michael Walzer, "Moral Minimalism" in *Thick and Thin: Moral Argument at Home and Abroad* (Notre Dame, Indiana; University of Notre Dame Press: 1994), pp. 1–19.
42 See Walzer, *Obligations*, pp. 138–142.
43 Walzer, *Obligations*, pp. 4–5 and 139.

role in our moral development.[43] Walzer's view, I think, is that it is only through our engagement in these groups that we come to articulate the principles, goals and values by which we stand, and learn to justify our actions to others in terms of these principles, goals and values. Our participation in these groups, then, is the means by which we develop and exercise our capacity to commit ourselves and stand by our commitments. In the large and bureaucratic modern state, our political life cannot play this role—as perhaps it might in a small participatory democracy. Since Walzer analyzes obligations in terms of commitments, this licenses the conclusion that the large modern state must leave its citizens free to participate in secondary groups if it is to claim persuasively that they have political obligations at all.[44] Indeed, Walzer draws the more radical conclusion that the state must recognize that citizens sometimes have an obligation to disobey its directives, since secondary associations cannot play their character-building function if members think of their shared ideals as binding only insofar as they harmonize with state policy.[45]

This argument seems to me extremely interesting and perhaps correct. However, it turns on sweeping, controversial sociological theses which I am reluctant to endorse. I believe that there is a more solid and convincing argument for the conclusion that internalist commitments can only be undertaken in conditions of freedom. My argument proceeds in two parts. First I present an argument for the "refined voluntarist thesis" that we cannot be coerced into undertaking new internalist commitments. This argument does not rule out the possibility that we might come to have internalist commitments through more mildly restrictive forms of indoctrination and socialization. The second part of my argument is meant to show that this is not a serious problem for my theory, since the internalist commitments that arise in these conditions are provisional enough as to be unproblematic. This second argument is extended, and will not be complete until the end of this essay.

The first part of my argument is an application of one of Locke's central arguments for religious toleration. According to

---

44 Walzer writes, "This is surely the great strength of a pluralist citizenship: that it not only implicates the citizens in state policy, but generates real obligations and an authentic patriotism by recognizing a sphere within which they actually have scope for meaningful action." (*Obligations*, pp. 219–20.)

45 Walzer, *Obligations*, pp. 10 and 16–17.

Locke, it is futile to use coercive force to attempt to alter the religious beliefs of others, since coercion is effective only for controlling others' words and actions and not for altering their religious convictions. To quote Locke:

> The care of Souls cannot belong to the Civil Magistrate, because his Power consists only in outward force; but true and saving Religion consists in the inward perswasion of the Mind, without which nothing can be acceptable to God. And such is the nature of the Understanding, that it cannot be compell'd to the belief of any thing by outward force. Confiscation of Estate, Imprisonment, Torments, nothing of that nature can have any such Efficacy as to make Men change the inward Judgment that they have framed of things.[46]

Locke's argument seems correct. Since religious faith can be construed as a kind of internalist commitment, a similar set of considerations can be brought forward to show the futility of using coercion to impose internalist commitments on others. (I do not mean to imply that the *only* thing wrong with the use of coercive force in such instances is that it is ineffective. I mean only to show why coerced avowals of "convictions" do not commit us to anything.)

Recall that obligations are the subset of internalist commitments which can be identified authoritatively by another, and internalist commitments are signaled to others by one's own significant actions. Under coercion, words and actions that would otherwise be significant do not provide a reliable, transparent register of one's convictions. When one speaks or acts under coercion, there is a standing explanation of what one is saying or doing that makes no reference to one's convictions. The explanation is that one is speaking or acting insincerely. Ordinarily, this sort of insincerity would cast doubt on one's fitness as a member of a community of conscience. Such a community is only possible if members generally signal their convictions sincerely, and trust other members to do likewise. However, if one is coerced into giving an insincere signal of one's convictions, this does not represent the betrayal of a community of conscience, since one clearly is not in this sort of community with one's coercer. Those who use coercion thereby

---

46 John Locke, "A Letter Concerning Toleration," paragraph 10.

announce that they are in some other, more nefarious sort of relationship with those whom they aim to coerce.

Now, some will object that this Lockean argument rests on nearly as controversial an empirical thesis as Walzer's, since there might well be a way of deploying coercive force to change people's convictions. This objection misses the force of the argument. As I stressed above, convictions are the sorts of things one revises or abandons only when one has good and sufficient reason to find them mistaken. Convictions certainly do not change simply because they are inconvenient. When we seek to determine whether an evaluative judgment counts as a conviction or not, we attend among other things to its origins. If a deliberate program of coercive force were to succeed in altering John's characteristic actions and utterances, we would not conclude that John had adopted new convictions. If the threatened harm were slight and the "conviction" central to John's public identity, John's insincere disavowal of the conviction might cast doubt on his capacity for true conviction. If the threatened harm were more serious, we might interpret John as someone whose capacity for true conviction had been repugnantly short-circuited by the intrusive manipulations of another agent. John's judgments would not be his *own* in the sense required to count as a conviction. The change in John's characteristic actions and utterances would be best explained as a reaction to torturous pain—or the threat of the same—and not as the result of what John himself takes to be a fresh insight into the good.

I have suggested that shared internalist commitments structure a valuable class of human relationships—relationships which I have called associations, and which are marked by shared knowledge or shared seeking for knowledge of the good. It might be more apt to call these *communities of conscience*—since, as Walzer repeatedly stresses, the word 'conscience' literally means shared knowledge.[47] One way to get at the futility of the coercive manipulation of "convictions" is this: We cannot enter into a community of conscience with another by coercively forcing the other to avow our convictions, since in so doing we would not be treating the other as a knower, and thus could not subsequently see the other as a fellow knower or fellow seeker of knowledge. I will argue below that those who are genuinely in this sort of community together have a strong claim on the completion of each other's

47 Walzer, *Obligations*, pp. 5, 121, 131.

internalist commitments. One could not come to have this sort of claim by attempting to alter the avowals of another through the application of coercive force.

IVD: Internalist Commitment and Restrictive Socialization

Even if it is true, as I have argued, that internalist commitments cannot be undertaken in coercive or totalitarian conditions, still this does not show that one's internalist commitments must be formed in a setting that is free in a fuller sense—a setting that provides for full political freedoms and for an unrestricted view of alternative conceptions of the good. It does not seem to me that they must be. It seems to me a requirement—even, or especially, in a liberal society—that a broad variety of communities of conscience be granted license to school their children in their own distinctive views of the good. Any political society that refuses to grant this license cannot be counted as tolerant. Furthermore, minor coercive threats are almost inevitably deployed during socialization to impart characteristic patterns of behavior on children, and a somewhat restrictive schooling is routinely deployed to convince children that these patterns of behavior are good.

These ordinary facts about how many of us have become who we are might seem to pose a problem for my view. It might seem that if we come to judge certain things valuable because we have been socialized to view them as valuable, our judgments cannot be called our own in the far-reaching sense required to count as convictions. This clearly would be too restrictive a criterion of conviction, since it would lead to the implausible conclusion that those whose beliefs have been shaped by a restrictive traditional schooling necessarily lack convictions. We might be tempted to think, for better or worse, that these are precisely the people who are most full of conviction.

Does this mean that we can be obligated to stand by the values in which we are schooled, even if our upbringing has been quite narrow and restrictive? I believe so. Do we violate our obligations if we abandon the characteristic values in which we have been schooled? I believe that we might or might not, and that one must know a great deal about a particular case to decide.

A good deal of the rest of this essay will be devoted to elaborating and justifying my answers to these two questions. The gist of my position is that obligations are more provisional than they are often taken to be. The class of obligations I am interested in are subject to change with changes in one's convictions. As I have argued, convictions cannot change whimsically, but they can change occasionally for good and thoroughly considered reasons, under the influence of a new and enlightening perspective on the good. Thus, a narrow traditional upbringing can foster genuine obligations, but these obligations are not rigid lifelong limitations on permissible action.

The problem under discussion is hardly unique to the internalist. It is at least as pressing for those who favor a promissory account of obligations. On the promissory account, obligations are binding if they are undertaken voluntary, and it is the very fact of voluntary agreement which makes them binding. This implies that if at the onset of adulthood we were to enter a voluntary agreement to adhere to a particular way of life and an associated conception of the good, that choice would bind us for the rest of our lives, even if the choice were made under the sway of a restrictive socialization. As in the case of ultimate obligations, so too in this case a past promise seems like the wrong sort of reason to fulfill the obligation in question. Here again, I believe, the promissory account subtly misdescribes the reasons that we think ourselves to have to meet our obligations. We lack a good reason to adhere to a way of life if we come to reject the conception of the good which gives shape and meaning to that way of life. Nor can the voluntarist dodge this problem by insisting that agreements made under the influence of a restrictive socialization are not voluntary; such agreements differ only in degree from the most voluntary agreements of which humans are capable.

PART V: AN ANALYSIS OF SPECIAL NON-PROMISSORY OBLIGATIONS

I will now formalize the internalist analysis of special non-promissory obligations that I have been developing:

> To attribute to person P a (special non-promissory) obligation to ø is to assert that P is committed (in the internalist sense) to some principle, goal or value which gives him reason to ø.

On this analysis, an assertion about P's obligations is a claim about where P has reason to stand. To substantiate such a claim, one must show two things: (1) that P is best interpreted as committed to some particular principle, goal or value; and (2) that this principle, goal or value cannot be followed, met or served without øing.

I turn now to a *prima-facie* difficulty with this analysis. Unlike a commitment, an obligation is usually thought of as something one owes to *other persons*—usually to others who have been encouraged by one's own actions to form legitimate expectations about one's behavior. Does this mean that my analysis leaves out a term for the person to whom the obligation is owed?

I claimed above that special non-promissory obligations are the subset of internalist commitments that can be attributed authoritatively by another person. Given this view, I was able to give an exhaustive analysis of these obligations by analyzing third-person attributions of them. Attribution of these sorts of obligations is appropriate only for those who have particular knowledge of one's internalist commitments—that is, only for those who have been witness to the history of one's significant actions.

It is not just anyone, then, who can speak authoritatively about one's internalist commitments, hence not just anyone who can insist on their fulfillment. But even when we have taken this consideration into account, my analysis might seem inadequate. The trouble is that an attentive yet disinterested observer might be able to speak authoritatively of one's internalist commitments, yet such a person does not have the same sort of authority to insist on their fulfillment as one's collaborators, or one's fellow believers, or one's friends or family members.

As I see it, the authority to demand that others remain true to internalist commitments is not epistemic at heart. Rather, it is the corollary of the authority that one grants to others to speak definitively about their convictions. I noted above that the readiness to grant this authority—that is, to interpret others as sincere, reflective and continent—can be regarded as a kind of background social capital of interpersonal trust, and that this trust makes it possible to form associations. It is only if we grant people this authority that we are able to engage with them in an effort to specify shared convictions in light of which we can dependably coordinate our activities. Within an association, this extension of authority exposes one to more substantial harms, and thus it represents a more substantial form of trust.[48] It is within the setting of associations, I believe, that it makes clearest sense to talk of others as being betrayed by a failure to fulfill internalist commitments.

There is a weak though non-trivial sense in which almost anyone might be thought betrayed by almost any violation of a special non-promissory obligation, hence a weak though non-trivial sense in which almost anyone might have standing to rebuke another for failing to keep a special non-promissory obligation. Violations of special non-promissory obligations tend to erode the valuable social capital of trust in the sincerity, moral seriousness and continence of others, and this in turn tends to undermine the possibility of creating and sustaining communities of conscience. This represents a harm to everyone and a non-trivial betrayal to all who

---

48 If it is appropriate, as I think, to call this a form of trust, this underlines a dimension of trust which is not captured in Annette C. Baier's extremely interesting writings on trust. Baier conceives of trust as one's reliance on another's goodwill towards oneself. I think that sometimes, trust involves a reliance on the dedication of others to speak truly—i.e. to make careful judgments and to represent those judgments sincerely in their speech. This sort of trust is important within all sorts of social intercourse aimed at mutual enlightenment, including enlightenment about what is good. When engaged in these sorts of intercourse, we give a provisional credence to the assertions of others, and this credence is misplaced if others forward their judgments carelessly or insincerely. When the topic of conversation is practical—i.e. when we are discussing how we ought to act—we also rely on others to exemplify their own considered judgments in their future actions. Now, it is certainly true that this sort of trust involves reliance on the goodwill of others, since people are sometimes motivated to misrepresent their own beliefs or intentions in order to harm or to manipulate others. However, one might utter careless or insincere judgments because one is inattentive, lazy or otherwise lacking in devotion to the truth. One might also lack the self-control to exemplify one's own considered judgments in one's future actions. Thus, the trust I have in mind involves a reliance on others' seriousness of mind and self-control.

   For Baier's discussion of trust, see "Trust and Antitrust," in *Moral Prejudices: Essays on Ethics* (Cambridge; Harvard University Press: 1994) pp. 95–129, esp. p. 99. See also the next three essays in this book.

49 This is analogous to the way in which broken promises tend to erode the valuable social capital of trust in promises, and give a ground for complaint not just to the recipient of the promise but to everyone who relies on the general readiness of others to accept promises as guarantees of future performances. To take a more colorful analogy: The boy who cried wolf likely eroded the general social capital of

have sought to preserve and enhance this social capital.[49]

However, if this is the only sense in which one would be harmed by another's violation of a special non-promissory obligation, it is not at all clear that one has a good reason to insist upon fulfillment of the obligation. It depends largely on whether one affirms the principle, goal or value from which the obligation springs. If one shares the conviction, one might speak in the name of that conviction in insisting upon fulfillment of the obligation.[50] If one does not share the conviction, one might well have good reason to prefer that the obligation be violated, despite the corrosive social effects of such violations.[51]

A person P's violation of a special non-promissory obligation represents a far more serious betrayal to those who are in association with P in a more robust sense. The people I have in mind are those who not only share the conviction from which P's obligation stems, but also have relied and continue to rely on P's affirmation of the conviction in order to engage with P in coordinated activities informed by these convictions. In such circumstances, P's violation weakens the association and casts doubt on the value of group activities in a subtle yet pervasive way.

To see this point, we must revisit what it is to interpret P as having violated a special non-promissory obligation. It is to attribute a relatively isolated instance of *akrasia* with respect to princi-

---

readiness to come to the aid of others in need, and not just the particular readiness of others to come to his aid. The story's tidy moral is deceiving. It could have been his friend, or his enemy, who ultimately supplied the wolf's lunch.

50 This is the most attenuated sense in which one might be said to be in association with another. Cf. Walzer, *Obligations*, p. 5: Walzer allows here that he is chiefly interested in obligations which arise in social, religious or political groups, then writes: "These can be obligations to the group as a whole (including oneself), or to the other members, or to the ideal the group stands for or claims to embody. In practice, none of these occur in pure form; obligations are generally, perhaps necessarily, admixtures of the three. But they are often described exclusively in terms of the last."

51 Presumably, however, one would most prefer that the other's convictions change so as to cancel the obligation. These musings help to illuminate our mixed response to displays of courage of conviction by those whose purposes contravene our own—e.g. by enemy soldiers. We acknowledge the value of their integrity and their example, but we would prefer that their courage be exhibited in a conscience-driven conversion to our cause and to the conception of the good that informs it.

ples, goals or values that P has affirmed and continues to affirm in his considered judgments. This attribution is in competition with two other alternative explanations of P's actions: (1) that P never really affirmed the relevant principles, goals or values in question (perhaps because P is insincere or lacks deliberative seriousness); or (2) that P lacks the self-control necessary if his judgments are to amount to real convictions. When P's associates reject these alternatives and maintain that P broke a non-promissory obligation, they rebuke P but they simultaneously assert their continuing association with P. I noted above that in the attribution of convictions, and by extension of non-promissory obligations, first-person avowals are given a certain delimited authority. Here too an extremely important test of whether P broke an obligation is whether P continues to avow the convictions which associates took him to have and which his actions betrayed.

I observed above that this grant of authority is a kind of trust that makes association possible, and that this trust is not unlimited—it is broken off when it requires unacceptably strained interpretations of the actions of others. When P's associates assert that P broke an obligation, they extend their trust to P, and the measure of this trust is the implausibility of the interpretation of P that they must accept in order to sustain this trust. If it is extremely implausible to interpret P as having a continuing internalist commitment to the distinctive principles, goals or values of the group, then P's actions have placed a considerable strain on the association. In such cases, alternative readings of P's actions are unlikely to be dismissed entirely; they remain as shadow interpretations of P—open interpretive possibilities to be embraced if P's future actions cannot easily be explained by any intentional interpretation that incorporates P's avowed convictions at face value.

An association can only sustain so many broken obligations. Each time that an associate strays from putatively shared principles, ideals or values, this further strains the trust that associates have in each other, by giving each associate a reason to doubt the sincerity, deliberative seriousness or capacity for self-control of others. This erosion of trust tends to go hand-in-hand with an erosion of confidence in the supposed truths jointly affirmed by members. This is so for two reasons. First, one powerful test of a putative truth is whether it compels conviction in those who dwell on it. Second, associates grasp the group's distinctive values and work out their precise implications in conversation with each other, and if there is reason to doubt the sincerity or deliberative seriousness of other group members, there is also reason to doubt any conclusions reached in the course of good-faith conversations of this sort.[52]

The same erosion of trust tends to cast doubt on whether the past coordinated activities of the group really did answer to the description under which members took them to be worthwhile. This, I think, is the most direct and dramatic sense in which the failure to fulfill an internalist commitment can constitute a betrayal of one's associates. In the moment that it throws into doubt the depth of one's internalist commitment, it also casts doubt on just what they have been doing and whether it has had the value they believed it to have. It tinkers with their life stories. It is a different activity—and arguably a far more valuable one—to farm fields and raise children with fellow members of a commune who share ideals of simple living and self-sufficiency, than to do so with people who merely give every appearance of affirming those ideals. It is a different and arguably more valuable activity to organize a jazz band or a poetry discussion group with others who find their participation intrinsically valuable than with others who are motivated by extrinsic considerations. It is different and arguably more valuable to administer a philosophy department with colleagues who find the teaching of philosophy intrinsically worthwhile than with others who convincingly pretend to find it valuable. One can neither describe these activities nor evaluate them definitively without reference to the motives of one's collaborators. To do so would be nearly as misguided as it would be to characterize and evaluate one's sexual activities without reference to the motivations of one's partners.

In the context of associations, then, to "break" an obligation is, roughly speaking, to be false to a shared vision of what is right, valuable or good. When one breaks an obligation, one gives other group members grounds for doubting whether they have indeed succeeded in living the life they wished to lead, believed themselves to be lead-

---

52 These considerations begin to bring out some of the characteristic dangers and paranoias of association. While I think that these dangers are real and frightening, I do not think that they constitute a reason to shun mutual association. I think instead that they constitute an argument for humility and restraint in attributing obligations and in insisting upon their fulfillment.

ing and hoped to continue leading. One might also cast doubt on the adequacy of their convictions. These are the rather complex senses in which others might be involved in one's special non-promissory obligations and harmed when these obligations are broken.

VC: Marital Fidelity as a Non-Promissory Obligation

Like fellow associates, so the parties to intimate relationships seek to guide their shared activities in light of convictions that they have come to affirm and struggled to make precise together. This means that intimate relationships too depend upon, and provide an important social setting for, special non-promissory obligations.[53] I will draw upon examples from the sphere of intimate relationships to show that my proposed analysis can account for our talk of certain interpersonal obligations, and that it can do so better than the rival promissory account.

Suppose Albert asserts that by sleeping with another man, his wife Betty has broken an obligation to him. On my analysis, what Albert means is that Betty has expressed a commitment to a shared ideal—let's call it the ideal of conjugal intimacy—yet failed to live up to this ideal.

This might seem too impersonal a reading of Albert's claim,

---

53 I do not mean to suggest that intimate relationships are nothing more than associations. As I see it, one key distinction that sets intimate relationships apart from other associations is that intimates need not share each other's convictions in order to have special standing to speak up for those convictions. This is not because intimates are exposed to special harms if convictions that they do not share are disregarded or abandoned. It is rather that part of what it means to be an intimate—at least on one compelling conception of intimacy—is to be the midwife and the advocate of another's deepest convictions. Our intimates are the midwives of our convictions in that they help us to bring our evaluative judgments into words and to reflect on their adequacy—that is, they help us in the sort of reflection that is needed if we are to have real convictions. Our intimates are the advocates of our convictions in that we place a particularly extensive trust in their claims about our convictions and their practical implications. We extend this trust because they have indicated, and we believe, that they are concerned with our preservation and flourishing under a description of us that we ourselves find acceptable and perhaps ennobling, and that includes a large number of our core convictions. Many of the particular fears and vulnerabilities of intimacy can be read off of this account: for instance, the fear of being reshaped in line with alien values, and the vulnerability to manipulation by the self-interests of another masquerading as selfless concern for a friend.

since it seems that Albert means something else as well—namely, that Betty has broken a commitment to *him*. This intuition would be easy to account for if the obligation in question were promissory. On the promissory account, Betty owes the obligation to Albert because he is the one she promised. Her promise was an assurance that she would sleep with no one else, and she has wronged Albert by ignoring the fact that she had provided him with an assurance concerning a matter of great importance to him.

We can bring out what is wrong with this promissory account by attending to a common expression by which Albert might be imagined to express his outrage: "How could you have done such a thing!" The emphasis here is at least as much on 'How' as on 'done'. This expression quite realistically locates the source of Albert's outrage not in what Betty did, but in the fact that she could have done it. What Albert wants is not merely that Betty not have slept with another man, but that she not have taken herself to have good reason to sleep with another man.

The problem with the promissory interpretation of Albert's claim is that it describes an unfamiliar and I think unattractive form of intimacy. I suppose it is possible to imagine Albert and Betty's relationship is such that Albert's primary complaint is that Betty did not adequately acknowledge the importance of promise-keeping. However, it is far more plausible to think of Albert as objecting to the fact that Betty failed to recognize—that is, to be appropriately moved by—a picture of their shared life which he affirmed as valuable, and believed her to affirm also. Albert is personally harmed by Betty because her action throws into question whether the life he has been leading is the one that he believed himself to be leading, wished to lead and hoped to continue leading.

One thing the internalist interpretation brings out is that in many social spheres, mutual commitments penetrate more deeply than outward behavior, and that consequently there is no possibility of an empirical verification that they have been or are being kept. This, I think, gives impetus to the misdirected and unfulfillable desire for proof of fidelity that is so pervasive a companion of love relationships, and that is brilliantly illuminated by Stanley Cavell in his discussion of *Othello*.[54] I view this potentially tragic

---

54 Stanley Cavell, *The Claim of Reason* (Oxford; Oxford University Press: 1979), pp. 481–496.

desire as the dark side, or the failure, of the trust I have portrayed as essential to association and to intimacy.

To return to our example, Betty might make a number of different kinds of responses to Albert's complaint, and these too are best understood on the internalist model. First, she might admit that some momentary temptation overrode her commitment to Albert, and that she continues to affirm the guiding ideals of the relationship, and hopes to be able to reenter it. Again, it seems to me inapt to think of this as the reassertion of a promise. As noted above, one can sincerely and appropriately promise to do that which one takes oneself to have no standing reason to do, yet the relationship cannot be repaired if Betty takes herself to have no standing reason to affirm and act on the guiding ideals of the relationship. What is needed is a sincere reaffirmation of these ideals.

Betty might also respond to Albert by agreeing that she is committed to an ideal of conjugal intimacy, while denying that her action represents a break with this commitment. She might argue, for instance, that conjugal intimacy does not consist in sexual exclusiveness but in consistent loving support—something, she might add, that Albert has failed to deliver. This could lead to a reexamination of the ideal to which Albert and Betty believe(d) themselves to share a commitment. Their common life might either be reestablished on the basis of a more adequate understanding of their mutual commitment, or it might disintegrate for lack of commonly affirmed values. Again, these eventualities are distorted if one thinks of the first as the clarification of a mutual promise and the second as the discovery that they had misunderstood each other's promises. Their interests in each other runs deeper than promises can reach.

A third possibility is that Betty might claim that she reconsidered her commitment. If her reasons for reconsideration strike Albert as insufficiently weighty, this strains Albert's trust in his wife's capacity for true commitment, since (internalist) commitments are the sorts of things that do not change except for good and weighty reasons. The relationship may or may not be able to weather this damage, but it cannot go on quite as before. The likely damage is not just that Albert might find it hard to trust Betty's promises, as might be expected on the promissory account. It is that Albert will be unable to trust his wife's sincerity and deliberative seriousness in the entire range of conversations within which they seek to articulate values that they jointly affirm as authoritative for their shared activities.

PART VI: THE RADICALISM OF INTERNALIST OBLIGATIONS—IBSEN'S NORA

I have argued for the "refined voluntarist thesis" that we cannot be forced coercively to take on special non-promissory obligations. Unlike the bare voluntarist thesis, the refined voluntarist thesis allows for the possibility that one's particular obligations might be the predictable, unchosen results of a restrictive and traditional upbringing. It would be a mistake, however, to conclude that the internalist position is conservative. Internalist obligations are subject to change with changes in one's convictions—provided at least that these changes do not impugn one's capacity for conviction. No matter what one's upbringing, one might at any time gain a more piercing insight into one's commitments and their sources, and this insight might at any time expose one's commitments as the undesirable results of a dogmatic or narrowly parochial socialization. In such a case, one could deviate from one's publicly expressed commitments without impugning one's capacity for true conviction. Indeed, one's deviation might stand as evidence of this capacity.

This will undoubtedly strike many readers as the most objectionable element of the internalist account of obligations. I believe, however, that we do sometimes recognize that the phenomenon of an individual awakening, or conversion, that alters one's obligations. Henrik Ibsen's *A Doll's House* can be read as a dramatic representation of just such an awakening.[55]

It would be obtuse or worse to take up Ibsen's scathing depiction of the marriage of Nora and Torvald Helmer, and of the debilitating bourgeois aspirations and anxieties which propel it towards crisis, and to respond with . . . a moral judgment. That is not my intent. What I want to do, instead, is to examine the complex relationship between Nora and Torvald, and the dramatic shift in this

55 Here as elsewhere in this essay, I am deeply indebted to Stanley Cavell, who provides a valuable and suggestive discussion of this play in *Conditions Handsome and Unhandsome: The Constitution of Emersonian Perfectionism, The Carus Lectures, 1988* (Chicago; The University of Chicago Press: 1990), pp. 108–115.

relationship at the play's end, in order to support my contention that interpersonal obligations are more obscure and tenuous than they are often believed to be. I draw upon Ibsen's play because I doubt that my view could be supported convincingly with the sort of abstract, thinly described case which philosophers are prone to use. These cases often lack the obscurity and complexity of realistic human relations, and these same obscurities and complexities are friendly to my position. I believe and hope that I am not pressing Ibsen's play into an alien service. Perhaps I am simply in the grip of a theory, but to my mind no great subtlety is needed to find in Ibsen's play an expression of disgust with the dominant social conception of morality as propriety in promises and contracts.[56] It seems to me almost equally obvious that Ibsen is gesturing towards a more personal and more subversive morality—one that premises genuine interpersonal bonds on shared convictions of the sort I have been discussing. At any rate, I will read the play this way.

As Nora recognizes in the play's denouement, her relationship with Torvald is quite like the relationship she had with her late father. When she lived in her father's house, she accepted all of her

---

56 It is clear that Ibsen's Nora challenges the bindingness of the obligations that can be read off of her marital vows. She also challenges the conventional understanding of contractual relations, and her marriage falls to pieces over precisely this question. When Nora is confronted with the fact that she forged her dying father's signature on a bond in order to secure a loan needed to fund her husband's recuperation from a grave illness, she insists that she acted out of love for her husband and a desire to spare her dying father any worry, that she has harmed no one because she has faithfully kept up with loan repayments, and hence that what she has done cannot be judged wrong. Her creditor, Krogstad, challenges her assessment:
Krogstad. The law cares nothing about motives.
Nora. Then it must be a very foolish law.
Krogstad. Foolish or not, it is the law by which you will be judged, if I produce this paper.
Nora. I don't believe it. Is a daughter not to be allowed to spare her dying father anxiety and care? Is a wife not to be allowed to save her husband's life? I don't know much about law; but I am certain that there must be laws permitting such things as that. Have you no knowledge of such laws—you who are a lawyer? You must be a very poor lawyer, Mr. Krogstad.
Henrik Ibsen, *Four Great Plays by Ibsen*, translated by R. Farquharson Sharp, introduction and prefaces by John Gassner (New York; Bantam Books: 1958), p. 24.
57 Ibsen, *Four Great Plays by Ibsen*, p. 63.

father's tastes and judgments, or at least pretended to accept them; since she married, she has accepted or pretended to accept all of Torvald's tastes and judgments.[57] There is a great deal to Nora's charge. It goes without saying that Torvald has been paternalistic towards Nora, though it is perhaps misleading to compare her marriage to her relationship with her father. Torvald's paternalism is not the temporary and relatively benign paternalism of the parent who aims at the child's maturation. It is a perpetual paternalism—perpetual because self-perpetuating.

Torvald aims to spare Nora all need for complex practical judgment, by sparing her all worldly responsibility. He aims to preserve Nora in her childlike innocence and naivete, and of course in her beauty[58], so that she might be displayed on demand for Torvald's pleasure and for the amusement of guests. To this end, he assumes responsibility for reigning in Nora's wayward appetites. He forbids her from eating sweets so as to keep her teeth from rotting. He tightly controls her allowance so as to curb what he takes to be her native spendthrift tendencies. Naturally, Nora chafes at his rules and does not heed them, but she never questions his right to impose them, so that their principal effect is to shade the marriage with a pervasive hypocrisy.[59] This suits Torvald. There is always a fresh infraction to be discovered, and he positively welcomes Nora's pecadillos as confirmations of her native incapacity for self-control, hence as proofs of the continued need for his paternalistic guidance.

This is what the relationship looks like on its surface. However, Nora knows the marriage to have a hidden shape—one that makes her acquiescence seem to her tolerable and sometimes even sublime. The audience is let in on Nora's secret early in the play. Nora's long-lost childhood friend, Christine Linde, avers with

---

58 Torvald apprehends his wife's beauty with a self-satisfied colonial gaze: "Why shouldn't I look at my dearest treasure? — at all the beauty that is mine, all my very own?" (*Op. Cit.*, p. 55) He has an invasive aesthetic. At one point, he goes so far as to recommend to his wife's friend that she take up embroidering rather than knitting, because the motion is so much more graceful and becoming. (*Op. Cit.*, p. 54)

59 When Torvald asks Nora whether she hasn't been breaking his rule forbidding her to eat candy, she says, ""I should not think of going against your wishes." She has just hidden a box of macaroons. (*Op. Cit.*, p. 6)

60 Ibsen, *Four Great Plays by Ibsen*, p. 11.

mixed envy and condescension that Nora has known nothing of "the burdens and troubles of life," and that she is really still a child.[60] Nora protests that like Christine, she too has made great sacrifices to ease the burdens of others, and thus she too has "something to be proud and glad of."[61] She confesses that she secretly arranged a loan in order to finance a trip to Italy which the family doctor believed necessary to save Torvald's life. On the doctor's recommendation, she did not tell her husband that his condition was grave and that the trip's purpose was his recuperation. Since returning from Italy, Nora has managed to keep up with repayment of the loan by diverting money intended for her clothing purchases, and by doing copying work late at night. "Many a time I was desperately tired;" she tells Christine, "but all the same it was a tremendous pleasure to sit there working and earning money. It was like being a man."[62]

In Nora's eyes, then, the marriage has a secret and satisfying symmetry. Torvald believes that he has ventured out into the world of business in order to support his wife and protect her from the hardships of life, but in fact Nora has forayed into the world of business contracts and wage labor in order to preserve and protect Torvald's life. Arranging and repaying this loan has been Nora's defining activity—the activity that has constituted her as an adult rather than a child. In this activity, she has demonstrated the rough dimensions of her (internalist) marital commitments: she has shown herself ready to risk her reputation, and to sacrifice her material pleasures and comforts, for the well-being of her husband. She is convinced that Torvald's commitments to her well-being perfectly mirror her own.

Nora's secret lends irony to nearly every word she says to Torvald. In order to convince Torvald to go to Italy without letting him know of his grave illness, she presents the trip as her idea, and she demands that he treat her as other husbands treat their wives. To the play's audience, this provides a covert demonstration of Nora's self-sacrificial devotion to Torvald; to Torvald, it provides fresh evidence that she is not to be indulged in her "whims and caprices."[63] Nora continually covers up her diversions of money

---

61 Ibsen, *Four Great Plays by Ibsen*, p. 12.
62 Ibsen, *Four Great Plays by Ibsen*, p. 14.
63 Ibsen, *Four Great Plays by Ibsen*, p. 13.

for loan repayments by posing as an irresponsible spendthrift, and this brings a nauseating scolding from Torvald: "Bought, did you say? All these little things? Has my little spendthrift been wasting money again?"[64] In her efforts to convince Torvald to rehire her secret creditor, and thus to avert great damage to Torvald's career, Nora remarks, "Everything I do seems silly and insignificant." Here again her words drip with irony: yes, everything she does *seems* insignificant, but if only Torvald were capable of trusting that her concerns were not really so shallow and insignificant, he might do himself a world of good. Torvald predictably hears her remark as a confirmation of his view of her. He replies, "Does my little Nora acknowledge that at last?"[65]

Throughout the first two acts, then, Nora presents herself as a vain and capricious child, yet she does so under the secret banner of self-sacrifice and responsibility. Words and actions that appear abject and self-deprecating have a private and ennobling meaning for her. The irony reaches its full pitch at the end of Act II, when Nora realizes that her game is up and determines to safeguard her secret for another day before taking her own life in an effort to protect her husband.

The plot here is complex. Nora's creditor, Krogstad, has placed a letter in Torvald's mailbox which tells Torvald of the loan, and further reveals that Nora forged her dying father's signature on a bond in order to secure the loan (she did so, she says, in order to spare him worries on his deathbed). Nora confidently expects that Torvald will respond to the letter by taking credit for the forged signature, permitting his own reputation and career to be damaged badly in order to protect his wife's reputation. This supposition follows naturally from Torvald's own self-representations. Just the day before, he announced that it would be "an insult" for Nora to continue thinking that he would be afraid of Krogstad's defamatory remarks. "Come what will," he adds, "you may be sure that I shall have both courage and strength if they be needed.

---

64 Ibsen, *Four Great Plays by Ibsen*, p. 4. Later, Torvald instructs her, "What are little people called that are always wasting money?" expecting to her his judgments echoed back like elementary school lessons. (p. 5.) Yet another scolding of his "sweet little spendthrift" prompts Nora to say ironically, "You haven't any idea how many expenses we skylarks and squirrels have, Torvald." (p. 6.)

65 Ibsen, *Four Great Plays by Ibsen*, p. 26.

66 Ibsen, *Four Great Plays by Ibsen*, p. 36.

You will see I am man enough to take everything upon myself."[66] And just hours before he opens the letter, Torvald says, "Do you know, Nora, I have often wished that you might be threatened by some great danger, so that I might risk my life's blood, and everything, for your sake."[67]

Nora looks forward to Torvald's sacrificial act as "a wonderful thing"—a wonderful thing that she both hopes for as a consummation of his love, and fears as an indelible and undeserved blot on his previously sterling reputation.[68] She makes a plan to kill herself so that Torvald will not be tempted to make personal sacrifices for the sake of her reputation, and she resolves to carry out her plan before he opens Krogstad's letter so that Torvald will have no chance to stop her.

Nora tries to distract Torvald from opening the letter for as long as she can, partly in order to prolong her time with her loved ones, and partly in order to choreograph a last public appearance before throwing herself into the icy river near her house. She is planning to perform an Italian folkdance for houseguests at a dinner party the next night, and she captures Torvald's attention by pretending that she cannot remember how to do the dance. ("I can't get on a bit without you to help me."[69]) She spins into a wild gyration that in no way resembles the Tarantella she is supposed to perform. This annoys Torvald, though again it serves him as confirmation that she requires his guidance in all things. He attempts to coach her, but her steps refuse to conform to his sensibility. Torvald scolds her: "My dear darling Nora, you are dancing as if your life depended on it."[70] Meanwhile she counts the hours to her death and realizes that only thirty-one remain.

The next night, after Nora's successful Tarantella, Nora realizes that she cannot put Torvald off any longer. He goes to his bedroom to read Krogstad's letter. I said earlier that given what internalist commitments are, nothing could count as a definitive empirical verification that one's internalist commitments are shared by another. I also said that this very fact helps to explain the intense longings for confirmation of shared commitment which accompany and threaten to destroy so many love relationships. Clearly,

---

67 Ibsen, *Four Great Plays by Ibsen*, p. 58.
68 Ibsen, *Four Great Plays by Ibsen*, pp. 45 and 66.
69 Ibsen, *Four Great Plays by Ibsen*, p. 46.
70 Ibsen, *Four Great Plays by Ibsen*, p. 47.

though, there are occasional "moments of truth" in which the words and actions of another provide unusually clear signs of his real convictions. Just as clearly, these moments are of utmost importance to those who suppose their lives to be intertwined by shared internalist commitments. Nora is on the verge of taking her own life in order to spare her husband's reputation, and she has planned to proceed on the supposition that his devotion mirrored her own, even though this will prevent her from witnessing the "wonderful thing" that could reinforce her supposition.[71] Perhaps her faith in Torvald is less than complete. Perhaps Nora had a premonition that Torvald's avowals of readiness to sacrifice all for her were mere bluster—a show of benevolence to gild his actual, selfish motives for enchaining her in his paternalistic rule. For whatever reason, she lingers in the hallway, muttering last goodbyes to Torvald and the children, long enough so that he is able to finish the letter and storm out into the hall.

It quickly become clear to Nora that the "wonderful thing" she has eagerly awaited and confidently expected during eight years of marriage will not occur.[72] Torvald has no intention of taking responsibility for her actions. He is willing to appease Krogstad in order to keep the entire affair hushed, and his greatest worry is that people might suspect that it was he who prompted Nora to forge her father's signature. He excoriates Nora as "a hypocrite, a liar—worse, worse—a criminal."[73] When she protests that she acted out of love for him, he tells her to dispense with "silly excuses."[74]

It is no good that once the crisis passes, Torvald announces himself anew to be Nora's protector and provider, magnanimously offering his "broad wings" to shelter his "frightened little singing-bird."[75] His actions have spoken more loudly of his true commitments than his belated pledge of restored faith possibly

---

71 Perhaps she was not so perfectly faithful as I suggest here. She did after all linger outside of Torvald's bedroom door, muttering goodbyes to Torvald and the children, for a long enough time that he is able to finish the letter and storm back out with his ill-advised reaction. Maybe this registers a premonition that his avowed readiness to sacrifice all for her was mere bluster, a show of benevolence to gild his real motives for enchaining her in paternalistic rules.
72 Ibsen, *Four Great Plays by Ibsen*, p. 66.
73 Ibsen, *Four Great Plays by Ibsen*, p. 59.
74 Ibsen, *Four Great Plays by Ibsen*, p. 59.
75 Ibsen, *Four Great Plays by Ibsen*, p. 62.

can. The revelation leaves Nora ready to "tear [her]self to little bits" at the thought of the eight years during which she has lived as the "doll-wife" of a man whom she has utterly failed to understand.[76] She gathers her things, returns Torvald's ring and walks out the door.

In the last moments of the play, Nora makes a scathing indictment of her marriage to Torvald, and this indictment can quite easily be read as a rejection of the promissory interpretation of marital obligations and as a semi-articulate insistence on the internalist interpretation. Nora says that she has ceased to love Torvald because she has seen that he is not the man he believed her to be. She does not insist upon the fact that he led her to believe he would act differently, or has been untrue to his word. She dwells instead on the fact that she has been vastly and catastrophically mistaken about his convictions, and that this mistake throws into question the nature and value of the life she has been leading. Their relationship does not have the symmetry she thought it had. His paternalism can no longer be traced to a selfless devotion to her protection.[77] And this means that the private and ennobling meanings that she has given to her outward shows of servility, helplessness and incompetence cannot any longer redeem her relationship. These same acts now appear to her as simple capitulations to a man who has sought to impress his will upon her for his own ends. He has regarded her as nothing more than a doll-wife, and she has played into his hands. "I have existed merely in order to perform tricks for you, Torvald. But you would have it so."[78]

Nora clearly breaks with her publicly avowed commitments to marriage and family. On the promissory account of obligations, it would be hard to resist the conclusion that she is obligated to stay with Torvald, and that she breaks her obligation when she leaves. This same interpretation appears quite implausible on the internalist account, since we need not view her departure as impugning

---

76 These fragments of dialogue come from the closing scene of Act III of "A Doll's House." *Op. cit.*, pp. 64 & 67.

77 Perhaps they really have shared certain values, but only ugly and second-hand ones. She has shared in his sense of worldly power: "It's perfectly glorious to think that we have—that Torvald has so much power over so many other people." (p. 17) And she has shared his concerns for material comforts and for appearances of bourgeois respectability. Nora shows by her actions at the end of the play that these are no longer values for her.

78 Ibsen, *Four Great Plays by Ibsen*, p. 63.

her capacity for conviction, and in fact are tempted to see it as the moment in which it first becomes possible for Nora to have true convictions.

Nora's departure does not impugn her capacity for conviction because her upbringing, her social world, and her marital relations have given her very little opportunity to articulate her convictions and expose them to critical scrutiny. Nora's understanding of marital relations arose within a highly restrictive social world—one whose orthodoxies and traditions have hidden from her view the full range of possible marital commitments, and the full range of lives she could lead. Within her marriage she has had neither opportunity nor encouragement to test these orthodoxies and to reflect on their adequacy. As a result, her convictions are largely unformed.

Nora leaves her marriage with the idea that she must attend to her own education, examining her received beliefs and determining whether they are worthy of acceptance. She recognizes that most people would insist that she is obligated to stay with her husband and children, but she explains, "I can no longer content myself with what most people say, or with what is found in books. I must think over things for myself and get to understand them."[79] When Torvald objects that her religion gives her reason to stay, she protests that she does not know what religion is:

> I know nothing but what the clergyman said, when I went
> to be confirmed. He told us that religion was this, and that,
> and the other. When I am away from all this, and am alone,
> I will look into that matter too. I will see if what the clergy-
> man said is true, or at all events if it is true for me.[80]

Nora finds herself lacking well-grounded convictions about how she ought to live. She is confident of two things, however. First, she is convinced that her current condition represents a cognitive improvement over her eight years of married life, since now at least she recognizes that her professed convictions did not deserve her affirmation.[81] Second, she knows that she cannot remain with Torvald, for that would make it impossible to set her-

---

79 Ibsen, *Four Great Plays by Ibsen*, p. 65.
80 Ibsen, *Four Great Plays by Ibsen*, p. 65.
81 When Torvald suggests that Nora is out of her mind, she replies, "I have never felt my mind so clear and certain as to-night." (Ibsen, *Four Great Plays by Ibsen*, p. 66.)
82 Ibsen, *Four Great Plays by Ibsen*, p. 66–7.

self aright. She has the "clear and certain conviction" that she does not love Torvald any longer, and that he is not the sort of man to whom she could bind herself.[82]

Nora's departure, then, does not seem whimsical or ill-considered; it seems instead to provide evidence of her reflective seriousness and determination to act on her convictions. Thus, it seems implausible to conclude on internalist grounds that she has broken an obligation. This seems to me to count in favor of the internalist account, since it seems to me at least as compelling to think that Torvald breaks his obligations than to think that Nora does.

What ought the internalist to say of Nora's departure? I see three possibilities. The internalist could say that despite her outward indications of commitment, Nora never really had an obligation to Torvald—either (1) because she entered her marriage without the freedom needed to see its true nature and implications, or (2) because she and Torvald never really shared a commitment to any set of principles or values regulating the terms of their common life. Alternatively, the internalist could say that (3) Nora did have an obligation to Torvald, but that it ceased in the play's last act, when she became aware of the ill fit of her marriage with her evolving self-understanding. I will argue briefly that (1) provides an inadequate account of obligations, and that the internalist should opt either for (2) or for (3). Along the way, I will attempt to show how internalism leads to one of two rather radical conclusions about obligations: either it leads towards skepticism about the possibility of knowing what obligations any given person has, or it undermines the categorical force traditionally associated with obligations. I will also suggest that these radical consequences are not fatal to the internalist project.

I do not think that (1) is a plausible assessment of Nora's case. Given what internalist commitments are, it is hard to see any good reason why they could not arise against the backdrop of a restrictive upbringing. But even if the criteria for genuine conviction were tightened so as to exclude the sorts of beliefs that have informed Nora's marital conduct, this would raise a *prima-facie* difficulty with the internalist account of obligation. The difficulty is that Nora's position at the time of her marriage does not seem so exceptionally disadvantaged. Like Nora, so most of us are in thrall to one or another restrictive nexus of social norms and opinions; most of us absorb values unreflectively from those around us. It is always possible that these values would appear inauthentic from some more stubbornly independent vantage point. This account of Nora's case presses one toward the conclusion that most of us are incapable of holding obligations most of the time, and further, that people who live in highly traditional societies are always incapable of holding obligations. Such a conclusion would not represent a theoretical account of obligations but a thorough debunking of them.

The internalist might also argue (2) that Nora was never obligated to Torvald because, as is now evident, she never shared with Torvald any principles, ideals or values regarding their marriage (or at least none which imply that she ought to stay).

It is not hard to see how this position might be elaborated. At the end of the play, Nora realizes to her astonishment and disgust that in eight years of marriage, she has never once had a serious conversation with Torvald. "We have never sat down in earnest together to try and get at the bottom of anything."[83] Torvald has been content to arrange their domestic life in line with his own opinions and to hear her echo these opinions uncritically. He has insisted on taking Nora's words and actions as confirmations of his favored illusion of her as a helpless and incompetent child. Torvald, then, cannot speak authoritatively of Nora's commitments.

Even if Torvald could identify Nora's internalist commitments, he would lack proper standing to demand their fulfilment. Nora does not betray Torvald in the subtle ways that the members of associations can betray each other. His ideals have not been betrayed by her, since he never sought her affirmation of them.[84] His warrant for holding his ideals has not been shaken, since he never regarded Nora as a worthy partner in the pursuit of insight into the good. The nature and value of his past activities has not been thrown into doubt by her departure. He did not acknowledge the importance of her inner assent to their shared activities. Thus, while her departure ought to prompt him to question the value of their shared domestic life, it gives him no reason for supposing that

83 Ibsen, *Four Great Plays by Ibsen*, p. 63.
84 It is not clear that Torvald has really sought to test his values by his own lights either. He is enormously concerned with keeping up the appearances, so much so that in the moment in which he thinks that his marriage is irrevocably destroyed, his first thought is that everything must appear unchanged from outside. (Ibsen, *Four Great Plays by Ibsen*, p. 60.)

he has not been living the sort of life he took himself to be leading. Nora is the one whose biography has been tinkered with. She can claim more convincingly that she has been betrayed.

This assessment (2) of Nora seems to me extremely compelling, but it is not without its oddness. First, it rests upon a view of obligations which threatens to leave all of us in a perpetual state of doubt as to what our obligations actually are. This is because beliefs about our obligations would always rest upon our best conjectures about the true commitments and motivations of others.[85] Second, in order to conclude that Nora was never obligated, and that she merely discovered this fact at the end of the play, the internalist implicitly assumes that there is a fact of the matter about Torvald's true commitments—one which predates the play's seminal moment. There may be good reason to hold that one's true character and commitments are less determinate than this picture would imply, and that they are continually *given shape*—rather than merely *revealed*—by the unfolding succession of one's actions and interactions.

This rumination points us towards the last interpretation (3): Nora did indeed have an obligation to Torvald, but it ceased in the play's last act, when a series of revelatory actions and events changed the self-understanding of both partners, changed the way that each partner viewed the other, and destroyed the possibility of a harmonious common life between them. Perhaps this is what Nora is hinting at when she says that in order for Torvald to be something more than a stranger to her once again, both he and she would have to be "so changed" that their "life together would be a real wedlock."[86] This interpretation is perhaps preferable to (2) because it does not rely upon the notion that there is always a fact of the matter about what others are committed to. However, it pointedly undermines the categorical force which has traditionally been associated with obligations.

---

85 This line of interpretation connects the problem of obligation to that variant of the problem of other minds which Stanley Cavell draws from Shakespearean tragedy. On Cavell's view, for instance, Othello's tragic doubt about Desdemona's faithfulness (commitment?) provides a dramatic, psychologically revealing mirror of the sort of skeptical doubts about the existence of others minds which have troubled many philosophers. See Stanley Cavell, *The Claim of Reason* (Oxford; Oxford University Press: 1979), pp. 481–496.

86 Ibsen, *Op. Cit.*, p. 68. Of course, this passage is susceptible to a number of readings...

Ultimately, whether the internalist chooses to say (2) that Nora was never obligated to Torvald because they actually held no common values, or (3) that she was obligated but that her obligation ceased in the course of the play, the internalist view implies that one's obligations are far more provisional than usually thought—either because one's obligations might at any time be revealed as illusions, or because obligations are themselves continually subject to change.

Is this a damning fault of the internalist analysis of obligations? I believe not, and I hope that my discussion of Ibsen's Nora has elicited intuitions friendly to my view. At the very least, the internalist can explain why people might believe that obligations are more transparently evident and/or more categorically binding than, upon reflection, they actually prove to be.[87] On the internalist view, judgments about obligations are the tools with which shared ways of life can be collectively crafted. As such, these tools are apt to be invoked unilaterally—perhaps with the force of tradition, rhetoric, or the threat of coercion behind them—to shame others into conformity with the speaker's personal interests, or to create a predictability within social interactions which is incompatible with the uncoerced and reflective affirmation of all. And just as obligations are prone to such misuse, so they are prone to be misunderstood; indeed, the coercive misuse of claims about obligations is most effective if obligations are widely misunderstood as easily identifiable and categorically binding dictates, on the model of promises or vows.

Internalism implies, on the contrary, that obligations—even those affirmed by a free and highly reflective individual—are always subject to reassessment. No obligation is ever entirely fixed in stone, because there is no moment in one's life at which (2) full knowledge of others or (3) full reflection upon all relevant considerations has been achieved. Of course, more can be *demanded*. But within the important class of social groups that I call associations, such demands are well-founded only if they find some foothold in the commitments of those to whom they are addressed.

---

87 These ideas are rather hard to put down on paper coherently. For as the internalist understanding of obligations gains a foothold, obligations are recognized as less categorically binding than once thought. Internalism is critical. For the internalist, the line between theory and practice is exceedingly thin.

Bibliography

Allison, Henry E., Kant's *Theory of Freedom* (Cambridge; Cambridge University Press: 1990).

Ameriks, Karl, "Kant on the Good Will," in ed. Ottfried Hoffe, *Grundlegung zur Metaphysik der Sitten: Eine Kooperativer Kommentar* (Frankfurt; Vittorio Klostermann: 1989), pp. 45–65.

Aristotle, *Nichomachean Ethics*, translated by Terence Irwin (Indianapolis; Hackett Publishing Company: 1985).

Austin, J.L., *How to Do Things with Words* (Cambridge; Harvard University Press: 1962).

Baier, Annette, *Moral Prejudices: Essays on Ethics* (Cambridge; Harvard University Press: 1994).

Baron, Marcia, "The Alleged Moral Repugnance of Acting from Duty," in *The Journal of Philosophy*, Vol. LXXXI, No. 4, April 1984.

Brandom, Robert, *Making It Explicit: Reasoning, Representing and Discursive Commitment* (Cambridge; Harvard University Press: 1994).

Buchanan, James M., *The Limits of Liberty: Between Anarchy and Leviathan* (Chicago; University of Chicago Press: 1975).

Carroll, Lewis, "What the Tortoise Said to Achilles," *Mind*, Volume 4, 1895, pp. 278–80; reprinted for centennial in *Mind*, Volume 104, Number 416, October 1995, pp. 691–3.

Cavell, Stanley, *The Claim of Reason* (Oxford; Oxford University Press: 1979).

Cavell, Stanley, *Conditions Handsome and Unhandsome: The Constitution of Emersonian Perfectionism, The Carus Lectures, 1988* (Chicago; The University of Chicago Press: 1990).

Foot, Philippa, "Virtues and Vices" in *Virtues and Vices* (Oxford: Blackwell; 1978), pp. 1–18.

Frankfurt, Harry G., *The Importance of What We Care About* (Cambridge; Cambridge, University Press: 1988).

Freud, Sigmund, *Therapy and Technique*, edited by Philip Rieff, editor, (New York; Collier Books: 1963).

Gauthier, David, *Morals by Agreement* (Oxford; Oxford University Press: 1986).

Gilbert, Margaret, "Agreements, Coercion and Obligation" in *Ethics*, Vol. 103, No. 4 (July 1993), pp. 679–706.

Gilbert, Margaret, "Modelling Collective Belief" (*Synthese*, volume 73, no. 1, October 1987), pp. 185–204.

Gilbert, Margaret, "Walking Together" in Peter A. French, Theodore E. Uehling, Jr., and Howard K. Wettstein, editors, *Midwest Studies in Philosophy, Volume XV: The Philosophy of the Human Sciences* (Notre Dame, Indiana; University of Notre Dame Press: 1990), pp. 1–14.

Guyer, Paul, *Kant and the Experience of Freedom* (Cambridge; Cambridge University Press: 1996).

Hardimon, Michael, "Role Obligations" in *The Journal of Philosophy*, Volume XCI, No. 7 (July, 1994), pp. 333–363.

Herman, Barbara, "Making Room for Character," in Stephen Engstrom and Jenniger Whiting, eds., *Aristotle, Kant and the Stoics: Rethinking Happiness and Virtue* (Cambridge; Cambridge University Press: 1996), pp. 36–60.

Herman, Barbara, *The Practice of Moral Judgment* (Cambridge; Harvard University Press: 1993), pp. 1–22.

Hume, David, *A Treatise of Human Nature*, edited by P.H. Nidditch with analytical index by L.A. Selby Bigge (Oxford; Oxford University Press: 1978).

Ibsen, Henrik, *Four Great Plays by Ibsen*, translated by R. Farquharson Sharp, introduction and prefaces by John Gassner (New York; Bantam Books: 1958).

Kant, Immanuel, *Anthropology from a Pragmatic Point of View*, translated by Mary J. Gregor (The Hague; Martinus Nijhoff: 1974).

Kant, Immanuel, *Critique of Practical Reason*, translated by Lewis Beck White (New York; MacMillan Publishing Company; 1956).

Kant, Immanuel, *Critique of Pure Reason*, translated by Norman Kemp Smith (New York; St. Martin's Press: 1929).

Kant, Immanuel, "The End of All Things" in Perpetual Peace and Other Essays, translated by Ted Humphrey (Indianapolis; Hackett Publishing Company: 1983), pp. 93–106.

Kant, Immanuel, Groundwork for the *Metaphysics of Morals*, translated by James W. Ellington (Indianapolis; Hackett Publishing Company: 1981).

Kant, Immanuel, *The Metaphysics of Morals*, translated by Mary Gregor (Cambridge; Cambridge University Press: 1991).

Kant, Immanuel, "On a Supposed Right to Tell Lies from Benevolent Motives," in *Kant's Critique of Practical Reason and Other Works on the Theory of Ethics*, translated by Thomas Kingsmill Abbott (London; Longmans, Green and Co. Ltd.: 1873).

Kant, Immanuel, *Religion within the Limits of Reason Alone*, translated by Theodore M. Greene and Hoyt H. Hudson (New York; Harper Torchbooks: 1960).

Kekes, John, *Moral Tradition and Individuality* (Princeton; Princeton University Press: 1989).

Korsgaard, Christine M., "From Duty and for the Sake of the Noble: Kant and Aristotle on Morally Good Action" in *Aristotle, Kant and the Stoics: Rethinking Happiness and Duty*, edited by Stephen Engstrom and Jennifer Whiting (Cambridge; Cambridge University Press: 1996), pp. 203–236.

Korsgaard, Christine M., *Creating the Kingdom of Ends* (Cambridge; Cambridge University Press: 1996).

Locke, John, *A Letter Concerning Toleration*, edited by James H. Tully (Indianapolis; Hackett Publishing Company: 1983).

Locke, John, *Second Treatise of Government*, edited by C.B. Macpherson (Indianapolis; Hackett Publishing Company: 1980).

MacIntyre, Alasdair, *After Virtue: A Study in Moral Theory* (Notre Dame, Indiana; University of Notre Dame Press: 1981).

MacIntyre, Alasdair, *Against the Self-Image of the Age: Essays on Ideology and Philosophy* (Notre Dame; University of Notre Dame Press: 1978).

Moran, Richard, "Self-Knowledge: Discovery, Resolution and Undoing" (unpublished manuscript).

Nagel, Thomas, *Mortal Questions* (Cambridge; Cambridge University Press: 1979).

Nietzsche, Friedrich, *On the Genealogy of Morals and Ecce Homo*, translated by Walter Kaufmann and R.J. Hollingdale (New York; Vintage Books: 1967)

O'Neill, Onora, Constructions of *Reason: Explorations of Kant's Practical Philosophy* (Cambridge; Cambridge University Press: 1989).

Plato, "Meno," translated by W.K.C. Guthrie, in *Collected Dialogues of Plato*, edited by Edith Hamilton and Huntington Cairns (Princeton; Princeton University Press: 1961), pp. 353–384.

Rawls, John, *Political Liberalism* (New York; Columbia University Press: 1993).

Rawls, John, *A Theory of Justice* (Cambridge; Harvard University Press: 1971).

Royce, Josiah, *The Philosophy of Loyalty* (Nashville; Vanderbilt University Press: 1995).

Ryle, Gilbert, *Collected Papers Volume II: Collected Essays 1929–1968* (New York; Barnes and Noble: 1971).

Scanlon, Thomas M., "Promises and Practices," in *Philosophy and Public Affairs* (Summer 1990), pp. 199–226.

Schopenhauer, Arthur, *Philosophical Writings*, Wolfgang Schirmacher, editor (New York; The Continuum Publishing Company: 1994).

Sherman, Nancy, "The Place of Emotions in Kantian Morality," in Owen Flanagan and Amelie Oksenberg Rorty, eds., *Identity, Character and Morality: Essays in Moral Psychology*

(Cambridge; MIT Press, 1990), pp. 149–170.

Simmons, A. John, *Moral Principles and Political Obligations* (Princeton; Princeton University Press: 1979).

Simmons, Keith, "Kant on Moral Worth," *History of Philosophy Quarterly*, Volume 6, No. 1 (January 1989), pp. 85–100.

Solomon, Robert C., *The Passions* (New York; Doubleday: 1976)

Stocker, Michael, "The Schizophrenia of Modern Ethical Theories," in *The Journal of Philosophy*, vol. LXXIII, no. 14 (August 12, 1976), pp. 453–466.

Taylor, Charles, *Human Agency and Language: Philosophical Papers I* (Cambridge; Cambridge University Press: 1985).

Taylor, Gabriele, "Integrity" in *Proceedings of the Aristotelian Society*, Supplementary Volume LV (July, 1981), pp. 143–159.

Walzer, Michael, *Obligations: Essays on Disobedience, War and Citizenship* (Cambridge; Harvard University Press: 1970).

Walzer, Michael, *Thick and Thin: Moral Argument at Home and Abroad* (Notre Dame, Indiana; University of Notre Dame Press: 1994).

Williams, Bernard, *Ethics and the Limits of Philosophy* (Cambridge; Harvard University Press: 1985).

Williams, Bernard, *Moral Luck* (Cambridge; Cambridge University Press: 1981).

Wittgenstein, Ludwig, *Philosophical Investigations* (Third Edition), translated by G.E.M. Anscombe (New York; Macmillan Publishing Company, Inc., 1958).

Index

actions
vs. events, viii, 8, 77, 80
characteristic, 19-20
impulsive, viii
aesthetic value, 24, 54, 56
affects. *See* desires; emotions;
   inclination; sentiments
aggregations, 140-44, 147
   vs. associations, ix, 131, 139, 150
   and obligations, 192-93
   See also groups, social
agreement. *See* consent
akrasia, 112, 112n, 149-50, 176, 180-
   82, 203-04
alienation, 193n
Allison, Henry E., 12n, 26n, 50n
Ameriks, Karl, 16n-17n
apathy, 63
apologies, 162n
Aristotle, 5, 27-28, 53, 81, 97, 158
   &58n
asceticism, 54
assessment. *See* moral assessment; self-
   evaluation; praise
associations, xii, 144-57
   vs. aggregations, ix, 131, 139, 150
   comprehensive, 145, 150-54
   and freedom, 198-200
   goal-directed, 145-50
   non-comprehensive, 154-57
   and obligations, 193-94, 198-206
   See also practices; groups, social

assertions, 109-11, 114
Austin, J. L., 107-09, 114-15, 160,
   162
authority,
   to attribute commitments, 164-66
   to attribute convictions, 186-89
   to attribute obligations, 190-91,
      201-206
   of professions of convitions, 177-
      82, 201-206
autonomy, xi, 28-29, 47, 56, 153n. *See*
   also freedom; self-control

Baier, Annette C., 202n
Baron, Marcia, 20n
behabatives, 108n, 162n
beliefs
   and freedom, 194-200
   as opaque contexts, 92-3
   professions of, 121-24
   shared, 136-39
beneficence, 3, 6, 61-63, 65-66, 70n,
   73, 77-80, 94, 159. *See also*
   duties to others
Brandom, Robert, 115n, 137-38

capriciousness, 180-81, 213
Carroll, Lewis, 75, 76n
categorical imperative, the, 11, 16-
   17, 19-21, 63-64, 81. *See*
   also the moral law
Cavell, Stanley, xiii, 207, 209n, 220n

229